MANAGING
YOUR CITY OR TOWN

or
A Reference Guide for
the New Public Offical

KENTON G. GRIFFIN

UNIVERSITY
PRESS OF
AMERICA

Lanham • New York • London

Copyright © 1988, 1994 by
Kenton G. Griffin

University Press of America,® Inc.
4720 Boston Way
Lanham, Maryland 20706

3 Henrietta Street
London WC2E 8LU England

Library of Congress Cataloging-in-Publication Data

Griffin, Kenton G.
Managing your city or town : a reference guide for the
new public official / by Kenton G. Griffin.
p.   cm.
Includes index.
1. Municipal government—United States—Handbooks, manuals, etc.
2. Municipal officials and employees—United States—Handbooks,
manuals, etc.   3. Public administration—United States—Handbooks,
manuals, etc.   I. Title.
JS331.G78   1993   352.073—dc20   93–44355 CIP

ISBN 0–8191–9403–4 (cloth : alk. paper)
ISBN 0–8191–9404–2 (pbk. : alk. paper)

The paper used in this publication meets the minimum requirements of
American National Standard for Information Sciences—Permanence
of Paper for Printed Library Materials, ANSI Z39.48–1984.

TABLE OF CONTENTS

APPENDICES

FIGURES

INTRODUCTION

This book is written by an experienced and trained city manager. This is not a rehash of academic subjects commonly found in collegiate public administration degree programs. Rather, it is focused upon those subject areas that the city official must deal with on a daily basis, the more practical aspects of public administration.

This book is intended as a reference for students of public administration, new city officials, both appointed and elected, and specifically for the new city manager. Although it is not designed to be all encompassing of the subjects and problems a public administrator will face, it is written to give the reader a flavor of practical public administration of a small city. A sense of humor is a vital ingredient for the successful management of a city and for one's sanity.

The text is divided among 27 chapters with individual chapters devoted to each of the departments that would normally be found in a city's governmental structure, i.e. the police, fire, water and street departments, etc. There are also chapters addressing such topics as advice to elected officials, personnel training, purchasing, budgeting, and public relations.

Aside from the text, a like number of pages in appendices are included to serve as models, samples, and/or idea-starting documents for the readers to put to use as they see fit. Sample ordinances, job descriptions, personnel policies, disaster plans and engineering specifications make up most of the appendices. There are also addresses of state/ city organizations and codes of ethics included as appendices.

This guide is designed to fill a void; there is no such text currently in publication. Students of public administration and all other new city officials need a practical reference source for the daily operations of their city. On the job training is great, but mistakes are sometimes costly; and oftentimes the mistakes cost the citizens the most.

References in the text to a council or commission are intended to be generic, i.e. completely interchangeable and could include selectmen, supervisors, aldermen, etc. References to city, town, and/or village are also intended to be interchangeable. Likewise, references to gender are intended to be asexual; any he could be a she, and vice versa.

MANAGING YOUR CITY OR TOWN

A REFERENCE GUIDE FOR
THE NEW PUBLIC OFFICIAL

PREFACE

This book is intended as a reference for students of public administration, new city and town officials, both appointed and elected, and specifically for the new city or town manager. Although it is not designed to be all encompassing of the subjects and problems a public administrator will face, it is written to give the reader a flavor of practical public administration. A sense of humor is a vital ingredient for the successful management of a community and for one's sanity.

Special thanks to Nancy Daniels who patiently served as my editor.

Dedicated to my wife and family: Candy, David, Greg and Trevor. Without their support this would not have been possible.

KGG

Chapter I

SMALL CITY GOVERNMENT -
AN OVERVIEW

The management and administration of any city government in our dynamic world are very complex challenges. A public administrator must have a broad and general understanding of every aspect of city government, as well as the services that government is to provide to the citizens. As a city manager, you need to know enough about every aspect of your government to represent that government to the elected officials and the citizens of your city, the press and your contemporaries. Because a city manager is a generalist, however, you also have to ensure your staff is knowledgeable and capable. The members of your staff are the technical experts; you must be able to rely upon them to handle the nitty-gritty details of their respective departments.

A city manager is a 'jack of all trades and a master of none.' The 'masters' are, or should be, the department directors. They should be masters of the jobs, duties and details of their individual departments; but they probably will know very little about any other department. This is where an effective city manager comes in; your job is to mold this group of technical experts into a team with one goal in mind - the delivery of the best possible services to your citizens at the lowest possible cost. If you can succeed in this goal, you will truly be a master city manager, a jack of all trades.

Depending on the size of your city, the geographical location and its proximity to other cities and their sizes, your city will have a certain personality. It may be a full service city that must deliver every traditional public service to its citizenry. It may be a city that delivers every service except electricity. Your city may be a suburb of a large metropolitan area, only delivering street maintenance and general administration to your citizens. Or, your city may fall anywhere in between.

Chances are, your city has been operating just fine without you for many years. That doesn't mean it has operated efficiently or that you cannot improve upon this operation and service delivery. It does mean that you should not walk in the door to your new employers acting as if you are the savior of their city government. You need to approach your new city, and its elected officials who hired you, confident that you can do a good job for them and yet humble enough to learn from them and the citizens what they expect of you. You can have the greatest revelation ever of how to better manage this city's government; but if the city is not interested in changing its method of operation, you had better sit on your revelation.

In the ensuing chapters I hope that you will find some technical information which will help you in the management and administration of your city. The appendices are as important as the chapters; there are several sample documents and idea starters that may help you help your citizens. I also hope that you will consider some of my philosophy that is offered in the text. I don't claim to have all the answers; but I do believe experience is the best teacher, and learning is a never ending process.

Although this book is targeted toward city managers, there is a great deal of information herein that can prove useful to elected officials, as well as appointed ones. It is very important for elected officials to take the time to learn about their city in particular and how their city fits into the overall scheme of government within their state. Because of the wide variations on these specifics, there is little I can say about this subject other than it is something that needs to be researched for each city in each state.

Some key questions that may help in this research are:

What forms of local government does my state recognize?

Does my city have a charter? Is it a standard charter shared with several other cities, or was it a special act of the state legislature?

Does my state recognize "Home Rule?" What exactly does "Home Rule" in my state mean? (In general terms, "Home Rule" means that a state allows a city to rule within its own corporate boundaries. The details of this concept vary widely from state to state.)

How often does the state legislature meet in my state?

How often do they change the laws affecting local governments?

Another area that both elected and appointed officials need to be very familiar with is the specific duties of each official within the city. If your city has a charter, these duties will be spelled out very clearly. Within a page or so of this charter you will know exactly what your duties are. By reading a few more pages, you can find what the charter states are the duties of the other officials within your city. If you do not have a city charter, hopefully there are still job descriptions written for each position in some form of official document. My experience has been that many hard feelings and interpersonal conflicts arise out of one or more officials usurping the duties of another official. This is in violation of the city charter or job descriptions. If everyone will take the time and the trouble to read and learn these different duties, perhaps some of these conflicts can be avoided.

Chapter II

YOUR MOST IMPORTANT JOBS

If you don't remember anything else that is in this book, remember that the single most important thing you can and should do as a city manager is to get involved and become a part of your city. If you can't do this, it will probably make you a much weaker manager in the long run. If you are not a 'joiner', get over it and join anyway.

Why should you get involved in your city? Because it gives you an independent base of support. It lets the citizens know that you have a mortgage to pay, children in school, a 'Honey-do' list at home, and all of the other problems they have facing them. I guarantee you, the contacts that you make by getting involved will reap you benefits ten fold.

If at all possible, live in your city. Whether you intend to buy a home or rent, do it in your city. There is a lot more to being a part of the city than just going through the motions. Be a taxpayer who pays a part of your own salary.

What should you join? Its really up to you and what you want to do. Do not join something just to join and then not show up at the meetings and activities. Joining means doing and getting involved!

I suggest you select a church within your city and attend regularly. When you attend, let the other church members know you are their city manager. Then, they will come to you with their problems and complaints, instead of your getting a nasty phone call from them, or worse, their calling one of your elected officials. Don't be boastful about being their manager. Remember, you are their public servant. They 'pay your salary.' You'll learn to hate this phrase, but they believe it. Often times I have felt like asking them if they want the 25 cents that they contributed refunded; but if you say that, it will come back to haunt you. If you can just exercise a little patience, soon you will not hear, "I pay your salary" from the people that know you and understand how hard you work.

Let me digress for a minute. If you do not intend to work hard at this job of being a city manager, you had better find another profession. You must be willing to be on-call 24 hours a day, 365 days a year. The only time you are not expected to respond is when you are not in town; and then, you had better have had the foresight to make your Public

Safety (Police and Fire) Dispatchers aware that you are not available. Tell them, too, what poor sucker, I mean subordinate, is standing in for you. The job of city manager is an all encompassing, completely consuming career. You must guard against it monopolizing all of your time. You need to spend time with your family and with the public. If, however, you think you can work from 9-5 Monday through Friday, go get another profession. I mean it!

Select some kind of civic group and join it. What's a civic group? (Don't ever be afraid to ask dumb questions; there are not any, just dumb answers.) Kiwanis, Jaycees, Lions, and Rotary are all considered civic groups; there are many others. You may want to visit all the clubs that meet in your city before you decide which one to join. You may already be a member of one in another city, and then it is just a matter of transferring your membership. From a scheduling standpoint, it has been my experience that it is best to belong to a group that meets for breakfast or lunch. You will find that many, many times your evenings are not your own; you may have to attend a meeting for your job on short notice. Consequently, your civic group meeting would fall by the wayside.

Select some type of youth program to assist, especially if your own children are involved. Maybe you can be a Boy Scout leader, a Girl Scout troop leader, a Little League assistant coach, or something to let the citizens see that you are an all right guy or gal. I recommend against taking on the load of the full-fledged coach or the Scoutmaster for the same reasons I do not endorse belonging to an evening meeting club; there are times that you are not going to be able to attend, and on short notice. If you want to build a great reputation with the parents who are tax paying and voting citizens, be the Little League Soccer Coach, call a practice, and then do not show up because you have to be in an emergency special session of the city commission. Then throw in, just for good measure, that none of your assistants happen to show up that night. You will become a very popular person in nothing flat. Your name will be on the lips of every parent in the area. Got the picture? It's not a good one.

When joining clubs/groups in your city, do not neglect membership in your professional associations. At a minimum, you should be a member of the International City Management Association (ICMA) [777 North Capitol Street NE, Washington, D.C. 20002-4201], and its state and regional counterparts. Furthermore, your city should pay for your dues to belong to this group. You'll find that apart from annual conventions, there are generally very few meetings to attend by belonging to ICMA. The important thing is that you will receive professional newsletters and magazines to help you stay current in this most dynamic of fields.

If you are interested in belonging to other professional groups, I would recommend that you check into the American Society for Public Administration (ASPA) and/or the American Society of Local Officials (ASLO). The American Management Association is another very fine organization, but it is very expensive when compared to the dues of these other organizations.

The next important job, next in this listing but equal in priority to the first job, is that you have to build a team. You must build a team between you and your commission/council including the mayor. Don't fall into the trap of the mayor's being a separate entity from the rest of the board. He is the chief elected official of the city and therein has certain privileges and responsibilities apart from the other board members, but he is a member of the commission/council as well. Anyway, the point is, he must be a part of your commission team.

You also must build a team of your entire staff. Teamwork is the best way to handle every problem. If you are not knowledgeable about a certain subject, I'll bet any money that someone else on your team knows all there is to know about whatever the subject might be - - a good reason for the team concept. Your staff team will have several smaller teams within the overall team. I cannot over stress how important it is for you to develop a team comprised of you and your supervisors and you must provide them an atmosphere in which they can learn, grow, succeed, and fail. (Yes, I said fail; and that doesn't mean they should be disciplined when they fail. You must evaluate each situation for the disciplinary action warranted, if any. If they never fail, how will they know how sweet success is?) Ask questions, give answers, be creative, become a planner, an organizer, a person of action, and perhaps most importantly, an evaluator. Furthermore, you must encourage your supervisors to develop a team within their own department/staff. At the same time all the city employees make up one large team to provide the best possible services to the citizens at the lowest possible cost.

You also must foster this team-like network between you and the citizens. Never discount the ability of the citizenry to sway the elected officials on any given subject. Also, do not underplay the importance that citizen volunteers can play in your city. I can assure you of one thing: if you have not developed a team with the citizens that fosters a volunteer program, there will not be many citizens volunteering.

Now would be a good time for you to take your first look at the Professional Codes of Ethics in Appendix J. As a City Manager, you have chosen a profession with high standards. Are you prepared to measure up?

Chapter III

PERSONNEL

A written set of personnel policies can keep a city, and its manager, out of a lot of trouble. There needs to be set, written procedures stating how certain given situations are going to be handled. Sometimes a court will order that a given policy be changed in a given personnel system but will not fine or otherwise punish the entity for the error in their personnel system. When no written system exists, however, there is an opportunity for attorneys to have a field day. To help you avoid this pitfall, I have included a sample of a merit plan and the ordinances to enact a personnel policy and a merit plan in Appendix C. Careful reading of Appendix C will provide very specific information on all aspects of handling your personnel.

A merit plan is a written set of personnel policies addressing virtually every normal predicament that might arise in a city government. I am certain there is at least one personnel problem in your city that has arisen and is not addressed herein. I have, however, tried to cover the most common problems. In addition to the personnel policies, a merit plan also deals with a logical system of awards for 'above the call of duty' job performance. This particular merit plan also includes an employee evaluation system.

When dealing with employee evaluations, it is of the utmost importance to understand that you must compare apples to apples and oranges to oranges. In other words, when deciding which city employees are going to get a merit salary increase this year, you have to compare employees against each other only if they have been rated by the same person (rater). The way I have used the enclosed merit system is as follows: (Pay attention; if used improperly, the whole system becomes a farce.)

If I had $ 20,000 in a given year to utilize for merit pay raises, I would divide that number by the total number of city employees. I then take this dividend and apply it to each department, multiplying it by the number of employees within that department, minus the department supervisor who was placed into a separate category with the other supervisors. These departmental totals then tell me how much money can be used for merit raises within each department, respectively. I subscribe to the philosophy that 5% is as small a pay raise as anyone ought to get, so the aforementioned totals may vary a little as to how much money is actually used in that department.

Then, the evaluations of all city employees are divided by department, with the supervisors being taken into a separate category and further divided by raters if there is more than one rater within a department. Your police and fire departments are probably going to have more than one rater; most others will not. The Merit Board then reviews the evaluations by department, and I explain to them that we have sufficient money within the department under consideration to give 'x' raises. In smaller departments only one raise is given, in larger departments three or four. The supervisors are all considered as one entity, getting the same weight as a separate department. With about twelve supervisors, we usually had enough money to give only two to three merit raises to supervisors. In some departments there may not be any one person that was evaluated as particularly outstanding. In that particular year in that department there may not be any merit raise given. In another department that may be entitled to three raises, perhaps in a given year there are four people equally outstanding; that department may get four merit raises that particular year, instead of the three it was ideally and mathematically allocated. The latter phenomenon must be watched closely so that it is not over implemented. It almost never can be implemented in the supervisory category in order to preserve the integrity of the merit pay raise system.

Another thing that needs to be considered with regard to general personnel policies is the maintenance of a file on every employee of the city, as well as retention of this file for a substantial period of time after the employee leaves the city's employ. In some states, employment records are permanent and may never be destroyed. Does your city have job descriptions for every job? Does your city have a related salary compensation plan?

You will note the enclosed merit plan covers a lot of different areas. I want to focus attention on some of them and encourage you to read the merit plan in its entirety, adapting it to fit your particular situation and city.

Safety is one of the most often overlooked areas of administering city government. In order to keep your employees safety conscious, and therefore cautious, you must continually preach and teach safety. Another method of keeping safety ever present in your employees' minds is doing an in-depth study and evaluation of every accident/injury that occurs in your city, judging whether and how it was avoidable, among other things. Disciplinary action against the employees involved may or may not follow; but having a formal employee-administered hearing on the matter and subsequently reporting on that hearing will do wonders to prevent this accident/injury from recurring. Review the section on the Safety Panel in the merit plan.

Every city vehicle that might have occasion to be stopped in a normal traffic lane on any street ought to have a flashing and/or rotary beacon as a part of its standard equipment. Now you know police cars and fire trucks/cars have rotary beacons as a matter of routine. But what about your sanitation department 'packers,' your water crew vehicles and your street department trucks? Every one of these vehicles is probably going to have to be in the traffic lane, slowing or stopping the flow of traffic in the normal routine use of the vehicle. As a safety precaution, the city should invest $50, or less, in an amber colored rotating beacon to be turned on when this vehicle is blocking traffic.

The men and women that work in and with those vehicles cited above, as well as many other employees within your city government, are also probably going to experience walking in and out of the traffic lane during their work. If they have access to, and are forced to wear, orange colored safety vests, the chance of their being hit by a passing motorist will be markedly reduced. I have found the biggest problem with these vests is making people wear them, once they are a part of the city's inventory. I believe the wearing of these vests can be instrumental in saving the life of an employee. You just have to communicate this importance to the employees involved.

You will also observe that the merit plan in the appendices identifies salary ranges by job title. A job title should be further defined by a job description. Sample job descriptions are provided in Appendix B.

A buzz word in municipal government circles today is 'risk management,' or 'reducing risk exposure.' This is particularly related to trying to reduce the city's liability risk, especially with respect to insurance risks and premiums. But it also addresses such areas as workers' compensation risks.

In other chapters I will point out that some departments are a risk to the city by their very nature; i.e., the police, certain aspects of parks and recreation facilities, sanitation workers, etc. One of your jobs as a manager is to reduce those risks through education of your employees and other means.

Sometimes you can transfer the risk to another entity. An example of this would be to contract out sanitation services, discontinuing the use of city employees in this role. (I will discuss this concept further in Chapter VII, Privatization.) The city, in such a move, has transferred any possibility of workers' compensation claims to the private company now contracting to handle collection and disposal of the citizens' garbage.

An alternative method is to retain the risk but manage it closely so that the actual risk is reduced. In this example, the city would still handle sanitation collection and disposal services performed by city employees; but the city would make the employees very safety conscious to reduce the possibility of one of them being injured.

Another tack is to eliminate the exposure. This is what some cities are doing when they close their parks and other recreation facilities. They are eliminating any possible liability claims against the city by eliminating access to the source of those claims.

Preventing the loss is a multifaceted tool for dealing with risk management. Perhaps a city can eliminate a part of the source for liability claims, thus preventing the losses hitherto experienced from that source. An example of this is removing asphalt in playground areas and replacing it with mulch. It is much more difficult for a child to be hurt from falling on a mulched surface as opposed to an asphalted surface.

Talk with your city attorney and your city's insurance carriers about what you can do to manage the risks within your city and thereby keep your insurance premiums down.

Another area related to risk management, and also related to personnel policies, is the possible violation of an employee's civil rights because of poorly written, or outdated, or nonexisting personnel policies. This is an area in which your city attorney can help you. You, as a city manager, need to stay abreast of court rulings that may affect your city and its employees.

One specific problem that comes to mind in this area is the way your city's personnel policies deal with a pregnant female employee. Does she get sick leave before and/or after her delivery? How do her doctor's orders interface with your personnel policies? Is this subject even addressed in your personnel policies? If not, you had better stop reading this, turn to the sample merit plan, and start drafting a change to your existing personnel policies.

Do you handle a married woman's personal problems differently than an unmarried woman's? If you do, you are asking for trouble. Do you hire an unmarried man with dependent children, but refuse to do the same for an unmarried woman? If so, you are asking for trouble.

Another problem that periodically arises in local government is determining who is allowed to speak to the 'press' and when. You should have such a policy in writing, and you should ensure that it is discussed and briefed to all of your employees on a periodic basis. For example, heaven forbid that this occurs, but for discussion purposes let's say a child dies in a car accident. You can bet the local TV stations are going to be there before you, as the city manager, even know about it. Now what happens when the police and firefighters start bickering and something like, "If you had gotten here sooner, he wouldn't be dead" slips out? The press will pounce on that like a bear on honey. Then that gets on the news. Then your elected officials see and hear the controversy. Your phone starts ringing off the hook. Later investigation by the coroner determines the child was killed on impact by the vehicle and no one after the collision could have done anything to save him. Does the press pick up on this report? Ten to one they do not! You're faced with a public relations scandal because your emergency services personnel "did not get to the scene quickly enough."

The proper response to this situation is: 1) No bickering on the scene among any employees. Any bickering will result in the participants being removed from the scene immediately by the ranking employee present. 2) Do not ever allow your people to publicly (within earshot of the press) jump to any conclusions. 3) Any statement sought by the press should be met with the 'canned response': "The Chief of Police will prepare a statement and read it at the Police Station as soon as possible, within an hour at most. Please go to the station and await his statement." (The press probably won't leave the scene; but as long as none of your employees will speak to the press, you have accomplished your goal.) 4) The prepared statement may be made by any one of a number of people that you and/or the elected officials have designated as being authorized to make press statements. It may be a department supervisor such as the Chief of Police; perhaps it is only the City Clerk or even the Mayor. Regardless of who it is, the initial statement should state the facts as they are currently available and advise the press "that more information will be forthcoming when we become aware of it." No conclusions should ever be drawn in an initial press release; conclusions that later prove erroneous can get the city into trouble. 5) If the situation is of such a nature that no official statement can be made at that time, then the official statement has to be, "No comment." There is nothing wrong with that, although the press won't be wild about it. The person making the release announcement can add that he will advise the press when he has information he can release. "But until that time, the City can make no statement on this matter." See also Appendix C, Section XVII. paragraph D, Restricted

Information and Sample Ordinance A, Appendix C, Personnel
Regulations, Section 1.05, Disclosure of Information.

You, as a manager, must be able to listen to and accept
constructive criticism from the citizens, and perhaps more importantly
from the elected officials for whom you work. That doesn't necessarily
mean that you have to change the way you do things, but it does mean
you need to honestly and open-mindedly listen to the way they feel it
ought to be done. More difficult than this, however, is that you also
need to be able to take this constructive criticism from your
subordinates. In fact, you need to foster an atmosphere within your city
organization that promotes this sharing of ideas and making
suggestions, even when the boss is the one handing out the directives.
Someday, someone is going to invent a better mousetrap. You must
allow them the opportunity to try, even when your mousetrap is the one
that is being redesigned.

Some cities have the unfortunate situation of having one or more
groups of their employees being represented by a labor union. I say
"Unfortunate," not because the union is there, but because the
employees felt that they needed a union to represent them and take care
of their needs and desires with respect to their relationship with the
city's management. That's you, or your predecessor. It is also the
elected officials and your department supervisors, but mainly its you -
the city manager.

You are the city manager. You are supposed to know your
employees. What kind of manager are you when your employees have
to go to an outsider to talk about what they want and need? Enough of
the guilt trip. My point is: If you do not have a labor union in your city
now, and if you take care of your employees in the annual budget go-
rounds with your commission/ council, and if you train your
supervisory staff to take care of your employees, you probably will
never have to wrestle with a labor union.

If you already have a labor union in your city, convince your
elected officials to hire an attorney especially for negotiating with the
labor union. Negotiation is a very specialized field that is best left to
experts. Generally, a labor union in the public sector is like oil and
water.

A big problem that all of us who are public entity managers need to
overcome is the misconception of the citizenry who believe
'government no longer delivers service'. Unfortunately, some citizens
really do believe this. This causes bad public relations in every sense of
the word. You and every city employee need to constantly provide

information and evidence (by actions and job performance) that your city's government is the best government in operation. Create a public awareness program to demonstrate to your taxpayers how many services they get in return for their small tax rate. This is important, lest we all end up wrestling with a 'Californian Proposition 13.'

Chapter IV

· ELECTED OFFICIALS

It has been my experience that the people who seek election to small city government offices generally have the most honorable intentions of wanting to serve their city and its citizens. I am not so naive, however, as to fail to acknowledge that some of these people seek office because of the inflation its gives to their ego to be elected by their fellow citizens. Be that as it may, the most important thing a city manager can do for elected officials is to be supportive of them and to provide them information before and/or when they need it, not after the fact. A good city manager anticipates problems and situations and does the necessary homework to prevent the embarrassment of him/herself and the elected officials.

By the same token, the most important thing that elected officials can do is to be supportive of their city manager, chief administrative officer, or whatever the title may be of the senior appointed official within their city. One of the key jobs of a city manager is to build a team with the elected officials. This team building is rather difficult, however, if the elected officials do not want to be a part of the team.

Most elected officials have some pet projects they would like to see the city adopt from time to time. City managers have this same affliction. The key is for no one to let these pet projects cloud their good judgment, nor get in the way of what is best for the citizens and ultimately the city. Many times elected officials will take potshots at the city manager or another elected official. The reason for these potshots may be any one of a number of things; but chances are, deep down, the 'shooting' elected official only wanted to ensure that he/she was getting press coverage.

The most successful cities I have seen are those in which personal differences are discussed 'behind closed doors.' As far as the press and the citizens are concerned, every elected official "loves" every other elected official in their city, as well as the city manager. And, the city manager "loves" every one of the elected officials. In any other arrangement, the ultimate losers are the citizens. Debate is important, and vehement debate allows everyone to know where each of the participants stands on the issues. But once the debate is over and a decision has been reached, it is time for everyone to take up the banner of that decision and support it for the overall good. If the decision turns out to be a bad one, address the issue in a professional, nonpersonal manner and get the decision changed. But don't fight the solution. When a decision has been made after open and honest debate, anyone who does not accept the decision is simply a poor loser. I do not mean to step on anyone's toes; but "If you are not part of the solution, you are part of the problem."

Some cities have partisan elections, and some do not. Regardless of whether there are partisan elections, some cities have primary elections in which candidates must be successful before they can seek office in the general city election. The best thing for a city manager to do concerning electoral politics is to stay completely out of them! Despite any personal feelings or friendships, city managers professionally can not afford to align themselves with any one candidate nor any one party. Whether the candidate or the party wins or loses, the city manager that involves himself in such a predicament is going to make enemies. A city manager must be able to serve any elected official who represents any political persuasion as long as that official has been duly elected by the necessary margin of the citizens.

Once the election is over, it is everyone's job to put the election aside and work for the common good of the city. Do not study the United States Congress as an example of how to put elections aside; many of the bills voted upon by the Congress are voted upon along party lines. Small city government can not afford to have decisions made along party lines, in my opinion.

I have seen a good deal of success realized by cities in which the elected officials work in concert with the appointed officials. Often times this takes the form of an elected official working closely with the city manager, or some other appointed official, in order to have some key project for the city come into reality. All the participants in such an arrangement must be careful, however, to not overstep the bounds of their respective jobs. For example, in a pure council-manager form of government, the city manager works for the council as a body, not for the mayor, and not for any one council person. All the other appointed officials work for the city manager. If the manager and a council person can work on a project without the mayor assuming, or worse stating, that the manager is doing favors for the council person that he/she wouldn't do for the rest of the elected officials, things will work great. If these fears of insecurity can not be overcome, then work between appointed and elected officials individually is virtually impossible.

The city manager must respect each of the elected officials, their jobs, and the work they are trying to do. At the same time, it is important for the elected officials to respect the appointed officials, especially the city manager, and the jobs they are trying to accomplish.

If this mutual respect exists and is verbalized, many problems will take care of themselves. If this mutual respect is absent, the city and each of the officials are in for a very difficult time.

Chapter V

TRAINING

Training is a very important and sometimes neglected part of any manager's job. If you are a city manager in a smaller city, chances are good that your city employees have only been afforded the opportunity for on-the-job training in their respective positions. On-the-job training is important and certainly necessary, but it should not be the end of training in local government.

For starters, your supervisors/department heads ought to be able to attend one-day supervisory classes/seminars. Check with local community colleges and your state municipal league organizations to see if such opportunities are offered. If not, try to prod them into making such classes available. You can bet your local industries send their supervisors to classes and seminars. Find out where, when and how. Your supervisors probably learned most of their supervisory skills from watching their supervisor and their manager. That is all well and good, but what about the short-range and long term planning? Have you ever watched your boss plan? Planning is something that often takes place only in the privacy of one's own mind. Your supervisors will get a tremendous amount of information, ideas and improved self-esteem by attending such a class once every six months or so. It keeps them fresh and growing. They will also make contacts with contemporaries in similar jobs in other cities/counties. These contacts are as important as the training itself. See also the Memorandum in Section XV. Paragraph F of Appendix C (City policy on educational expenses) and Section XX, Appendix C, Sections 10.01 C and D; and Section 10.04 B (Leave with pay to attend meetings and examinations).

Another form of on-the-job training that is sometimes overlooked is cross-training. Cross-training is the training of one person in another person's primary job. In job categories like the street department, cross-training is an every day and common occurrence for most of the jobs. How many people in your street department know how to run the street sweeper? If your answer is "Only one," you and your street superintendent are making a big mistake. What happens when the street sweeper operator goes on vacation, gets sick, or quits? Do you get the point? The same thing goes in every other job you have in the city.

If your clerical staff has a monthly/quarterly utility billing system, how many of them know how to do that? My experience has taught me that everyone on that clerical staff needs to know exactly how to produce every portion of the routine report process, including the city clerk. Additionally, the finance director and the city manager, yes, you, should have a general understanding of what it takes to operate the system, produce bills, the timing involved, the possible breakdowns or other SNAFUs (Situations Normal - All Fouled Up), etc.

Another example: if your city operates a water treatment plant or a wastewater treatment plant, how many of those departments' employees know how to operate that system and how to keep it operating? The answer might be only the department superintendent. Is that the right answer? No! Now you're getting the idea. Furthermore, in this last example, in order for your other water/wastewater department personnel to become state certified, they need to have some hands-on experience as to how their system works.

Once you get the internal department on-the-job cross-training going, then you need to consider if there are any departments wherein you should force the supervisors to cross-train across the normal imaginary department lines. For example, if only your shop/maintenance department personnel know how to sharpen lawn mower blades, chain saw chains, etc., I would encourage you to get your street department personnel cross-trained in these types of tasks. If you have a utility billing system, you should have the employees of your utility departments whose bills are actually being generated come into city hall and learn what happens to the information they collect out in the field. I am not advocating that each of your water technicians needs to know how to run the computer in order to make all the water bills print out, but I have found that the water techs, and especially those that work as meter readers, have a much greater appreciation and understanding for the job of the clerical staff once this little briefing and show-and-tell demonstration has taken place.

Another form of internal training that should occur in your city is that of leadership training for your leaders. Who are your leaders? You have to decide that. I would suggest that each of your department heads is a leader, as is their immediate subordinate, the assistant supervisor for each department. In the police and fire departments you have several people in leadership positions, everyone serving in a sergeant's position or higher and an engineer's position or higher, respectively. This leadership training may be conducted by you, the city manager, or you may pass it around among your supervisors with assigned subjects. You might even find some basic leadership skills classes/seminars being conducted in your local area.

After some basic leadership skills are taught (time management, scheduling, short-range planning, counseling, evaluating subordinates' job performance, and management styles), you might consider having each of your supervisors present a 15-20 minute class on what his department does and what current major projects are under way. You can have these classes in conjunction with your weekly staff meetings, one class per week. It not only teaches your supervisors about what is going on in the city, but it provides them an opportunity to polish presentation skills.

A sad but true training fact that you should consider, especially in smaller cities, is: How many of your city employees do not have a high school diploma or GED? If the answer is only one, you might consider giving encouragement to that one individual to go to adult education evening classes. Most commercial companies with this type of problem will pay for the tuition and/or books for an employee to complete this type of training. That is a decision you would have to make, in concert with your elected officials. My opinion is that this is money well spent. If, on the other hand, the answer is that several employees don't have a high school diploma, you need to take some drastic action to solve this problem. Improving the education level and abilities of your employees also improves the level of service delivery they are capable of making to your citizens. Everyone wins! See Appendix C, Section XX, Sample Ordinance A, Section 1.10 (Literacy tests).

Special job categories have special training needs. Water and wastewater/sewer department plant operators, police officers, and firefighters are examples of employees with such needs. If you as the manager of the city can help them satisfy these needs, you should do so. This help may only be providing them with a city-owned vehicle and gasoline to travel to and from classes. You may have a facility (community center) that you could provide the state/region to use to instruct these classes. This type of instruction, provided locally, will increase the probability of your employees attending the training.

In the conduct of any training, it is important to use effective and proven training techniques. Think about the different kinds of training you have experienced. The things that stick with you the most are those in which you were really involved. Hands-on and/or role playing techniques cause the participants to learn more and retain it longer.

Gimmicks, if well planned and executed, also aid in the learning process. For example, if you are teaching a select few individuals in your city how to handle a press interview, use a tape recorder and/or a video camera and recorder, conduct the interview and play it back. Let each interview be critiqued by everyone in the class. After doing this a few times, end the class by encouraging them to watch and/or listen to the news, trying to place themselves in the shoes of the interviewee.

Then have another class in a couple of weeks to check for retention and
improvement. If possible, keep the tapes from the first class and play
them back at the end of the second class. Hopefully you, and your
'pupils', will see a marked improvement in their handling of the
situation.

As an aside in this matter of handling press interviews, it is
important to look your best if you're going to be on television and to
sound your best at all times. Try to find out what the reporter is going
to ask you and rehearse your answers before going live. If a radio or
television reporter asks you a question during an actual interview that
he did not say he was going to ask ahead of time, you should beware of
dealing with this reporter in the future. Don't be afraid to respond by
saying, "I'm not prepared to answer that at this time" or something
similar. If you're going to be on television you should try to wear a pale
blue shirt, a conservative tie (if you're a male), and a navy blue sport
jacket/suit jacket. Chances are you will only be photographed from the
chest to the top of your head. Look directly into the camera when you
are speaking.

Another excellent use of the video camera and recorder is for the
fire department at the scene of a fire, preferably a practice burn on a
condemned house. Your senior fire officers can photograph the event,
then use it for critique and classroom training.

Can you think of other ways you can get more mileage out of one
training event?

Managing training time is very important. There are a lot of
problems generated by allowing one hour for training in a specific
subject and finding at the end of the hour that only half of the planned
material was taught. Plan your training time to the last detail. Make a
schedule of what subtopics need to be initiated and ended at what
times. Do not, on the other hand, discourage discussion and questions if
they are on the subject. What must be guarded against is tangential
subject discussion and 'war stories.' There is nothing wrong with
continuing a training session on a given subject to the next meeting, if
there is good subject oriented discussion and learning taking place.
There is plenty wrong, on the other hand, with having to continue a
class because you allowed nonsubject-oriented discussion to take over
the training session.

Physical and/or room arrangements are another important aspect of
training requiring advance planning and provisions. I am certain you
have been exposed to this type of suggestion before. If you want to
promote discussion, set the class up so the participants are sitting in a

circle. If you want to promote note taking, provide a desk-like surface. If you want to discourage discussion and primarily lecture on material, set the desks up in rows and lines, stand at the front of the room behind a podium and in front of a chalkboard.

Suppose your fire department training officer comes to you and advises that he is going to conduct a class on making the proper connections between a fire pumper and a water hydrant for the department's reserve firefighters. He wants to conduct the class in the classroom? What should you do? If he really wants the reservists to learn this operation, you might suggest that he conduct the training outside using hands-on teaching techniques with the related equipment. You might also suggest that he begin by having the task demonstrated by some regular duty firefighters, first at full speed, then again in slow motion as he narrates their activities to his class of reservists. Then he could use the regular (full-time) firefighters as assistant instructors to give the reservists hands-on training. The session could be closed by having the reservists demonstrate their skills in a timed test. I am not saying that you would necessarily ever be asked for your opinion in such a situation as described; but you might, and you should give some thought in advance as to how you would handle such an opportunity.

Sometimes you will be involved in a training class where you have problem participants. I hope these individuals are not your employees, but be that as it may. Problem participants are people who disrupt and/or detract from the training session. They probably do not want to be there and consider the particular subject matter a waste of their "valuable" time. Such participants must be dealt with quickly and effectively, or your entire training session will be undermined. One method of dealing with them is simply dismissing them from the class. This is not always feasible or practical. If you do use this as a solution, you still need to deal with the individuals later, teaching and discussing with them the finer points of maturity and consideration for others. Sometimes you can solve problem participants' problems by getting them intimately involved in the presentation process; perhaps they can serve as an example or demonstrator or become involved in some other manner. Asking them to explain their knowledge of the subject matter, and subsequently allowing the class to critique same, will also sometimes solve the problem.

Once a year, or so, I recommend that you get all of the employees into one room with you and listen to their complaints, concerns, suggestions and ideas. I am not certain this issue-area can be considered training, but it is an important aspect of managing. As a practical matter, it may be necessary to divide the employees into two groups; do it twice in order to provide the necessary coverage of police and fire services to the city as well as keeping the city hall's doors open and available, and so forth.

Anyway, listen to what your employees have to say. Answer those questions and concerns that you can; sometimes people are upset about something they don't understand. Once explained they are no longer concerned. Take notes. Promise to address the issues you can, and ask the elected officials to address those areas you can not. Then follow through! If you are doing your job as a manager, and consequently an advocate for your people (subordinates), you should get some of these concerns and issues brought up to you in your normal relations with them. If you keep yourself locked in city hall, you will not be able to get that pulse of employees' concerns.

Regardless, this annual bull session does a lot of good in clearing the air and letting the employees voice their sentiments. It is important that you preface the meeting by sincerely telling the employees that you want to know what they think; state that this is a 'no holds barred' meeting to find out what is on their minds. You must promise no retaliation for comments made, and then stick to your promise after the fact. You should also reiterate your position that you are always available to talk with each of them individually, if they would like to do this - - if, in fact, that is your policy.

You may want to structure these bull sessions so that the supervisors of the departments are not in the same meeting with their employees. If there is a supervisory/personnel problem, the absence of the supervisor at this session may be the fastest method for you, the manager, to learn about this. A section similar to 10.5.4, Appendix C, Section XX, Sample Ordinance B, Consultation with Employees, in the Merit Plan Ordinance legalizes this process.

Chapter VI

BUDGET

You probably have a basic understanding from your college budgeting classes of what a city budget is and how one is formulated. It is not (supposed to be) a yardstick to measure the performance of the city manager; although this is what it often becomes. A city budget is a tool to be used in operating the city. If you don't want your budget to become your performance yardstick, then don't adopt the philosophy that every budgeted appropriation has to be spent to the last penny. By the same token, if you see a need for a piece of equipment that will improve your city's efficiency and performance and you have money appropriated and available to purchase the equipment, do so. Or at least ask your commission/council to do so. Equipment is cheap when compared to labor; equipment is a one-time purchase, whereas labor is continual. If you can buy a piece of equipment that will save your clerical staff one hour of work each week, buy it. Inside of a year, you will have saved over a week's work.

You have to find out what the policy is in your city and your locale, what is accepted, and what is expected. My experience has been that once appropriated, the city manager can authorize/make those purchases for equipment and items costing up to a few thousand dollars. Major items, however, like a vehicle, should probably be officially voted on by the elected officials in one of their regular meetings. (Vehicles are generally purchased on state contracts, but it's important to have the official support of the commission/council when buying a vehicle. See Chapter VIII on Purchasing.)

Your city government may have several budgets within the city budget; or if you don't, perhaps you should. I am referring to enterprise funds. An enterprise fund is a specific department's budget that is designed to be totally self-sufficient. Certainly most city departments do not have the capability of having their budget so structured, but utility-type departments can and should be self-supporting.

Your city's water department is a prime candidate for an enterprise fund. Let's explore this concept in detail through the example of the water department. Your water department should generate sufficient revenues to totally and completely offset their expenses. In actuality, the water department should make a little more money each year than their expenses in order to allow for future capital purchases, both replacements and new.

If the water department has a fleet of eight trucks, chances are it needs to buy at least one replacement truck each year, retiring one currently in service. If your city is growing at all, it's very probable that your water department may need to add to its fleet in the next year or so. All these purchases should be paid for from the revenues generated by selling the water to your customers/citizens.

The water and sewer departments also have a unique fiscal requirement. They have major capital investments in their treatment plants and in their delivery or collection (pipes in the ground) systems, respectively. These departments, therefore, need to have separate capital replacement/improvement funds to keep these capital investments properly maintained, and to be able to build new, additional systems as the demand warrants.

Hopefully your city already has these separate funds established. If they do not, you need to establish these funds post-haste. You can call them whatever you like. They are a capital replacement type of fund that works like this: When someone builds a house or business building, he has to pay a 'tap fee' to the water utility and a separate fee to the sewer utility. These fees pay for the installation of the water meter in the water utility and allow the property owner to dump into the city's sewer collection pipes. This fee should be calculated by your engineer so that it pays for the cost of constructing the system.

If, for example, you have a water treatment facility that is approved/designed for 1,000 residential connections, your water tap fee should be calculated such that 1,000 of these tap fees would build a new water plant and place all of the delivery pipes into the ground to get the water to another 1,000 residences at some point in time in the future. Your engineer can make those calculations for you. You should have these calculations re-checked periodically in order to keep pace with inflation and some changing costs. This tap fee must be adopted by your commission/council, via an ordinance. (Any time you are dealing with money, establishing fees, taxes, etc., the legislation necessarily should be an ordinance.)

In some cases, you may have a water treatment facility built for your city by a developer. If a developer is going to build a subdivision, especially if it is located a little distance away from any current water treatment facilities you have (be they potable or sewerage), it is not uncommon for the developer to build the plant to service his new subdivision and then 'give' that plant (those plants, if he builds one potable and one sewerage) to the city. In actuality, and remember this, he is not giving the city anything. He is building a water treatment facility instead of having to pay tap fees for each house he connects on to your water or sewer system.

If this opportunity arises in your city, there are several things you must consider. First, the plans need to be reviewed and approved by your city's consulting engineer before a contract is ever signed, let alone a spade of dirt being turned. The new water treatment facility to be built must be connected into your current water or sewer system. A plant that is independent is going to cause you problems down the road. The new treatment facilities should be designed to complement those facilities you already have in the city, and they all should work in concert with each other. If this new subdivision is relatively small, the city may want to form some sort of TEMPORARY partnership with the developer in order to have the new treatment plant built larger than the developer currently needs, but big enough to aid in the city's overall water or sewer plan.

I am discussing this information in the budget chapter, because if it is not handled properly during the planning and construction stages, believe me, it will adversely affect your budget in the future.

When working with the budget, the first thing you must do is identify your sources of revenue and estimate the gross income you will receive from each of these sources. There is a tendency to work on the expenditures side of the budget, and then make the revenues fit whatever the expenditures are calculated to be. Although this may seem attractive at the moment, a little common sense will tell you that this is going to buy you big Trouble down the road; note the capital 'T'.

The most common source of revenue for local governments is real property taxes: that is, the tax people pay based upon what assessment is placed upon the land they own within your corporate limits. In actuality, it is the value of the land and any improvements thereon, most commonly a house. Property taxes are handled in many different ways, depending upon your state's legislation. In some states, the assessment is supposed to be the actual value of the property. I say, "supposed to be," because for a house just sold, the assessment will be the sale price. If the house has not sold for a few years, the assessment may be the last sale price, which may no longer be the real value of the building and property. Whoever the tax assessors in your locale are, they have the right, arguably the duty, to reassess a property that has not been recently sold to determine its fair and current market value. In some states, the assessed value of the property is based upon a percentage of the fair market value, for example 80 per cent. Many states have different exemptions available to property owners which lower the effective assessed value of the property and thereby lower the tax they pay. Examples of these are: homestead exemption, disability exemption, current mortgage exemption, etc.

In some states, the assessment of property is performed on a county basis by a state or county official known as the property assessor, the property valuation assessor, or some similar title. Sometimes this assessor is a subordinate of the county clerk. Sometimes assessors are elected officials. Sometimes they are appointed, in which case they are usually subordinate only to their appointer. Some states allow cities the right to have their own assessor or to utilize the services of the county-level assessor. Some states require the cities to pay the county-level assessor for utilizing his information, and other states provide that service to cities at no charge.

Often, states have the assessing official collect the taxes for the city, forwarding a tax revenue check to the city monthly, or so. Other states only provide information to the city, and the city is responsible for collecting its own taxes. Since property taxes probably comprise between 20% and 90% of your budget, you need to find out what your city's particular system is and your part in the process.

While we are on the subject of tax revenues, I am going to digress briefly and discuss property taxes in some detail. Property taxes are generally called 'ad valorem taxes,' Latin for according to the value taxes. Property taxes are payable annually, at some fixed date. Usually a discount is offered if the tax is paid 'early,' but after the tax bills have been sent out. A penalty is added if the tax is paid after the fixed date. Interest is generally added to the amount of the tax and the penalty, compounded monthly, for every month the tax continues to go unpaid. Many cities file liens against the property and property owner for unpaid taxes.

A lien is a legal device that effectively "clouds" the title of property, so that that parcel of property can not be sold without the lien being satisfied, i.e. paid off and subsequently released by the city that filed the lien. (Sometimes attorneys do not do a complete or thorough title search, and a property is sold without the lien being satisfied. This is not supposed to happen. If it does, however, the city still has a lien against the property; and in fact the new owner has bought property with a 'clouded' title.) Liens are not foolproof. The property retains the lien against it, regardless of who the owner is. So, if your city files a lien against the property, you are ultimately going to get your tax paid with penalty and interest. You should also seek from the property owner the lien filing and release fee that your city paid.

If your city files a lien against parcels of property with outstanding taxes due, I would discourage your city from allowing the attorney for the city to file suit against the delinquent property owners in order to collect the lien. Unpaid property taxes entitle the city/county to file a foreclosure law suit against the property owner in most states. Civil lawsuits are very expensive; chances are any money the city gained from a court's finding against the property owner, would be offset by money owed to the attorney for the city for his time. If, on the other hand, a bank or other mortgage company files suit against a property owner as a part of their foreclosure, the city will probably be named as a codefendant in the suit; this is OK, as it is necessary for the city to be so named in order to collect the outstanding taxes due. This position of codefendant should not cost the city any legal fees.

As I mentioned above, property taxes are payable annually. It is, therefore, the duty of the owner to ascertain the amount of the tax owed and to make payment. In most states this has been interpreted to mean that the city/county technically does not have to notify the property owner that a tax is owed, nor how much the tax is. The city/county should make every effort to provide this information to the owner; but in the case of 'lost mail' or absentee property owners, the law is on the side of the city/county.

Most property tax assessments are as of January 1st of the current tax year. This means that for a house under construction on January 1st, the assessment on that particular piece of property may be for the value of the land only. The house might be finished by March but will not be reassessed until next January.

Once assessed, it probably will not have a tax levied on it until the following April, or later. Consequently, a city may not realize any tax revenue off of a house until 12-18 months after it is constructed. This is a real problem when you consider that your city must deliver services (police, fire, street maintenance, perhaps garbage collection if it is tax supported, etc.) for a year or more without receiving any tax revenue in exchange for these services. What do you do about this problem? That's a good question. Some cities have initiated impact fees for just this reason. Most cities, unfortunately, take no action, other than delivering the services without receiving revenue for same.

Another term related to property tax is millage or millage rate. The millage is the rate at which the actual property tax is calculated. For instance, if a house and property are assessed at $100,000.00, the tax will be calculated using that assessment and the millage rate. The millage rate may be, for example, $0.43 per $ 100 of evaluation. In the example before us, the ad valorem tax owed would be $430.00. It is important to bear in mind that your city will have one millage rate; but your citizens will also have to pay a millage rate to the school board, to the county, as well as perhaps the state, one or more special taxing districts, and so forth. So, the tax rate of your city is not the whole picture.

Several different variables will impact the taxation structure within your city, not the least of which are the feelings of your elected officials. You may have, or need, several revenue sources in addition to property taxes. Most of these sources are controlled by state legislation, inasmuch as cities must be given the right to utilize these sources by state enabling legislation. If your state has 'Home Rule' legislation already in place, additional taxing authority legislation may not be necessary. Talk with your city attorney or league of cites to be sure. By way of information, however, I want to give you a partial listing of such revenue sources. If your city has more needs than your current revenue sources can supply, you may want to discuss the possibility of using some additional revenue sources that your city does not already have in place.

Revenue Sources
Personal property taxes
Utility company franchise fees;
     these might include electric, natural gas,
     telephone and cable television companies.
     (See the end of the Privatization Chapter.)
Utility company sales taxes
Occupational or business licenses
Payroll taxes
City sales tax, piggybacked on state's sales tax
Alcoholic beverage sales licenses
City license fees/taxes for automobiles
Insurance policies taxes
Building permit fees (Generally should be encumbered only to
     support the operation of the Building Department.)
Zoning fees (Generally should be encumbered only to support the
     operation of the planning department.)
Fines and forfeitures (This one can cause headaches, if not used properly. Encumber these revenues to pay for police officer training, or something specific that is not going to impact upon the budget regardless if many or few are collected. Don't make it seem you have to have your police go out and write tickets in order to make your budget work!)

Impact fees (designed to make growth within the city pay for itself.
    Revenues from these fees must be encumbered and an exact
    audit trail maintained.)
Street light taxes or assessments
Hydrant fees
Parking fees; not to be confused with parking fines.

I have not addressed the issue of intergovernmental revenues. You
probably studied about these in your budget classes as well. The classic
intergovernmental revenue was Federal Revenue Sharing monies. This
program was retired in 1986. Your state may have gasoline or cigarette
tax revenue sharing, or other sources. Sometimes revenue sharing has
strings attached; i.e. gasoline tax revenues must be spent on road and
drainage work only. Other revenue sharing does not.

I also have not addressed grant monies. Grants are, in many ways,
almost a thing of the past. Some cities are still quite successful at
getting grants for special projects, but most are not. The big reason is
that all governmental entities are having to tighten their belts. This is
not to say that you should not try to get a grant from your state or from
the 'Feds' if there is some program or project your city needs and grants
are available for it. A common grant currently available is for the
codification and safekeeping of small city government ordinances and
records. Another common grant in some states is the fluoridation of
your city's potable water supply. Talk with your state's municipal
league and your contemporaries. You will soon see if there are any
grants currently available for which your city may qualify. If you
studied Community Development Block Grants (CDBGs) in school as
a classic grant, that is generally a 'used to be.' CDBGs still exist, but the
restrictions and strings are such that it is very difficult for a small city
to qualify. You should know, however, that there are many private
foundations which offer grants for different projects and programs. If
you have something you think a private foundation might be willing to
support, you should pursue a grant inquiry with them. The worst they
can tell you is no.

Target Budgeting is a tool and a 'buzz word' of the budgeting
process. It is also referred to as program budgeting. You hopefully
studied target budgeting in your budget class as well. If you didn't, you
need to become familiar with it. Target budgeting is a process by which
you pay for major, if not capital expenditures by allocating monies for
that purchase/project over a period of years. Thus, the city is paying for
things through an internal savings account, as opposed to borrowing
money to do so. An example might be the purchase of fire trucks. For
example, you may target budget fire truck purchases so that you can
buy a new engine/pumper every five years, retiring the one in service.

When retiring vehicles from your city service, however, do not neglect the possibility of selling this equipment to another city less fortunate than yours or even selling the equipment at public auction. These little sources of miscellaneous revenue help out over time.

Pooled financing is a relatively new concept generally touted by the state city league. It is a very sound process of taking the borrowing needs of several cities and combining them into one large package. Financing for a larger package is much more marketable to investors than are the smaller ones. If your city has a need to borrow a large sum of money for a capital project, check with your state municipal league to see if they have such a program in effect and what the next timetable for it will be.

If you decide to borrow money from one of your local banks, you should know that you can do so at markedly reduced interest rates because your city government is tax free. Consequently, the bank does not have to pay any tax on the money loaned to you, so you shouldn't have to pay that extra finance charge to the bank.

Bonding is another method for a city to borrow money in order to fund a capital project. The pooled financing programs mentioned are a form of bonding. If, on the other hand, your city wants to do its own bonding, the best advice I can give you is to have your elected officials hire an experienced and good bond attorney (a specialist, yes, in addition to your regular city attorney), and perhaps a special bonding agent from a financial company. If you need to bond, I strongly encourage you to check out your local league of cities' pooled financing capabilities first. It will save you time, money and headaches.

If you have the luxury of not needing to borrow any money, you may in fact have a surplus to invest and thereby earn additional money for your city. Investments can be very tricky. Investments of taxpayer dollars can be even more tricky. If you have money to invest, discuss this issue with your elected officials and get their thoughts and directives on how and where to invest the money. As a practical matter, your finance director, or treasurer, is probably going to do the actual investing, but the city manager has the ultimate responsibility for this investment, as directed by the legislative body. I have found that federal securities, such as Treasury Notes and Treasury Bills, are the safest investment for public money. Beware of funds, even GNMA Funds. (GNMA stands for Government National Mortgage Agency. GNMAs are certificates sold by the government to fund a group of existing mortgages. The bearer of a GNMA receives interest payments on these mortgages.) If you purchase, and actually receive a GNMA Certificate that is one thing. If you buy into a GNMA pool, or Fund, you may be buying trouble. Some unscrupulous investment brokers have been known to sell more of a GNMA pool than actual GNMA Certificates exist. When this occurs, the money you have invested is unprotected.

When investing it is also important to consider how long a period your city can afford to have the money invested. Some investments include a penalty if the money is withdrawn ahead of a specified timetable. This is not a problem with federal securities. Although they have a specified maturity date, they can be bought and sold virtually at will; they are very 'liquid investments.'

As a manager, you should also be concerned about the amount of cash the city has available, and more importantly, where and how it is maintained. The cash flow of your city may, at times, cause the city to have more than $100,000 in the checking account. The point here is, under the Federal Deposit Insurance Corporation (FDIC), the money of any one investor is only insured up to $100,000, should the bank fail. I am not, by any means inferring that the local bank in which the city maintains its checking account is in danger of failing. But, as a matter of protecting taxpayer dollars, it is very prudent to keep the cash on hand below this $100,000 threshold. If this is not a feasible for your city, due to its size and routine demands upon checking account assets, the city can force the bank to pledge certain securities that the bank owns, as collateral for the city's money. The bank may not be real happy about this request, but you will be assured that the taxpayers' money is fully protected.

Beware of 'budget busters'. Budget busters are those items that exceed the appropriation that your legislative body allocated for them. In the mid-1980s, one budget buster was the insurance premium to renew a city's policy. Often times the construction project underway in your city is a budget buster. Sometimes professional consultants are budget busters, the engineer or the attorney for the city. It is not easy, but it is your job to keep a close eye on these things. Control them if and when you can, but report their current status at your elected officials' regular meeting, routinely. Very little will hurt you more, as a manager, than to report to the legislative body that a particular expenditure item in the budget has markedly exceeded its appropriation, unless you have kept the legislators informed right along that this was going to happen, or was getting close, or had just happened and it was just a question now of how big it was going to get.

While discussing this problem of budget busters, let me discuss the process of the budget structure. Most states require that your budget be published in a certain form in the local newspaper before it is adopted and/or before the budget becomes effective. This publication should be

accomplished in the broadest terms possible, because this publication is
your 'official' budget and because publication charges are calculated by
size. See the budget ordinance in Appendix A, Section I.

As you put your budget together, you will probably calculate your
expenditures by individual line items, or by project. Your budget may
be over 100 entries long before you are able to arrive at a budget total.
If you publish this entire listing, your publication costs are going to be
astronomical, conservatively speaking. Furthermore, if any single line
item within that budget is exceeded, you must then adopt a new
ordinance amending the original budget and republish the amended
budget.

If, on the other hand, you officially adopt a department-level
budget, you may only have six or ten entries therein. Each entry is
actually a subtotal of several other entries. Your publication costs are
decreased, and the chances of exceeding any published subtotal are
decreased. Still, if you would exceed one of these published subtotals,
your state law probably requires you to adopt a new budget ordinance
amending the original budget ordinance, and you would also have to
publish this amended ordinance.

Your line item, or project line budget is an important tool, but it
should be used as an informal in-house tool and not an official tool. If
your elected officials want to have their periodic review by line item,
this is not a real problem. I just think it safer and more economical for
the official budget to be a functional summary budget, and not a
detailed, monstrous document that will cause more problems than
necessary.

Recall that a few minutes ago I mentioned how insurance
premiums were sometimes budget busters? Many states responded to
this by legislation allowing their respective city leagues to implement
pooled insurance programs. These pooled insurance programs operate
in a similar fashion to the bonding programs mentioned earlier. There
are often several different insurance pools within one league of cities.
For example, there may be a health insurance pool, a liability insurance
pool, a workers compensation insurance pool, and an unemployment
insurance pool. Your city, if it is a member of the league of cities, may
be entitled to participate in one or all of these pools. My experience
with these pooled programs has been very good and a big cost saver. I
recommend you look into these programs if your city is not already a
member.

One sizable problem facing city managers and city finance
directors is that of knowing exactly how much money the city currently

has. One method of solving this problem is the use of purchase orders & encumbrances. Purchase orders are a set process whereby nothing in your city can be ordered, nor bought, without a purchase order form being completed and approved, processed and posted to the financial accounts. The approval may only need to be made by the department head, but it necessarily allows the city to make this entry into their financial system. This entry then becomes an encumbrance. An encumbrance is a lock on a certain sum of money, as if this money has already been spent. In effect, it ear marks this specific sum of money for the specific purpose identified in the purchase order, and it can not be spent for any other purpose. If your city does not have such a system in place, I highly recommend that you work closely with your finance director and try to implement one. It will not be easy, and it will take a lot of training of your subordinates; but it will provide you with better information. The lack of this purchase order and encumbrance system is akin to writing a check from your checking account and then taking all the money out of the bank before the check gets to the bank. Now do you understand?

Preparing your city's budget for presentation to the legislative body is, and should be, a lengthy process. It is, however, only part of the process. Your elected officials must have time to review this document, question you and/or your department heads about requests, and enact the budget ordinance, once they are satisfied with a final product. I thought a budget timetable might be useful to you. Generally, key dates within this time-table are set by state legislation or local ordinance. By taking those dates, and the effective date of the budget, you can work backward and establish a timetable with specific sequence dates so that you don't get caught without enough time to do your job.

Figure 1. Timetable for Preparation of
Municipal Budgets

Completion Date

_____ 1. Collect budget input from department heads, elected officials and others.

_____ 2. Prepare proposed budget. Forward it to the legislative body for them to review with the "budget message."

_____ 3. Schedule any required "Proposed Use Hearings", preferably in conjunction with a commission/council meeting. Publicize the date, place and time of this hearing.

_____ 4. Schedule a work shop session for your legislative body to work on the budget, if desired.

_____ 5. Conduct public hearing(s).

_____ 6. Have the first reading of the budget ordinance. (May need to publicize in advance, depending on your state's legislation.)

_____ 7. Have the second reading of the budget ordinance. (May need to publicize in advance, dependent upon your state's legislation.)

_____ 8. Publish budget ordinance with notice of availability of budget summary for public inspection added to the bottom of the ordinance. (This advertisement may need to be accomplished prior to the second reading of the budget, depending on the laws in your state.)

_____ 9. If you have to amend your adopted budget at any time during the year, or at the end of the year, several steps within this process will have to be repeated, to include but not necessarily limited to, steps # 6, 7, & 8.

_____ 10. After the budget has been used for the year, your city's records will probably have to be audited, to comply with your state laws. If you are required to be audited, you will probably have to publish the audit or a summary thereof in the local newspaper, once the audit has been presented to your city's legislative body.

The budget message is your cover letter generally explaining the big picture of this proposed budget, including the major program goals. This budget message may be a letter from the mayor to the other elected officials, rather than from you. You should follow the precedents that have been established, and considered the desires of the people involved, as well as the duties set forth in the city charter.

Chapter VII

PRIVATIZATION

Privatization is another current buzz word. It simply means changing traditional governmental services from being delivered by the city government to having those services delivered by a private contractor. A common example of this is the way many cities have gotten out of the garbage collection business. The garbage within their cities is now being collected by a private contractor. Sometimes such arrangements are still funded through tax dollars, while other times the city is removed from the picture completely; each property owner must contract with the garbage contractor individually to remove and dispose of the garbage from their property.

Privatization is done for any number of reasons. Sometimes a city is too small to make owning its own equipment feasible or practical. For instance, a city of 2,500 citizens probably is not large enough to own their own garbage packer trucks and to do their own garbage collection. Primarily, this is because it would not take a full work week for one truck to collect this much garbage. What would the garbage department employees do for the rest of the week? This is similar reasoning to very few cities owning their own street paving equipment; they just don't use it enough to justify owning it. Its much more economical to hire a paving company the one or two times a year that the city is going to perform resurfacing projects.

Sometimes privatization is used to augment city forces, for instance, to put in a new water line. If it is a very small job, the city's water crew can probably do it easiest and fastest. If the line is of any consequence, it will be done much more quickly and efficiently by a contractor. Technically, this is an act of privatization.

Sometimes privatization is done to transfer the city's risk to another entity, thereby getting the city out of the business and away from the liability risk. An example of this might be some aspect of the parks or recreation process. Several cities owned golf courses a few years ago. Since the insurance crisis of the early 1980s, these golf courses have been sold to private entities, usually a citizen board created to purchase the golf course in order to keep the golf course open. Swimming pools have been treated similarly in some communities.

Some people (citizens) believe that government is, by definition, inefficient. Their argument, therefore, is that private industry always can deliver a service to the citizens more cheaply than can the government. Sometimes this is true, only because of the nature of government. What I mean is, a private industry can come into a city, providing a service to the citizens but paying their employees minimum wage, or barely above, with little or no benefits. No one complains that the privately owned business is not taking care of its employees! Let a city government pay some of its employees minimum wage, however, and everyone is up in arms that "the employees are being taken advantage of," etc. Given this example, one can easily see how a private industry could come into a city and deliver a hitherto traditional city service at a cost below what it would cost the city to deliver that same service.

If, on the other hand, all things are equal, the city should be able to deliver the service at the same or a lower cost than the private industry. If the city can not, there is a management problem. Cities are tax exempt, so there is one break private industry does not have. Cities are only supposed to break even when providing services; whereas private industry has to make a profit, or their owners/stockholders will be quite irate.

We must also consider that some forms of government services are quite unique. Most services are provided by private industry because the private industry sees that they can make a profit. Cities, on the other hand, deliver some services because they are for the common good and there is no profit to be made from delivering this service. Consider how much profit could be made from the money spent on repaving a street, or having a fire department, or a police department.

This is not to say that we, in government, can not learn some things from private industry. Sometimes we can deliver services more efficiently than we are currently by looking at the management of that service from an objective viewpoint.

Cities can often substitute volunteers for paid city employees in some positions, thus reducing the costs to tax payers; for example, a city hall receptionist might be a group of volunteers, one of whom works each regular work day at no cost to the citizens. If you have a volunteer program, you should ensure that you have some type of annual recognition program to thank the volunteers for their assistance. Perhaps presenting them with a special pen or desk set with the city crest on it, or something like this, just to let them know their work is appreciated.

Another method of reducing taxpayer costs is by encouraging self-help and/or do-it-yourself type projects. Some cities have a program where the city buys paint for citizens to paint the water hydrants in their neighborhoods periodically. A central collection point for recycling newspapers would reduce the amount of garbage collected and the lower cost of disposing of this extra weight, is another example.

Some communities have retired executive programs through which retired business executives are available as consultants at no cost.

Make no mistake; government is a monopoly. This does not mean that you need to be dictatorial and unfeeling. Your citizens are customers of many different city services. The fact that they cannot seek these services from elsewhere, short of moving out of your city, should not be a consideration on your part. You should provide the best possible service at the lowest possible cost, attempting to keep as many citizens happy with those services as possible.

Because of the nature of government, when things go wrong some citizens look to the government to fix them, even when the government is not really involved. An example of this might be the delivery of cable television service or electrical service. Your city may not be involved in either; but if the citizens get upset with the cable television company or the electric utility company, guess whom the citizens will call. The city hall! One method of keeping the city involved in the delivery of these noncity services is by having a franchise program.

By forcing utility companies that deliver services in your city to negotiate and 'buy' a franchise from the city, the city has influence over the utility company and can become an advocate for their citizens in disputes. Franchises are generally contractual agreements between the city and the utility company lasting several years. Each year, the city receives a franchise payment, or series of franchise payments, from the utility company in exchange for the utility company's right to operate within the city. These franchise payments are generated out of the company's revenues, often treated like a tax by the company and therefore are in fact paid for by their customers who are your citizens. Without a franchise agreement, however, it can be argued that the city does not have as much influence over the utility company and therefore can not 'protect' the citizens from the utility company.

Chapter VIII

PURCHASING

Your state probably has some formal bidding law on the books, governing bidding requirements when dealing with public monies. This law will state that if your city is going to purchase some object or service that is going to cost, or might cost, more than a given amount of money, perhaps $7,500.00, your city is required to advertise in a newspaper for and accept bids from anyone who wishes to deliver this product or service to your city. This advertisement must include the specifications for this product or service, or directions as to how those specifications can be obtained if said specifications are too lengthy to be published with the advertisement. This advertisement must also state the final date and time after which no bids will be accepted and when such bids are going to be opened in public and read.

This process, obviously, is very structured, but it is not difficult. I recommend conducting the public opening of the bids prior to the meeting of your commission/council, so that you/your staff can review the bids submitted and make a recommendation to your elected officials, concerning the bid. Generally, the low bidder is awarded the contract to deliver this product or service to your city, unless your review indicates that this particular bidder is not capable of providing same, or has had problems in providing same to other governments, or some other negative reason(s) why the low bidder should not be awarded the contract. The contract may, or may not be a written agreement, dependent upon the complexity and longevity of the bid award and the desires of your city. The staff's review of the bid submitters should include checking with references supplied to the city by the bidders prior to arriving at a recommendation.

The only exception to the above bidding requirements occurs when the product you are desirous of purchasing for your city has already been bid and approved through your state purchasing office or a GSA contract. A GSA contract is a contract negotiated by the federal government's General Services Administration for a specific product to be purchased by a federal governmental agency at a specific price. Such items as vehicles and office equipment (typewriters and calculators) have often been negotiated in advance by federal purchasing officials. Items similar to those, as well as computer systems and other commonly used items, have often been negotiated through the GSA. If you are considering making such purchases, check with vendors to see if they have a GSA price already in place which you may use. Your state should supply you with a list of the items already negotiated by them and a list of the vendors available to deliver that product. If your city doesn't already have such a file, talk with your state's office for local government liaison, and see if such a list exists. Oftentimes, this list is maintained on microfiche and updated very regularly, monthly or even more frequently.

Another avenue available for purchasing equipment is that of state or federal surplus property programs. Check with your state to find out more information. In such a program, you really have to look at the equipment to be purchased. Sometimes it is used, so well used that it is not worth much. Other times, this is equipment that has been confiscated or never actually used, and it is in excellent condition. Some equipment, such as desks, can be used by someone else, and then used by your city; there is nothing wrong with them at all. By participating in such a state or federal program, you can save your city a great deal of money in equipment costs. You should know that many of these programs require you to keep the equipment in use in your city for a specified time after you purchase it from the surplus program.

Many states have laws that require public entities and agencies such as city governments to maintain an inventory of the public property owned and used by the city. This inventory is required to be updated periodically and checked to be sure equipment has not been lost. A vehicle would certainly not be lost without someone noticing it, but a tool box full of expensive tools very well might not be noticed. Common sense tells you that inventory inspections are important. State law may require it. Generally accepted accounting principles (GAAP) do require it.

An inventory list is made up of the fixed assets in your city. There is generally a cutoff dollar figure (maybe $200.00); items that cost less than the cutoff amount are not placed on the inventory. You may consciously decide that a specific item that does not meet this cost test should be placed on the inventory any way, if it is something highly pilferable or otherwise important; your official city seal is an excellent example. Auditors and other CPAs are generally experts on inventory procedures. Talk with your finance director and the last independent auditor that looked at your city's books to get their input on the state of your city's inventory system.

You may wish to implement an identification sticker system that would ease your periodic inventorying work. These stickers are commercially available from many companies and list your city's name and a specific number. Each number then becomes equal to a given piece of equipment. You may want to assign a series of numbers to a given department, thus aiding you in returning equipment to its rightful department when it inadvertently becomes separated. If you elect to implement a sticker program, it is important that you follow through with this sticker program each time you purchase some new piece of equipment. Otherwise, you may put equipment into use without getting it on the inventory. When this occurs, the equipment might be stolen; without it being on the inventory, no one would ever miss it.

Centralized purchasing of commonly used items (office supplies being one general category) can save your city a tremendous amount of money. Purchasing in large quantities, purchasing from proven, less expensive vendors, and planning in purchasing saves money, too. If you are going to need a case of file folders to redo the files at the end of the year, you should purchase them in advance, at sale price if possible, and in the largest quantity feasible to save your city the most money. If, on the other hand, you run down to the drug store to buy as many file folders as they have, then to the grocery, and then to ..., you will not be saving as much money as you might by buying what you need in quantity from the big discount warehouse.

Chapter IX

PUBLIC RELATIONS

As I have alluded to several times thus far, public relations are very important to your city and consequently to you as the city manager. It is not enough for you to do a good job; nor is it enough for your employees to do a good job. The citizenry, the public, has to perceive that you are doing a good job in order for the loop to be complete. Unfortunately, there are those, not just in local government, who have such a knack with the public that the public perceives they are doing a great job, even when they are not. I am sure you have had some classmates or acquaintances that fall into this category somewhere along the line. My goal has always been to do an excellent job for the citizens and to try to let them know I am doing a good job.

As I have also mentioned before, one way of keeping a good public perception of the city staff is to keep the elected officials happy, informed, and looking good to their constituents. Don't overlook this important aspect of public relations.

Other important things have also already been mentioned: Looking good in front of the television camera, participating in civic clubs, and generally communicating with the citizens of your city. As a public employee, you are being evaluated everywhere and every time you are seen. Try to always put your best foot forward, and some of these other suggestions will naturally fall into place.

I have found that most citizens who take an interest in their city government feel more comfortable, and therefore are easier to please, when they know what their city is doing and how their tax dollars are being spent. I am aware that the state law requires you to publish your city budget and the auditor's report, but you need to share more than that with the citizens. Some citizens, frankly, don't read the 'stuff' in the legal notice section of the newspaper and might not understand it if they did.

If you have a weekly newspaper serving your city and/or the general area, you may want to contact the publisher or editor to see if they would allow you to have a weekly or biweekly column in their paper. In this column, you could tell your citizens what your city is doing, what projects are being considered, decisions made by the commission and projects currently under way. You should not write this column as a reporter, nor should it be a rehash of your last commission/council meeting, but rather an informational and unofficial report of the current status of your city.

If a cable television company serves your city, it may be possible to negotiate, as a part of the franchise agreement (see the end of budget chapter), having the regular commission meetings televised and aired on one of the cable channels. With or without this cable television coverage, the informal newspaper column cited above could prove most beneficial.

Many cities are publishing quarterly or monthly newsletters delivered to each residence and business within the city to accomplish this same purpose. If your city is a smaller city within a larger metropolitan community, this may be a more viable alternative than a column in a big newspaper that services literally hundreds of small cities. If you and your elected officials decide this is the way to go, it is important that the format and the image you produce and convey to the citizens is what you want it to be. Don't send out a hand drawn logo on a poorly reproduced cheap white paper, or that is exactly the image the citizens will associate with their city. By the same token, you don't need to spend a fortune on printing and typesetting. Computer assisted desk-top publishing programs produce an excellent 'typeset' product. A good quality copy machine with some better than average paper stock will result in a high quality piece of work for you to distribute to your citizens. This extra effort will produce a product of which everyone can and will be proud.

Another important aspect of public relations in small city government is the manner in which your employees respond to the citizens. You must train the city employees to know who their boss really is. Is it the mayor, the commissioners, the city manager (you)? All of these people are their bosses, but technically every citizen is their boss, too. City employees know that the elected officials have a big say in determining their pay, benefits, etc. City employees in a manager-council form of government know that they work for the city manager, who in turn works for the elected body. But city employees tend to forget that they, and their bosses, work for the citizenry. You need to constantly remind them of this. See Appendix C, Section XX, Sample Ordinance A, Section 1.07 (Code of Conduct [For Employees]).

When a citizen flags a city truck down on the street and inquires when the city is going to fix the hole in their backyard made by a problem in the drainage ditch, the city employees in that truck need to ask the person's name, phone number, and address. The employees need to find out if the citizen has reported this problem before and assure the citizen that they will see that corrective action is taken.

Then, those employees need to report this to their supervisor who needs to report it to the street (drainage) department supervisor. The street supervisor needs to go out to the site, assess the problem and have the hole fixed, assuming it is in fact an actual fault of the city caused by a flaw in the drainage design. (The fact that the city employees flagged down by the citizen are not from the street department should not have any impact on this process. The same steps should occur.) All this time, the street supervisor needs to be keeping in contact with the citizen generating the complaint, apologizing for the inconvenience, and informing the citizen of the corrective process under way. Technically, if all your employees and subordinate supervisors do their job, you, as the city manager, may never be involved in this complaint resolution. If you do get involved, it is probably because some communications broke down or the job is just not getting done. In that case, you must reopen the communications channels, get the job done, and see to it that the citizen is satisfied.

Another job, that you need to be sure to do is showing citizens what a good deal their city government is for the amount of tax dollars it costs them. This job needs to be a constant process and needs to be undertaken by everyone, from the highest elected official all the way down to the garbage collectors and city hall janitor. Part of the method of accomplishing this is through providing your citizens with information about what their city government is doing for them. The other side of that street is that all of you must listen to the citizens to find out what projects and programs they want the city to undertake. Some current programs may need to be revamped or dropped altogether. Different new programs and projects need to be implemented. Don't over respond to your citizens, though. Don't launch a brand new program or project or install a new traffic control sign because one citizen asks for it, no matter how forceful the request is. Generally, new programs or projects, or the possible installation and placement of a new "Slow, Children Playing" sign, or something similar, should be matters decided by your elected officials as a legislative body, not decided by one official, nor by you as the manager. Let your system work.

Chapter X

GENERAL GOVERNMENT DEPARTMENT

As city manager, the general government department is your bread and butter, your personal staff to assist you in carrying out the plans and programs directed by the elected officials. This department will generally include your finance director or treasurer, your city clerk, and a clerical pool to include your secretary and the city's receptionist.

The finance director or treasurer is generally going to be a trained accountant who will handle the city's fiscal record keeping. If you use your accountant properly, however, he/she can be an indispensable friend, confidant and co-worker. A good finance director can make you look good to the elected officials, and in turn the elected officials will look good to the citizens. Or, a poor finance director can make you look like a fool; then the elected officials will amplify that characteristic attributed to you to their constituents. So, either everybody is happy, or the city manager is a doo-wah! It all depends on the finance director.

The city clerk is generally considered the departmental supervisor for the general government department; the finance director is somewhat an equal to department supervisors and sometimes a superior to them. Like the finance director, the city clerk can make you look good to the elected officials, or make them think the city staff does not know what time it is. I'm telling you this to impress upon you how important it is to have superb people in these jobs, to have good working relationships with them and they with each other. The city clerk will usually direct and control the work load of the general government department clerical staff, with the exception of the city manager's secretary. There may be occasions when the your secretary will need to seek assistance from the city clerk's staff in order to get a job done in a timely manner. Consequently, there needs to be a good working relationship between these two people, too.

Generally speaking, the city clerk's primary function is that of secretary to the elected officials' body (commission/council). Consequently, the clerk is responsible for recording the minutes, the maintenance and retention of all pending and/or adopted legislation, and the assembling of information comprising and supporting the agenda. Your job as the manager is to provide the clerk with sufficient support for those tasks to be quickly and easily accomplished. This is not the area of city government that you want to allow to become tardy in any sense of the word. The remainder of the clerk's time and talents should be used to achieve the city's common goals as directed by you, the manager.

The city clerk is also the official keeper of the city seal. The city seal is an embossing device that is used to certify an official city document, similar to wax seals used in the days of kings and serfs. Every city ordinance, resolution, municipal order, contract, set of minutes, etc., should be sealed. If the document is signed by the mayor and attested by the city clerk, then the city clerk's signature should have the seal over it.

In some respects, the city clerk has more stated duties than does a city manager. The city clerk's position is generally considered a 'constitutional officer.' That is to say, the state's constitution may state each city shall have a city clerk. No state constitution states each city shall have a city manager. Consequently, many traditional city services are specifically identified as tasks that must be accomplished by the city clerk: the issuance of business licenses, the verification of official city documents (plats, contracts, etc.), and other duties which may vary from state to state. Remember, however, in a council-manager form of government, the city clerk works for the city manager. Just because the city clerk is the specified official responsible for the administration of a city election does not mean that the city manager is not equally responsible. In other words, a city manager is responsible for everything that goes on in the city government, regardless of this responsibility being explicitly or implicitly assigned.

Frankly, managing and administering city government is a difficult job at best. It is, therefore, exceptionally important that all of the employees that routinely work together or in proximity with each other have a good working relationship. They do not have to love each other, but they do need to be able to work together. When this situation does not exist, the tension in the atmosphere is generally a humongous distracter that must be addressed. You, as the manager, need to be on the lookout for the development of this type of atmosphere and put a screeching halt to it if you observe it beginning to deteriorate. Sometimes, a gentle counseling of the parties involved will solve the problem. Other times, an interdepartmental transfer is necessary. Sometimes suspension, as a disciplinary action when appropriate, will help. As a last resort, do not be afraid to terminate the employment of the unyielding instigator. It will be difficult for you and them, but the city government will be better for it. Unfortunately, a pure personality conflict is seldom justification for ending an employee's employment. Try to overcome the problem.

Computers, generally speaking, can improve the capabilities and efficiency of every employment position I can think of in this department known as general government, including you, the city manager. A word processing program alone can make a world of difference in the quality and quantity of correspondence a secretary can produce for the boss. I have found the word processing programs on computers to be an invaluable time saver when it comes to drafting legislation, meeting minutes, repetitive letters, and so forth. Anytime something lends itself to a given form or format, with that format in your computer, you can drastically reduce your drafting time.

Data base management programs can assist your clerical staff with maintaining the city's equipment inventory records. Data bases may also assist in budget reports and summaries. Without a computer, any form of a utility billing system (water bills, garbage bills, sewer bills, etc.) is a nightmare to try to manage. The new emphasis many cities place upon communicating with their citizens makes computer assisted publications a must in the software inventory of any city government.

To say that there are hundreds of computers available is probably not an understatement. You and your staff need to decide which type of system, or systems, can best suit your needs. Then, you have to be able to convince your elected officials that this is the best choice for your city, assuming your city does not already own a system. If you do already own one, I hope it meets your needs.

You are probably very computer-literate, as the lingo says. If you are not, however, it is not that difficult to become computer-wise. There is nothing wrong with reading a few books or periodical articles, on the subject, to help broaden your horizons. If you're in the market for a computer, ask some of the local dealers/vendors to explain which one of their systems is best for you and why. This will require you and your staff to determine prior to this what exactly you want your computers to accomplish for you.

You should know there are microcomputers (generally the same as personal computers, or desk-top computers), minicomputers and mainframes. Unless you are managing a huge city that has an electric, water, sewer and garbage utility with 10,000 customers (that is, households as opposed to 10,000 citizens which would only be about 3,800 households) each, you probably have no need to look into a mainframe computer. I would argue that many small cities will need no more than a couple of microcomputers to handle the majority of their problems. If you do have a utility billing system to manage, you probably will want a minicomputer to help you manage that system. You may want to invest in software that will enable a microcomputer to be used as a "smart-terminal" for the minicomputer, at times and also operate independently at other times.

When considering computers, I highly recommend that you try to buy the hardware and the software from the same vendor under the same service contract. It may cost a little more initially, but it will save you immeasurably down the road. There is somewhat of a scarcity of municipal government oriented programs in some types of software. I believe this is being overcome, but money spent on customizing a program to meet your city's needs may, in fact, be money well spent. Again, this is a judgment call you have to make.

When buying computers, you will find there is generally training offered for minicomputer systems, and seldom training offered for microcomputer systems.   The availability of training may be a consideration in deciding which vendor has the best material for you.

Your general government employees are probably going to be responsible for such things as utility billings and collections, tax billings and collections, city personnel files(including health insurance records, workers' compensation, payroll, etc.), city inventory files, and general clerical support of most of your other departments. Such things as the selling of building permits, the processing of code enforcement violations/complaints, and some of the governmental purchasing functions are all additional jobs commonly performed by the general government department staff. See Appendix B (Job Descriptions for Account Clerk, Accountant, Administrative Assistant, Clerk Typist I, Computer Operator, Secretary I and Executive Secretary).

One of your key jobs as the manager, as well as that of your personal staff, is the maintenance of good intergovernmental relations. Your city does not operate in a vacuum, nor do you. There are times when you need to ask what your contemporaries are doing in their cities. There are times when you need to work closely with the local county's staff. There are even times when you will have dealings with state and federal government employees, both from the executive branch and legislative staffers, and probably even some legislators. As in relationships with your chief of police, your finance director, the city clerk, your spouse, and ad infinitum... good intergovernmental relations take work and the ability to be flexible and open- minded.

Your city hall staff will no doubt be the initial repository of most citizen complaints, at least those that are received by telephone. It is of paramount importance that the employees that hear these complaints are courteous and not argumentative. Sometimes, the citizen just wants to vent on somebody, and this venting goes a long way in resolving the complaint. Your staff should take that venting, but only with a grain of salt. That is not to say, however, that any city employee shall be forced to take verbal abuse, much less vulgarity or profanity from any citizen. I always told my people that if some citizen began swearing at them to politely say, "Sir/Madam, I am not allowed to listen to this kind of abuse. I am going to hang up now. Good-bye." If this tack is used, the employee should not be vehement, nor slam the phone down. They must be polite, but they do not have to take that kind of humiliation, in my opinion. Set your own policies.

Anyway, once the complaint has been noted, I have it sent to the supervisor of the individual against whom the complaint was lodged. If this supervisor cannot handle the situation to the citizen's satisfaction, then train the supervisor to come and talk to you about the matter without the citizen present. If the complaints are in general terms, train your city clerk to handle them. You as the manager, should strategically place yourself in a position where you are the appeal-level available to your citizens after they have dealt with one of your subordinates. This creates a position wherein the elected officials' body (commission/ council) becomes the third step in a complaint process, and hopefully you can drastically reduce the number of complaints that get to the elected officials by satisfying the citizen before the complaint goes that far.

Hopefully, no citizen complaint in your city will ever get this far, but it is possible that the citizen may formally appeal a decision made by you, the manager, to the city commission/council. If this is the case, you should be certain the citizen understands that any appeal or rehearing of a council/commission decision at a later date, requires a verbatim transcript of the original meeting. In general terms, this means they will need to hire a court stenographer to come and transcribe the commission meeting, or at least that portion dealing with the pertinent subject matter. This is also the case when an employee is appealing a disciplinary action to the council, should that unfortunate circumstance ever come to pass. Likewise, a developer that may be unhappy with a council's ruling/decision, etc. also needs to be aware of this requirement.

Consequently, a caveat has been developed that I advocate being printed on the bottom of the first page of every agenda of your decision-making bodies.

Any person who desires to appeal any decision from this meeting will need a record of the proceedings, and for this purpose may need to ensure that a verbatim record of the proceedings is made which includes testimony and evidence upon which the appeal is based.

This leads us to an unpleasant area of city government, and that is litigation. Because the city exists, there are dissatisfied citizens and disgruntled developers, and a myriad of other people who are going to sue the city in an effort to 'teach the city a lesson,' 'get some of my tax dollars back,' or for numerous other reasons, many of which are quite illogical. You, as the chief administrative officer of the city, are the individual that is probably going to have the majority of these lawsuits served upon you by your friends in the local county sheriff's office. Oftentimes, you are going to be personally named in the lawsuit. Do not let it shake you! Do not lose any sleep over it! Do your job to the best of your ability. Always let your city lawyers talk to someone else's lawyers (Don't you talk with the other guy's lawyers.), and make certain your city has a good liability insurance carrier.

In January 1992, the Americans with Disabilities Act became effective. Although at the time of publishing this handbook administrative rules and regulations have yet to be distributed, several experts have recommended that cities and towns add another notice to the bottom of their agendas, to further protect these cities from litigation, in this case from persons with disabilities.

Any person who requires special accommodations to attend or participate in a meeting of this Board is asked to contact Mr./Ms. _____, the City's ADA Coordinator, at least 24 hours in advance of the meeting they wish to attend.

Since we have just discussed some of the legal aspects of managing a city, you need to know about the creation and formulation of laws within a city. A law created by a city is known as an ordinance. Some other official city documents are called resolutions and municipal orders. Your city may, or may not use one or both of these.

A rule of thumb to remember: If you are dealing with money, your authorization should be an ordinance. Black's Law Dictionary defines an ordinance as-

A rule established by authority; a permanent rule of action; a law or statute. In its most common meaning, the term is used to designate the enactments of the legislative body of a municipal corporation. An ordinance is the equivalent of a municipal statute, passed by the city council, or equivalent body, and governing matters not already covered by federal or state law. Ordinances commonly govern zoning, building, safety, etc. matters of municipality. [1]

Sometimes, a person who doesn't understand this will attempt to utilize a resolution as the weight of law, because it is easier and faster to adopt, and subsequently rescind. Most states require that an ordinance be given two readings at two separate meetings of the legislative body. Furthermore, at some time in the process before the ordinance becomes law, it must be advertised in a newspaper. A resolution, on the other hand, can be adopted by the legislative body at the same meeting it is introduced. Black's Law Dictionary defines a resolution as:

A formal expression of the opinion or will of an official body or a public assembly, adopted by vote; as a legislative resolution. . . . The term is usually employed to denote the adoption of a motion, the subject-matter of which would not properly constitute a statute, such as a mere expression of opinion; an alteration of the rules; a vote of thanks or of censure, etc. Such is not law but merely a form in which a legislative body expresses an opinion...

Ordinance distinguished. "Resolution" denotes something less formal than "ordinance"; generally, it is mere expression of opinion or mind of council concerning some matter of administration, within its official cognizance, and provides for disposition of particular item of administrative business of a municipality; it is not a law, and in substance there is no difference between resolution, order and motion...
2

A resolution, in other words, is only a desire or the consensus of your elected body. It may change every time your elected officials change. An ordinance has gone through public hearings and is a much more formal document. In order for an ordinance to be changed or amended, the legislative body of your city must have another round of public hearings and the related advertisement. If you city is collecting utility fees on an administrative order or memo, stop it by asking your commission to adopt an ordinance setting the rates. If you do not have an ordinance in place, do a detailed calculation to allow your water, and/or sewer, and/or sanitation department to at least break even (already alluded to in Chapter VI). If you already have utility rate ordinances on the books, ensure that those rates are fair and equitable to the city and the citizens alike.

Money is one of the key areas that is to be controlled by the commission/council. If you are collecting utility rates on a resolution from the last commission/council or from an administrative memo, how is your council controlling and monitoring that money? They're not. Don't confuse this issue to think I am telling you every utility rate ordinance or other money-ordinance must be changed every time a new elected official assumes office. If an ordinance is in place, that ordinance has the weight of law and is not something that can be discarded without due process.

Some state statutes provide for the city governments within that state to utilize a document called a municipal order. A municipal order is an internal directive from the legislative body to the city's administrative staff. In effect, it has the same weight as a resolution, inasmuch as it is not law; nor does it require public hearing(s) and publication.

As I stated in the first chapter, it is imperative that the manager and all of the elected officials, at a minimum, know and understand the municipal laws of their respective state, as it applies to their particular city. 'Sunshine laws,' public bidding laws and requirements, budgetary requirements, the technicalities of the election laws, and all matters of public hearing requirements are probably the most important technicalities with which you all need to be intimately familiar.

I, personally, like to have a set of state statutes in my office (the city manager's office), to which I can refer regularly. At a minimum, you should check with your state city league and/or state bar association to see if either organization routinely publishes a synopsis of the state statutes concerning municipal government. Many states publish such a document after each general session of the state legislature. You need to know what actions need to be taken if, for instance, one of your elected officials resigns in midterm.

NOTES

1 and 2. Henry Campbell Black. 1979. Black's Law Dictionary, 5th Edition. St. Paul, MN: West Publishing. Pp. 989 & 1178.

Chapter XI

POLICE DEPARTMENT

Your police department can be, and probably is, your city's most visible public relations tool while simultaneously being your largest liability. Both of these features, public relations and liability, can be positive or negative in nature. At times, both features probably take on both aspects.

First, let's get down to basics. Every police department that I have been associated with has three types of officers: patrol officers, investigative officers and administrative officers. As in most of life, however, the lines are not neatly drawn. That is to say that all of these officers do each type of job at some time, even though their primary workload is in one specific area. Police science, or criminal justice, or criminal investigation, or any other general title you might place upon this vocation, is a very specialized and complicated business. The worst thing you, or anyone, can do is to try to armchair quarterback your police department in general, or your chief, specifically. If you don't trust the chief, then you had better work with him/her until you can trust the individual, get a new chief, or you get a new job! The city manager is not supposed to be the chief of police, nor the fire chief, nor the street superintendent, or any other one of your department directors.

Your job is to coordinate all of the departments into a team to deliver the best possible service to your citizens, at the lowest possible cost. If you want to be the chief of police, go back to school and get a degree in police science, and then get a job as a patrolman and work your way up!

Back to the beginning of basics; patrol officers are those that, generally speaking, have the most contact with the citizens. Patrol officers are the ones driving around in the marked police cars providing your city with that all important omnipresence of law enforcement. It is very important that these men and women present a good image to the citizens. They must look sharp. Their patrol cars must look sharp and be clean. They need to handle themselves in a professional manner at all times. Note that some police officers are covered by separate incentive plans. And, I think, perhaps most importantly they need to practice a city policy that must emanate from the mayor and legislative body, through the city manager, through the chief of police, throughout the department that no citizen is above the law - no one gets special treatment. A good method of ensuring all of the above occurs is to have a written set of standard operating procedure (SOP) within your police department that everyone follows at all times.

These SOPs necessarily need to be very complex and as all inclusive as possible. If your department has none, talk with your chief. Have him borrow some samples from other police departments, and have him start writing his own department's SOPs. You may also have him check with your state police for assistance. Although these SOPs will deal with virtually every type of incident the police may face, they will routinely be most used by the patrol officers.

As a matter of policy, if your department does not have SOPs, once your chief starts writing them, issue each subject matter within the SOPs separately and only issue one or two a day or five to eight a week. Purchase sturdy (because they're going to get a lot of use and need to last) three-ring binders for your officers to file each new subject matter as it is issued. By issuing one or two at a time, the officers should be able to read, absorb and begin to routinize the SOPs, as opposed to having volumes of subject matter papers dumped on them all at once.

One of these SOPs should be a requirement for each of your officers to call in on the radio the license plate number and location of any vehicle one of your officers chooses to stop, for whatever reason. Why? Several police officers have been shot, otherwise wounded, or outright killed by the occupants of a vehicle which that police officer stopped in a routine traffic stop. If an officer advises the dispatcher that he/she is making a stop, at a specific location, the dispatcher can keep "tabs" on that officer. If the dispatcher attempts to contact the officer and cannot, the dispatcher immediately knows where to dispatch another officer in order to verify the well-being of the first officer. If the second officer arrives, and finds there has been an incident, the second officer and the dispatcher know the license number of the vehicle with which the injured officer was last in contact. I hope you see the need for this type of SOP, and insist on its execution within your city's police department.

Let me digress a moment; if your department does not have written SOPs, chances are the implementation of these regulations will meet with some resistance. For the good of the department and the protection of the city, it is important that you and the chief weather this 'storm' of negative feelings and hesitation and put the written SOPs in place.

Investigative officers are generally referred to as detectives. This type of officer, without a doubt, is the most romanticized type of 'Cop,' as far as the television, movie and paperback novel industries are concerned. But, don't be taken in by all that. Being a detective is a lot of hard, tedious, boring work. Most detectives I know work about sixteen hours a day or more and get paid for eight. They are dedicated to solving crimes against the people and property within their city, and they get very little recognition. Now and then, a detective may make a bad decision and 'go to the other side.' I think this, too, is something that has been blown out of proportion by the leisure industries. If there is any doubt about the trustworthiness of any of your detectives, or any of your police officers in general, discuss it with the chief and have him do an internal investigation. Don't receive complaints about the honesty of your police department personnel from citizens and do nothing about those complaints. Look into the allegation(s).

Administrative police officers are those that administer the department. Imagine that! Your chief and division directors (captains, lieutenants, etc.) are examples of administrative officers. These officers spend most of their time in the police station(s), as opposed to being out on the road patrolling or investigating.

We must now address the issue of sworn and nonsworn police department employees. Most of the employees of the police department are going to be sworn police officers; those people that have had the state certified law enforcement officer training. Nonsworn employees are civilian personnel that work in and for the police department. Your chief's secretary, record clerks, perhaps a crime scene technician, etc., are all examples of nonsworn employees. A general divider: If they are authorized by law to carry a weapon, they are a sworn police officer, otherwise they are nonsworn. There seems to be a malady, however, that infects nonsworn employees of law enforcement agencies; sometimes these people work around police so much that they truly begin to believe they are police officers. They may illegally carry a concealed weapon. They may even begin to carry a badge that they will subsequently flash at someone, intimating they are police officers and the someone needs to do what he is told. Guard against this malady affecting your department.

I mentioned earlier the liability issue. As I am writing this book, liability insurance is one of the biggest financial crises ever to hit local government. Unfortunately, police departments within cities are one of, if not the single, largest liabilities the city has. Every time a police officer arrests (stops) someone, there is a potential lawsuit. This is one of the reasons that written SOPs are so important. For the protection of the city and the police department, all SOPs that address arrests should be approved by the city attorney prior to distribution to and implementation by the police officers, thus limiting the city's exposure.

Just because a police officer does everything properly is no guarantee that some individual is not going to sue the city and/or the police department on the premise that that individual, is going to make some money off of the proposition. Again, unfortunately, many insurance companies will pay a plaintiff to settle out of court because it is less costly than defending the case. It has nothing to do with who is right and who is wrong. It's important that you are aware of this.

Another related liability issue is the to be or not to be of reserve or auxiliary police officers. Reserve or auxiliary police officers are those citizens who volunteer their time, or are paid a very modest monthly fee, in order to augment the regular police officers. Reserve/auxiliary police officers can be of great aid to regular police officers when there is a large emergency, a parade, or some other gathering that brings crowds of people and/or confusion with it. Most attorneys I have talked with, however, are of the opinion that reserve police officers are just too great a liability for the positions to be continued in any city.

The key to this problem, generally, is that there is no state certification of training requirements for reserve/ auxiliary police officers; yet, as far as any citizen is concerned, that reserve/ auxiliary police officer is a police officer: "A rose by any other name..." Thus, the reserve/auxiliary police officer is carrying a gun, has arrest powers, and therefore is a liability, without the training provided to the regular police officers to limit this liability.

Next to the sanitation department, the police will probably be your largest source of workmen's compensation insurance claims. Just because this is the case, however, is no reason that you, your chief, and everyone else involved should not make a concentrated effort to limit these claims. Just as in the industrial work place, a lack of accidents and the related lost work time are a function directly correlated to the emphasis placed upon the prevention of these problems by management. You must preach safety to all of the city's employees and make your department directors, especially your chief of police, do the same thing. "Safety is no accident" is a very applicable statement. See Appendix C, Section XVI: Safety and Workmens' Compensation; Section XII: Disability Sick Leave and Workmens' Compensation.

Just for a moment, let's think about some of the sources of workmen's compensation claims from the police department. Arresting a drunk is always a potential problem as is any kind of pursuit, be it in the vehicles or on foot. Without a doubt, however, the biggest danger for the personal well being of the police officer is responding to a domestic disturbance complaint.

Since we can identify these high risk situations, it is important that the SOPs address the specifics of handling these problem situations, and that management reenforce these specifics through discussions, in-service training, and other opportunities.

One of the biggest problems for every police department is breaking in new police officers. The "rookies," as they are commonly known, do not know the city, do not know this department's SOPs, and may not have any real world experience to draw upon if he/she has just graduated from the state certified police training program. An excellent way around these problems and a multitude of others, is the field training officer program.

This program pairs a very seasoned officer, one that has gone through additional state approved training, with the rookie for a specified period of time, generally six to twelve weeks. The FTO, as the trainer is known, teaches the rookie about everything. The FTO also has the opportunity to rate the rookie in general duty performance and specific situations. If the FTO does not think the rookie is going to work out, the dismissal of the rookie during the probationary period may save the city incalculable expense and problems. It should be noted, if an FTO and a rookie do not see eye-to-eye, it is very common for the rookie to be placed with another FTO prior to a lasting decision being made concerning the rookie's future within that department.

The number of police officers within your department is very important in order that you can provide adequate and timely law enforcement protection to your city and citizens. The national average, cited in the 1988 Municipal Yearbook, published by the ICMA, is 2.52 police officers per 1,000 citizens of population. This figure relates to sworn law enforcement officers, not to administrative or other nonsworn departmental employees. You might also want to check the City-County Data Book, published by the U.S. Census Bureau; it lists major cities and the number of police officers per 10,000 citizens. Regional averages will vary somewhat. Averages do not tell the whole story, but they are indicative of norms. I recommend that you do your own calculations to see how your department stacks up to the national and regional averages. Perhaps you can do some comparisons between your department and neighboring city departments.

The point is, if your department does not rank well under these averages, I believe you would be wise to point this out to your elected officials, talking with them and the chief of police about how to handle this situation and avoid future problems from a shortage of police officers.

Because your city, like other cities, can not afford to have a police officer on every corner any more, you must look for ways to add to the eyes and ears of your police department without adding to the salary line item of your budget. One method of helping this situation has been mentioned in several places in this guide, that of teaching and training all the city employees that they are a team that must work together on every project and program, crossing traditional departmental lines for the ultimate good of the citizens.

Another method that will give your police department an officer on every corner is the use of block watch captains. A block watch captain is a citizen who volunteers to watch the block in which he/she lives. Ideally, block watch captains are usually homebodies, and are somewhat busybodies. I do not advocate using these terms in your departmental recruiting program, but they are descriptive of the type of people that do best in these voluntary positions: Someone who is home most of the time and someone who looks out of the window to see what is going on in their neighborhood, constantly. You say, no one is home all of the time. This is true. Another part of a block watch captain's job, therefore, is to attempt to get virtually 'round the clock' observation coverage of the neighborhood by coordination of the neighbors within each assigned block. Block watch programs do not advocate that any citizen sit up all night long and look out the window. What these programs do attempt to instill is an habitual watching of the neighborhood by the citizens/residents who live there.

No matter how often a police officer patrols through any given neighborhood or how many times other city vehicles go through this neighborhood, none of these people know the neighborhood as well as someone who lives there. If there is a strange car parked in front of a certain house, chances are neither the police nor any of your other employees will know it is a strange car. But, anyone who lives in that neighborhood/block and pays attention to the goings-on of the area will know that is a car that does not belong there.

A block watch captain is a person recruited to be the liaison between the neighbors and the city's police department. The block watch captain and his/her neighbors should take the lead in reporting mysterious incidents, people, and vehicles in the neighborhood to the police. The citizens should be trained in rapid identification techniques, not the least of which is noting the license plate number on that suspicious car parked down the block. No block watch captain should attempt to take the law into his/her hands, have a personal confrontation with a suspicious character, or anything like that. A block watch captain's most important tool is the telephone. No guns, clubs, or jogging shoes!

A block watch program can be fostered by placing signs up in the neighborhood warning would-be criminals that they are entering a block watch neighborhood and that they are therefore being watched. The block watch program can also host such things as block parties and other activities to make the neighborhood a more close-knit organization. The block watch captain can also encourage the neighbors to participate in the "Operation Identification" program that most police departments sponsor. In this program, social security or driver's license numbers are engraved onto valuables, making those valuables far less easy to fence when stolen.

The best block watch programs are those that are city-wide, or at least area (subdivision) wide. It does little good to have a block watch program in one block, with the next ten blocks in any direction not participating. Don't discourage the creation of a one block area, though; just encourage the surrounding blocks to jump onto the block watch band wagon.

If possible, you should have a police officer with the major additional duty of crime prevention officer. Part of this officer's job would be to meet with neighborhood groups and promote the block watch and operation identification programs, thus making it tougher for criminals to be successful in your city. Another key function of this crime prevention officer should be performing home security surveys for your citizens at no cost. These surveys aid in teaching the citizens how to make their home more burglar proof.

The relationship between the chief of police and the city manager must be excellent. Like marriage, such a relationship takes a lot of work on the part of both players. And, like marriage, oftentimes a poor relationship arises out of lack of or poor communications. Talk with your chief. Get to know the person. Work together so you learn to trust each other. If you can not do these things, you are destined for trouble.

I will discuss radios and vehicles in more detail in the chapter of the same name, Chapter XXVI. For implication of development on expanding police departments and one solution thereto, See Appendix A.

NOTE

1. International City Management Association. 1988 Municipal Yearbook, Washington, D.C.

Chapter XII

FIRE DEPARTMENT

The fire department is another department that can bring a great deal of good feelings toward the city from a public relations standpoint. Very few people have any ill will toward a well trained, competent and friendly fire department.

Like the police, fire fighters have state certified training standards that they must attain and maintain. A lot of a fire department's training can be done by your own chief and his officers. Your department may want to work with one or two other departments in your area in order to provide an all-around training staff from in-house, readily available personnel.

The fire department performs the obvious task of fighting fires, but an even more important task is that of fire prevention. Most fire fighters will tell you they would much rather go into a business, or a home, and tell the owner what corrections need to be made in order to prevent fires instead of responding to an emergency call once the building has caught on fire. Fire prevention and safety inspections of every commercial and industrial structure in town need to be a routine part of the fire department's duties. These inspections will normally be done by the fire fighters on duty under the direction of the fire prevention officer.

The fire prevention officer has the additional duty of reviewing construction and development plans for all proposed buildings in the city. For both of these functions, the fire prevention officer must work very closely with the building official, the city engineer, the planner, and the development director (if your city has one). In some cities, the fire prevention officer is a part of the building department staff, as opposed to the fire department. You have to make the decision on where this individual can best perform his/her job.

The fire prevention officer may have the title of fire inspector; these two titles are basically synonymous. A fire marshall, on the other hand, is generally a state-level official whose main job, as far as your city goes, is to inspect and evaluate fire scenes, assisting your own city's fire department in determining cause, methods of preventing reoccurrence, etc.

The fire department is akin to the police department inasmuch as their work is very complex and specialized. Work with and through the fire chief; do not try to be the fire chief.

Every fire department has it's own methods of operation. The fire department should have a written set of SOPs in order to keep all the fire fighters singing off of the same sheet of music, as it were. You may have fire fighters working 24 hours on duty, 48 hours off duty, and then repeating the process. Company-level officers may be on that same shift, or on an 8:00 AM to 5:00 PM shift, five days a week. Certainly, regardless of other work schedules, your battalion-level officers should be there during normal work hours, on normal work days; this includes your fire prevention officer. You should at least have a working knowledge of the routines within the fire department. You should know how often your people work, and for how long.

Your city's fire department probably will run rescue operations in addition to their firefighting and fire prevention duties. Rescue operations consist of such things as extricating a person from a wrecked automobile, saving someone from hanging off of the side of a cliff or building, and other such predicaments. If your city has any bodies of water within the corporate limits and if your fire department handles the rescue operations within your area, your fire department will need at least one boat to utilize in water-borne rescue efforts. A large, well equipped motor boat will usually do quite nicely. A cabin cruiser, even a small one, is overkill.

Your fire department also may provide emergency medical services (EMS) for your community. If in fact this is the case, you will find that your EMS calls for service are two or three to one, when compared to fire and other calls. I only advise you of this to caution you that one of your fire department's hiring requirements may be that the applicant is a state certified Emergency Medical Technician (EMT) or greater. If your department does not currently deliver EMS services to your city, at least with respect to transporting of sick and injured citizens and your department is considering implementation of this, you need to make certain that the 'big picture' is looked at in its entirety. The transporting of people requires backup equipment, personnel, and vehicles while one or more other vehicles are transporting a person out of the city to a hospital in a nearby community.

One of the more mundane but nevertheless important duties of your fire department is water hydrant flow tests. These tests need to be performed on a strict periodic basis in order to detect and correct problems that might hinder the fighting of a fire in a particular area.

Since fire fighters obviously need to know exactly where water hydrants are located when approaching a fire scene, you may want to have your fire fighters install a little device on the street that will aid them in this important quest. You can purchase street mounted reflectors in different colors. You have probably seen white and yellow ones mounted on state and interstate highways, to mark the center and edge lanes of the pavement. You can purchase blue reflectors, and have your fire fighters install them in the middle of the driving lane adjacent to the location of the water hydrant on the side of the pavement. This will then tell the fire fighters they are approaching a hydrant far before they can see the hydrant, especially after dark.

The number of full-time fire fighters in your department is important, in order to ensure that you can deliver adequate and timely fire protection services to your citizens. The national average, according to the Fire Protection Handbook, [1] is 1.5 fire fighters per 1,000 citizens; this does not include administrative staff, but does include company-level officers. The 1988 Municipal Yearbook, published by ICMA, cited the national average at 1.65 fire fighters per 1,000 citizens. [2]

As I noted in the similar discussion involving police in the last chapter, regional averages vary; you must also consider such things as population density, effectiveness and efficiency of you fire fighting equipment, etc. The point is, do your own calculations and see how your fire department stacks up against the national and regional averages. If you are well under those averages, perhaps you need to discuss this with your elected officials and your fire chief in order to bring your department up to a higher standard.

The proximity of the fire station to the population center(s) within your city is also very important. The length of response time can have a major impact on your city's fire insurance ratings and consequently the fire insurance premiums within your city. The location of fire stations with regard to railroad tracks and citizens that could need the fire department's help are both important considerations when deciding to build a fire department building, be it the main or a secondary station. You see, oftentimes a train will be traveling on the railroad tracks when an emergency vehicle needs to get across those tracks. Logically, ideally, if railroad tracks divide your city, you should have a fire station on each side of town; the tracks would create a dividing line for responses, and so the trains would not impede the response time of the fire department in an emergency.

As mentioned before, I will discuss radios and vehicles in Chapter XXVI.

NOTES

1. National Fire Protection Association, <u>Fire Protection Handbook</u>, 16th Edition. Quincy, MA. 1986.

2. International City Management Association. <u>1988 Municipal Yearbook</u>, Washington, D.C.

Chapter XIII

PUBLIC SAFETY DEPARTMENT

Your city may have a public safety department. Such a department generally takes two forms. In one case, the police and fire entities become known as divisions, and their respective chiefs work for the public safety director who heads this department. A more recent development in this department is the total integration of the police and fire entities into a single unit. In such an arrangement, all the sworn personnel are known as public safety officers and are fully trained in all aspects of both law enforcement and fire science.

The theory behind the integrated public safety department is that it provides for more efficient use of manpower. There are those who argue that a traditional fire department's personnel are not fully utilized, and by having them cross-trained as traditional police officers, they can patrol the city while 'waiting for a fire.' I have never observed a fire department's personnel not being gainfully employed for the majority of their waking hours while on shift. If this became the case, I, as the city manager, would talk with the fire chief and see if, in fact, he had a lack of work for his firefighters to perform.

This dilemma of having an integrated public safety department has had volumes of essays written upon the pros and cons of the concept. If you are interested, I would suggest you visit your local library and explore the matter in more detail. The few cities I have had personal contact with that have moved to the integrated public safety department have confessed that it seems to work better in theory than in practice. I do not, however, feel that I have enough exposure to the matter to sit in judgment.

On the other hand, the concept of having a public safety director to administer the police and fire divisions is similar to the idea of having a public works director to coordinate the work of the water, sewer, streets and/or sanitation divisions. Such a position merely gives another level of management between the city manager and the police and fire chiefs. In some larger and/or more rapidly growing cities, this could be a very desirable goal. In other cities, it is merely a waste of manpower. Such decisions, ideas and arguments are why you, as the city manager, are being paid the 'big bucks'. You research, consult, and decide what is best for your city, and then see if your mayor and elected legislative body agree. If you can not convince them of your point of view, perhaps you don't have a very strong argument; or perhaps you march to a different drummer.

Chapter XIV

COMMUNICATIONS/DISPATCH SECTION

If you have a police and/or a fire department, your city will have to have some method of dispatching personnel and equipment from these two departments/divisions to crime or accident scenes. This dispatching is generally performed by a communications or dispatch section within one of these departments or within the public safety department.

This section's primary function is to answer emergency telephone calls directed to the police and/or fire departments, get the necessary information from the telephone caller, and send help to the scene as soon as possible. Help may be dispatched via radios between the dispatch section and the vehicles within the respective departments or by buzzers activated by the dispatcher that ring/buzz in the fire station, followed up by radio directions or some other methods.

In many, many cases, the cool, calm head of the dispatcher speaking with the panic-stricken caller has markedly alleviated the problems at the scene before the police officer or fire fighters arrive.

The person working in this section is commonly called a dispatcher, although the official title may actually be communications officer. The communications officers, more often than not, are carried on the city's personnel files as nonsworn employees of the police department, although some cities place the dispatchers under the control of the fire chief. A few cities have separate dispatchers, and consequently separate dispatch sections for both the police and the fire departments respectively. Unless your city is very large and the volume of calls necessitates separate communications sections, I believe this is a duplication of job effort and therefore ends up costing the taxpayers more money by paying two people to do the same job simultaneously in separate locations.

It may, however, be necessary for you to have two communications officers, or even more, on duty simultaneously, but they would be working in the same dispatch section, answering the same bank of telephones and utilizing the same radios.

Unfortunately, many dispatchers feel like they are the 'red-headed step children' of the public safety departments. This is most unfortunate because in actuality the manner in which a dispatcher handles an incoming request for emergency services can literally be the difference between life and death for a citizen. One of your jobs as city manager should be to ensure that the dispatchers are being properly treated by the chiefs and personnel in your public safety departments. Be sure that these dispatchers do not assume the attitude or opinion that they are treated as less than equals.

It takes a special type of person to be a dispatcher. He/She must be able to monitor four or more radios (frequencies) simultaneously while being able to answer telephones and speak intelligently and kindly with the caller. The dispatchers have to have a general working knowledge of things that police officers and fire fighters can and cannot do for the citizens. They have to know when a superior within the city's administration would be better able to help the caller, and they have to know when in fact the caller needs to call an attorney. A dispatcher must be able to keep a cool head, even in times of exceptionally high stress. A dispatcher has to be Miss/Mr. Congeniality on the telephone, even when the caller just cussed at them. Among many other things not mentioned, the dispatcher must be able to work eight hours at a time in a little room, looking at maps, radios and telephones when there may only be two telephone calls during the whole shift and one of them was the wrong number!

A relatively new, and valuable communications system that can have far reaching effects on your communications section is a public phone system commonly referred to as the "911 system." Perhaps you are familiar with this system from your hometown or other experiences. It is tremendously expensive to install and not cheap to maintain, but if your city doesn't have it, I highly recommend trying to get the system installed.   Time was when the Law Enforcement Assistance Administration, out of the U.S. Justice Department, funded the installation of these systems through grants. It is my understanding that most of this type of money has dried up, but you might check with your state law enforcement agencies and/or the Federal Emergency Management Agency in Emmittsburg, Maryland.

A 911 system is a communications system integrated into the telephone system in any given locality, be it city-wide, county-wide, or a particular phone company-wide. When anyone picks up their phone and dials 9-1-1, the phone rings into a dispatch center of some kind. Most 911 systems are designed such that when that phone call comes into the dispatch center, the phone number from which the call is originating shows up on a screen in front of the dispatcher. In some 911 systems, the address, where the initiating phone is located, also appears. If you have a choice, obviously there is a great benefit to having the address appear in front of the dispatcher.

Suppose someone breaks into your house. You pick up your phone and dial 9-1-1. Before you can speak, the 'burglar' comes into the room where you are and grabs you, or whatever. If the 911 system has the address on the screen in front of the dispatcher, the dispatcher can immediately send help to your address, possibly saving the life of the caller.

If the system is designed such that only the phone number appears, the dispatcher can use a book, commonly known as the criss-cross, and still decipher the address, but it naturally will take longer.

If your city doesn't have a 911 system, try to get one. If you are in an area with several other cities, try to get them to join in your quest, as well as the county sheriff, surrounding volunteer fire department boards, etc. It might save someone's life.

There are a myriad of radio and communication systems available. Some employ lighted maps of your City, and an intricate system of being able to pinpoint police officers and fire equipment locations at any given moment in time. If your communication system is in need of major repair, you might be better off to buy a new, or newer system. Check with area radio suppliers, ask them to evaluate your current system. You might also review some of the advertisements in professional and governmental periodicals for ideas about suppliers and types of systems. Make no mistake; they are all expensive. But a radio/communications system that does not work can get city employees killed or seriously harmed, and then you have workmens' compensation and/or litigation problems with which to contend. You conceivably could endanger a citizen's life as well if you can not make contact with a police officer or fire fighter when the citizen needs help. I don't mean to turn this discussion into a melodrama, but communications is a very sensitive and important part of city government. In this era of exponentially changing technology, do not underestimate the value of a good radio system, computer assisted dispatch, the ability to speak to a police officer or fire fighter on the scene with their radio through your telephone (phone patch capability), and cellular telephone sets augmenting the city's radio system. See Chapter XXVI for more information on radios.

Chapter XV

DRAINAGE

Drainage is probably the single most overlooked and down played 'department' within a city. In most cities it is a subsidiary function of the street department. There is nothing wrong with that, as long as you remember that drainage exists.

Drainage is becoming more and more of a problem with the onset of the 'asphalt jungles.' Why? Because there is a reduced pervious (absorbing) surface through which the water can seep. I don't know of too many parking lots, roads, houses, apartment buildings or tennis courts that the water will run through and ultimately get back into the ground water network, do you? So, what developers and builders are doing is forcing, for example, 100 gallons of water that used to percolate (seep down through) on an acre of land to percolate on the quarter acre that is still in a pervious condition. Three-quarters of that acre now has some kind of building/structure on it that is impervious or will not percolate. Will it work? This is the problem.

Part of your job is to ensure that the decaying infrastructure (drainage/storm sewer pipes) you have in place is as functional as it can possibly be. Is it clean? Is it blocked? Or, do you need to have a visit from the friendly roto-rooter man? A key factor is keeping these outfalls functioning. (Outfall is a buzz word meaning any gravity controlled water flow. There can be positive outfalls, i.e. the water flows downhill as it is supposed to do or negative outfalls where the water doesn't go anywhere because it would have to travel up hill. One way of keeping these structures properly functioning is a program of street sweeping. This needs to be a planned and routine program. For example, every third week this street gets cleaned; or every month that street is cleaned, etc. Not a haphazard "Oh! This street is dirty today, and it hasn't been cleaned in six months. I guess we ought to have the maintenance shop people try to get the street sweeper running before one of the commissioners/ councilmen brings it up at a meeting" program.

Another good indicator of drainage is observation. Go out and watch the storm sewer inlets during a rain. After a while, you can tell if the outfall process is working properly or if it has a glitch in it somewhere.

Some very important points to keep in mind: ask your city engineer what he sees as the drainage problems in your city. By the way, I will discuss city engineers vis-a-vis developer's engineers later in the development department chapter (XXIII). Find out from your planner and/or building official if your city has any homes or other buildings built in flood plains. How long have they been built there? What kind of evacuation plans are in place for those citizens? Has any thought been given to a project to alleviate the flooding problem?

"What's a flood plain?" I'm glad you asked. A flood plain is an area identified by the Federal Emergency Management Agency (FEMA) as an area that is prone to flooding. These flood plains have different ratings indicated by letters of the alphabet. If your city does not have a Flood Zone Map, get one from FEMA in Washington, D.C.

What possible project could stop a flooding problem? Oh come on now! At least you have heard of flood walls, haven't you? Or, the city might dig up all of the old, now undersized, drainage pipes and put in new larger ones. That would certainly help. Maybe the solution is to identify the particular flood plain that is not salvageable, move the houses out of there to higher ground, and make that area a big percolation pond. Your engineer will have all of these answers. Don't start something on your own, though. Make sure your council wants to explore the options available before spending a bunch of engineering fees on finding those options.

Drainage systems can generally be categorized into two types, open and closed systems. Open systems use open drainage ditches along the edges of roads and property lines. These are further identified by an absence of curbing on the streets. Most people do not like drainage ditches around their property. Beware, the crafty engineers have invented swales. A swale is nothing but a baby drainage ditch that is generally very gently sloping and grassed. Many subdivisions are designed with drainage swales throughout and with such subtlety, they often are indiscernible without the aid of a plat map which reflects the related drainage easements. Most subdivisions actually utilize a combination of open and closed drainage systems. The open portion may only have swales, while the closed system actually is the more readily visible. A closed drainage system is characterized by an underground piping system with curbs on the streets and a series of drainage inlets built into the curbs and street surfaces. Ultimately, the closed system should empty into some percolation or retention pond.

What's a percolation pond? A percolation pond is a depressed area in the ground. It may or may not be a body of water, depending on how well it drains, when it last rained, etc. This pond is probably man-made, and it is designed to allow the water to collect therein and slowly seep back down into the underground water network.

What's a retention pond? A retention pond is very similar to a percolation pond. The retention pond, however, is designed to retain a certain volume of water during/after a rain to allow the unnatural impurities (like oil, gasoline residue, paint, etc.) to settle out of the water before the water finds its way back into the earth's water systems. The retention pond may or may not be a body of water, just like the perc pond at any given point in time. As you know it protects the quality of both underground and surface waters which are often used for recreational swimming, boating, fishing, drinking water supplies, etc. Therefore, you can readily see why it is important that impurities be filtered out of incoming water supplies before they are mingled with the surface waters.

If a closed drainage system is utilized, there should be headwalls installed at certain intervals, or at least at the point of outfall into the open portion of the drainage system. Your engineer will determine precisely how many and where the headwalls should be. A headwall is a concrete structure, generally precast, that serves to hold the drainage pipe in place. You might think of it as a sort of abutment. Without it, over time, the drainage pipe will have a tendency to wander or slip apart from itself at joints. The design of drainage systems is a very complex science studied and practiced by engineers.

In an open drainage system of a larger scale, you may have ditches as deep as six feet or more. In this type of system, you periodically (once every two years or so) may need to go in and dig out the bottom of the ditch in order to return the ditch to its normal capacity. Over time, drainage ditches tend to fill up with dirt and trash that accumulates from the water bringing deposits down stream. Depending on how powerful the state environmental department is in your state, you may need to have a permit before you can start this maintenance work. You must also bear in mind that you have to have some place to dispose of the "spoil" that you take out of the bottom of the ditch. The spoil is the dirt, and other stuff, you are removing from the bottom of the ditch. You may have a landfill in your area that will take the spoil. This, too, may be controlled by your state's agencies, so ask questions before you are ready to start the work. Your city's engineering firm should be able to help and advise you on any permitting process necessary and where you can get rid of the spoil.

Nowadays, the drainage design is often subject to state and/or regional agency approval, in addition to any approval that your own Development Review Committee (DRC) must give. What's a

Development Review Committee? It's a group of staffers that preview development plans and develop the "party line" that is ultimately presented to the commission, showing what the staff believes the city should do and/or require of a development. The DRC can consist of any staffers you feel should sit on this board. I recommend that it include your planner, building official, a representative from your engineering firm, fire inspector, water superintendent and a senior police officer at a minimum. Regardless of whom you select to sit on this panel, you should solicit comments from every department supervisor on the plans submitted so that you have as complete a package of information as possible before you take recommendations to the commission.

The planner can probably serve as the chairperson and/or coordinator of the DRC. Aside from that function, he should also review the development plans in detail for zoning compliance, road right-of-way preservation, etc. The building official's job on the DRC is to review the specific building plans that are a part of the proposed development in addition to checking for zoning compliance and related areas within his/her expertise. The engineer's job is to check the engineering calculations made by the developer's engineer. Drainage retention and runoff is certainly a key part of this, but so are the sizings of the water lines, sewer collection lines, the hydraulics thereof, and so forth. The fire inspector's job is to aid the building official in checking the building plans for compliance with the fire codes. He/she also should provide input on hydrant placement within the proposed development, water flows from the sizes of water lines, use of sprinkler systems, etc. The police officer should review the proposed plans for general safety and security of the development as well as traffic patterns, etc. The water superintendent's job is to check for sizing of water lines, placement of lines, sufficiency and sources of water supplies, etc.

You should have maps of all the drainage systems within your city in your street department offices. These maps will enable your street department to better maintain the drainage systems. They will know where the closed drainage systems go under the ground, and where and how they interface with the adjacent open systems. If you do not have maps from the designers of these systems, call upon those employees that have been working with drainage for many years; they probably have a fair idea of what is underground and where it is. Have them map this information for future use. You may also be able to get information from the original developer's engineer, if you have knowledge of who that was, and if he is still practicing.

Drainage systems are designed to routinely handle a certain volume of water, in the form of rainfall. This volume is couched in terms of "storm events." Talk to your engineer to get the scoop on storm events and minimum subdivision design standards within your state. Basically, a storm event is the mathematical probability of a certain volume of rainfall occurring within a given time frame. For example, in some parts of the country, two inches of rain falling within one hour would be considered a 'ten year storm event,' that is to say that the likelihood of two inches of rain falling within one hour will only happen once every ten years. In other parts of the country, this same volume of rain, two inches within one hour, may be a 25 year storm event, or even a 50 year storm event.

Most states have minimum standards for storm events that a drainage system must be designed to handle. In some states this standard will be a ten year storm event, while in others the minimum standard may be a 25 year storm event. One key problem with this system is that if the subdivision was designed ten years ago, it is quite likely that the drainage management standards for ten years ago are not the same standards that exist today. Consequently, you may have repeated drainage problems in some older parts of the city just because the drainage systems were not designed to today's standards.

A related problem with this system is the classification of storms. Storm event records are maintained by the local office of the U.S. Weather Bureau. These records are based upon data collected and measured at their official weather bureau stations. If one of these stations collects 0.25 inches of rain, that is the official rainfall for that day/time/etc. Your city may be two miles away from this weather station, and your citizens' unofficial rain gauges may have measured two inches of rain for this same period. As far as anyone is officially concerned, the storm event was only equal to the accumulation of 0.25 inches within the specified time period. This is all well and good, but its difficult to explain to your citizens why the city's drainage systems are overflowing when the weather bureau says it only rained 0.25 inches. Just another reason why you get paid the "big bucks!"

Once you are ready to actually begin work on a drainage system, I recommend that you hire a contractor that has a 'grade-all' type of boomed excavation bucket. Grade-all is a brand name for this type of device, but its like Kleenex. If you say you want to rent a grade-all, everyone knows what you mean. It is not a road grader. It is an earth moving bucket on the end of a boom, such that it can reach out into a drainage ditch and scoop up a quantity of dirt. If you have a lot of big open drainage systems, you may want to consider buying your own grade-all device. But if you are only going to use it a month at a time every two years or so, I don't think you can justify the price. A used piece of equipment runs around $150,000, and a new one approaches twice that much. Another thought to bear in mind: If your staff doesn't use it very often, then they forget all the nuances of operating the machinery. If your people are using the equipment and they tear out an electrical line or some other buried utility service, you are responsible. If you hire a contractor to do the job and they tear out a utility line, they have insurance and it's their problem. Think about it before you ask your commission to expend enormous sums of money for this complex, not too often used, piece of equipment. See Appendix B (Job Description for Equipment Operators). See also Figure 2, a telescopic-boom excavation bucket vehicle.

Figure 2. Telescopic-boom excavation bucket vehicle

Chapter XVI

STREET DEPARTMENT

Aside from the less recognized function of maintaining the drainage systems within your city, the street department also has the obvious function of maintaining the streets. A key word here is maintaining. Don't let your politicians decide that your street department employees can do their own new construction. You just will not have the quantity of people, the equipment, nor the expertise.

Your street department will most probably spend the majority of their time patching potholes in the streets, cutting the grass on the road right of way in the summertime, marking the streets, erecting street signs and miscellaneous other jobs, not the least of which should be inspection. During any work on streets within the city by an outside firm, you should have one of your knowledgeable street department personnel on the job site watching what is happening. If you are paying a firm to do resurfacing, you not only want to ensure the quality of the work. To protect yourself from a billing standpoint, you also need to have someone on the site to verify the number of truckloads of asphalt hauled into the site and the weight of each of those trucks. You see, your bill is calculated, at least in part, on how many tons of asphalt you use.

In the case of new street construction in a new subdivision, although you are not footing the bill, you (the city) are going to be responsible for the street they constructed for a long time, probably forever. Consequently, you want to ensure that the work being performed is to your specifications. Your engineer will be able to provide you with specifications, if your city doesn't already have a defined set in place. Generally speaking, these specifications should be virtually the same, if not identical, to those of your state's department of transportation's specifications for road construction. Your knowledgeable employee's job on the work site is ensuring those specifications are followed and met.

As a rule of thumb, your specifications should call for the final course of asphalt (this may be the only layer you put down in most resurfacing jobs) to be laid thick enough to be measured at either one or one-and-a-half inch thickness, once it is compacted; and it must be compacted to work properly. Your engineer can give you more complete guidance, but the laying of asphalt at less than one-inch thickness, compacted, is not going to last very long and is therefore not a good idea!

Asphalt has different grades used for different purposes. Generally, the final course of asphalt will be known as 'Type I' or 'S-1;' and a subcourse grade may be known as 'Type III.' Different locales have different ways of addressing the issue, but you can speak their language by asking just a few questions.

When the subdivision is being developed, do not allow the builders or the developer to let dirt run into the storm sewer system; it will sit there, and you will have to come in and clean it out eventually. If dirt does get in the storm sewers, a very high pressure fire department-type hose for running water through that part of the system may help some; but the only real solution, I have found is a visit by your friendly roto-rooter man. The developer will tell you that the fire hose solution will solve the problem completely, but I know from experience that this just isn't so.

Another point to be careful of.... When you are resurfacing streets in your city, you will have occasion to have to raise manholes and other valve covers that are located in the street. First of all, don't let anyone tell you they can't raise the valve cover to be flush with the street; they simply haven't looked hard enough for the parts to do so. Generally, valve covers, and especially manhole covers, can easily be raised using devices called riser rings. Often times, the asphalt company will have access to these riser kits and can install them for you quite reasonably in conjunction with their laying of the asphalt. Square valve boxes do present a challenge, but they, too, can be raised to the new level of the road. Not raising these valve covers causes a big 'hole' in the road that most people will think is a pothole. You can make your subordinates and contractors do the job right. Just hold their feet to the fire.

Your resurfacing specifications should call for all of the valve covers, and/or the actual valves, to be raised prior to the street being resurfaced in that area. If you do not insist on this policy, you will end up with cuts and patches in your brand new resurfacing job where somebody had to dig into the new asphalt to raise the valve/cover. Because of this cut in your new asphalt, this area will have a tendency to allow water to get under the new surface course of asphalt. Soon, you will have a nice crack there, then a pothole. Won't that make you happy? Make them do it before laying down the surface course!

Do not allow a contractor to come into your city and just put down asphalt over top of the bad road surface that is already in place. In some cases, you will need to have the contractor put down some subcourse (lower grade) type of asphalt as a leveling course, to smooth out a road that has gotten quite uneven and consequently bumpy. In the case of a road that has a lot of cracks in it - if those cracks are not patched before resurfacing, they will reappear in the new asphalt within a year or so, prematurely to what new cracking would appear purely from the resurfacing. This is called 'reflective cracking.' One method of patching these cracks to avoid reflective cracking is a special fiberglass product designed specifically for this purpose. It is a cloth-like material patch that is placed over top of the crack and sealed onto the old surface of asphalt with a tar-like substance.

Another method of stopping this reflective cracking is to have that portion of the old asphalt removed from the street, and an asphalt patch placed in the hole prior to resurfacing the street with the new asphalt.

A relatively new product that will reportedly prolong the life of a new asphalt resurfacing job is an asphalt rejuvenator treatment. I feel that the name is kind of a misnomer as the manufacturer will tell you that it should be applied to either a brand new surface of asphalt or one that is not more than a year old. But the concept of the product is that it does not allow the asphalt to dry out so quickly, and therefore it prolongs the life. For example, it causes rainwater to run off the asphalt surface as opposed to soaking into the surface. This will retard the deterioration rate of the asphalt.

While I have no personal experience with either the fiberglass material or the asphalt rejuvenator products I have described to you, I want you to know that there are such products on the market in case you see a particular need of them in your city.

A useful technique I have found for helping you and your street superintendent plan for your annual resurfacing program is to take a map of the city and mark it for reference purposes. First, mark the roads that the state and/or county maintain. Then select a different color and mark the roads that you resurfaced last year. Try to go as far back as you can go, historically, and indicate by color coding which streets, or portions thereof, were resurfaced in which year. You need to bear in mind that main thoroughfare streets that get a lot of traffic will need to be resurfaced more often than a cul-de-sac that only has a few homes on it. But, with the map to help you, I have found that you have a better idea where to start, what probably is in need of resurfacing, and when to schedule it into the annual resurfacing program.

A caveat concerning the resurfacing of roads: As you plan your city's annual resurfacing program and you begin to prioritize which streets are in need of resurfacing, you need to bear in mind who is

responsible for the maintenance of those streets. Some streets within
your city are probably state highways, and therefore they are the
responsibility of the state department of transportation. You may find,
if you ask the state to resurface a road, that they have already
established their resurfacing program for the particular year in question
and can not honor your request for this year. You need to make a note
and remind them again next year, only earlier in the year, in an effort to
get that section of state highway in your city resurfaced.

Your city may also have some roads in it that are to be maintained
by the county highway department. The same procedure needs to be
followed to get it resurfaced. My point is: In this time of continually
dwindling local government funds, do not expend your city's monies on
the resurfacing of a road that is to be maintained by some other entity.
You may find that, out of the necessity of taking care of your citizens,
you will have to repair a pothole in a state or county road that runs
through your city; but that is a minimal expense compared to the cost of
resurfacing a section of highway.

The geographical location of your city will dictate the amount of
time your street department may spend patching potholes, during
certain times of the year especially. If your city is in the northern part
of the United States where you experience a lot of freezing and
thawing, you are going to have more pothole problems than if you do
not experience this weather problem. Regardless, there are several
ways to repair potholes. The most common is to fill the holes with
asphalt. You can use hot patch or cold patch. Hot patch is asphalt that
is at a relatively hot temperature. The longer it is hauled around and
therefore allowed to cool, the more difficult it is to use. Cold patch is
asphalt that is not heated. Generally speaking, the hot patch has more
lasting results than does the cold patch. Regardless of which asphalt
patch is used, it is necessary to tamp the asphalt once it is placed in the
hole.

Without this tamping action, the asphalt will not be compacted and
will ultimately work its way out of the hole; then your street department
personnel will have the same job to do over again. For small jobs, like
potholes, the tamping device may be a 'compactor.' A compactor is a
machine that looks a lot like a lawn mower; except that on the bottom
of it (where a blade is on the lawn mower) there is a flat piece of metal.
The whole machine vibrates the ground surface to accelerate the
settling effects of the asphalt, or whatever you are trying to tamp. For
very small potholes, your street department personnel may use a hand
tamp. A hand tamp is a tool consisting of a flat square of metal (6" x 6"
or so) mounted on the end of a handle, similar to a shovel handle. Once

the asphalt patch is in place, the worker merely beats it flat with the hand tamp.

Depending on how deep you have allowed the pothole to get, it may be necessary to fill a part of the pothole with lime rock or gravel before capping it with asphalt. This not only saves you money in material costs, but it also makes the 'fix' last longer. Again, if you do fill the hole with something before you put the asphalt in, that substance, too, should be tamped or compacted to prevent problems generated from settling after the hole is repaired. You should use at least enough asphalt to have one-and-a-half to two inches in thickness after it is compacted. Less than this will probably not hold; then, guess what? The street department is back fixing the same hole. In all fairness to your personnel, however, once in a great while a pothole patch may pop out for reasons other than an improper repair job, freezing and thawing, for example. But, generally speaking, a good patch job, well tamped, will last until the road is resurfaced, i.e. many years.

What is lime rock? Lime rock is a soft gravel-like substance that comes from the mineral lime. To look at it, one would think it is a cross between dirty white gravel and sand. Lime rock is a common product used in the construction of road beds.

Summertime grass mowing is one of the most time consuming jobs your street department will have. It is also a time when your less dedicated personnel will have their greatest opportunity to goof off and not get caught. A general caveat: Do not allow your supervisors to get in the middle of the manual labor part of the work so that they can not supervise. (By the current interpretation of labor law, as a result of Garcia vs. San Antonio, a supervisor can work no more than 20% of his/her time in manual labor and still be classified as a supervisor.) See Appendix B (Job Description of Designated Lead Worker).

In the case of lawn mowing, your street department supervisor, or street superintendent, or whatever you call him (now, let's be nice!), should not be cutting the grass, anywhere. He should be spot-checking his personnel as they work. At the same time he is driving around the city to check on the grass mowing, he can be looking for other problems within the city that need his department's attention: missing street signs, defaced street signs, newly formed potholes, clogged drainage systems, etc.

Speaking of grass mowing, you should know that there are several different types of mowers available. Some of these mowers can make a world of difference in the capabilities of your people to properly maintain specific areas. Although the initial cost may sound expensive, consider the repeated labor costs involved when these more sophisticated types of mowers are not purchased. Probably the single most useful and simultaneously unusual mower is called a 'boom mower.' There are two types of boom mowers; one is flat, and the other appears to be cylindrical and is called a flail mower. Both of these mowers have their cutting deck mounted on the end of a large boom that is controlled hydraulically from the tractor. They are excellent for maintaining ditches, hillsides, and other difficult to reach areas. (See Figure 3.)

Oftentimes, the only alternative to maintaining an area without a boom mower is to utilize your individual people with weedeaters, sickles, or scythes. You may or may not want to buy a whole new tractor with the boom mower fitted thereto; you could have the boom mower fitted to a tractor you already have in inventory. Regardless of what you decide, you must understand that because of the nature of the boom mower, the tractor must be counterbalanced with weights on the opposite side from the boom mower extension. Do not be chintzy on these weights, or you may find your boom mower, tractor and driver lying on the side of a ditch, or some other undesirable circumstance. See Appendix B (Job Description of Equipment Operator).

Another type of mower that is very useful is called a 'batwing mower.' This is generally a three-piece mowing deck that runs behind the tractor. The two decks on the outside fold up, similar to aircraft wings on those planes used on the navy's aircraft carriers; then the tractor can pull the mowers down a street and only take up a single lane of traffic. Once the tractor is on a wide right of way or similar large grassy area to be mowed, the two outside decks fold down; your driver now is mowing three times the width that he could mow with a normal bush hog type of mower. There are some batwing mowers that are only two decks wide, and then only one deck folds up. (See Figure 4.)

Another key area that your street department personnel need be involved in is the marking of your streets. Specifically, I am referring to the painting of stripes, arrows and lines on the pavement. If your city is large enough to have a street department, let me assure you that it is large enough to have a line striper painting machine to use on the streets. I say this because in one of the cities I managed, we didn't have this machine. When we finally purchased it, it was like a revelation. A striper is really a worthwhile purchase, trust me. With just a little bit of practice, your people will be able to do a first class job of striping your streets, your city parking lots, etc.

Figure 3. Boom mower

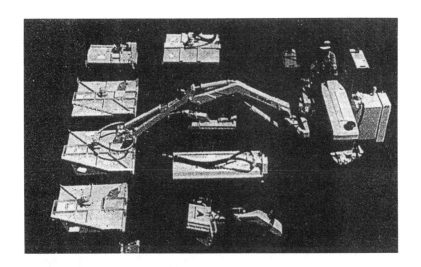

Figure 4. Batwing mower

A few warnings about striping. Before painting the street, you (actually your people doing the work) must be certain that the street surface is clean. Sweep it off and get all of the pebbles, sand, etc., out of the road. Use traffic cones and/or barricades to mark off the freshly painted area and keep cars off the paint until it dries. Also, be sure your people use traffic cones, flashing lights, red flags, orange-colored safety vests, and whatever else they can get their hands on to slow down the traffic going around them when the actual painting is going on. If there is an accident on the site where your people are painting, you can count on getting sued as being the cause of the accident. This is not to say your people are guilty; I'm just suggesting methods to reduce the risk. So, be sure there are enough people on the scene to control the traffic and do the work.

If, after the street has been striped, or the stop bar painted on, or whatever, you notice that the paint has worn off already, have your people go back to the scene with soap, water and a broom and wash off the place where they painted the markings on the street. Yes, I said wash it off! For lots of different reasons, an area that looks like it needs to be repainted in fact only needs to be washed off.

Another form of street marking, aside from painting, is the use of thermoplastic markings. As the name implies, this is a plastic marking that is installed with heat. It is very good and lasts much longer than paint, but it is expensive. There are contractors that put this thermoplastic type of marking down if you have selected intersections, railroad crossings, or school crossings that you believe warrant thermoplastic rather than paint. Your state department of transportation (DOT) may have this capability internally. It is also common for the state DOT to come in and mark a state highway, right after they have resurfaced it. So, if you do have a paint striper, don't be too anxious to use it on that newly resurfaced state highway.

An area that can cause you a lot of trouble in our litigious society (that means there are too many lawyers around and everyone wants to sue everyone for anything) is a missing traffic control sign, a missing stop sign for example. What happens when someone unfamiliar with the area comes to an intersection that has the stop sign torn down? They go right on through; if there is on-coming cross traffic, you have just generated some work for your police and fire (rescue) departments. My point is, you must impress upon all of your subordinates how important it is to be aware of the street signs they pass in the normal course of their travels in your city. If one turns up missing or knocked over or defaced, report it to the street superintendent immediately. Then, you, the manager, must make sure your street superintendent follows up on it promptly, or as soon as is reasonable depending upon what type of sign is missing. Your street department people can not see and be everywhere at the same time, so you must instill this team work approach to aid your city in keeping the streets properly marked.

Needless to say, in order to respond in a timely manner to a potentially hazardous situation, your street superintendent must keep a stock of some signs on hand; it should not be necessary to order a sign from a sign company, or local painter every time you have one turn up missing. You, on the other hand, as a business man/woman do not want a bunch of signs on hand tying up the city's money. Use your common sense, and make your street superintendent use his.

One caveat about street signs: it is important that many of these signs be of a reflective nature so that they are readily visible after dark with low light. It is not necessary for your street name signs to be reflective, but certainly your stop signs and other traffic control signs should be. Consequently, if you have a sign that has been defaced or has become faded over time, it may be necessary to order a new one, as opposed to having the sign repainted by your local sign painter. Some states have statutes dictating that certain street signs be reflective; check it out. If your city does not have The Manual on Uniform Traffic Control Devices book in their city hall, you should purchase one from the U.S. Government Printing Office. It is the 'bible' on street markings.

Before your street department installs a new street sign on a given street, ensure that they are aware of whose street it is and that they have a working relationship with the state DOT and the county highway department. Case in point: in one city at one particular intersection, there was a very small median in the road with a stop sign placed thereon. This particular intersection was heavily used by trucks (tractor-trailer type trucks), and this stop sign was always being run into, bent over, flattened/mangled, etc. The road belonged to the state, and we knew that. We would advise the state DOT that the stop sign was torn down or otherwise bent beyond recognition, but they would not respond too quickly sometimes. So, in the interest of safety, our street department would go erect a new stop sign. A few days later, the DOT sign boys would come into town, take our stop sign down, put it in their truck never to be seen again, and erect their own stop sign in its place. We would complain to DOT, and they denied it transpired. So, get your lines of communication between intergovernmental relations open, and functioning.

Your street department superintendent should keep an inventory on the location of every major traffic control sign within the city;

specifically, I am referring to stop and yield signs. This inventory will help your personnel if a sign turns up missing. Certainly, if a sign is missing, it is no longer there. Without the aid of an inventory, however, you may not realize any sign is missing. The inventory may also be required by your liability insurance company. If someone is involved in a traffic accident because they go through an intersection that is supposed to have a stop or yield sign there and it is missing, such an inventory may come in handy in the law suit with which you are about to be served. A missing yield sign is a different problem than is a missing stop sign, as an example.

A related problem your street department needs to keep under control is the blocking of the visibility of traffic control signs by low hanging branches of trees or other vegetation. This problem usually occurs during midsummer, after the plants have enjoyed a growth spurt. It is important to keep these plants trimmed back away from all of your signs.

Street lighting may be another major problem for your city. If the electric utility is privately owned or otherwise owned by some entity besides the city, your responsibility is markedly reduced to only ordering new lights when necessary, reporting lights that are not functioning, and reporting lights that are burning twenty-four hours a day. Again, you need to develop the team work approach to be able to determine when lights are burned out or when they are on all of the time. A logical department to assist you in reporting lights that are not burning at all is your police department. They patrol the streets during the hours of darkness, and they should notice when a street light is not working. All you have to do is convince the chief that his patrol officer really can take two minutes and jot down the street address, or the pole number, of a nonfunctioning street light. Report that to the shift sergeant, he/she reports it to the lieutenant, with a little luck, it can be reported to city hall for forwarding to the utility company. Your street, sanitation, water and possibly other departments, can tell you when lights are burning 24 hours a day, assuming you can get them to make note of their observations, as well as making those observations at all.

One of the biggest jobs of your street department, and often most neglected, is that of inspecting new construction in a subdivision under development. I addressed this issue in part under the Drainage Chapter as well as earlier in this chapter. But, the same general information goes. You are going to inherit the streets from the developer at some time in the future. Coordinate with your city engineer and ensure that the work being done is according to specifications. If your street department personnel do not have the technical skill to inspect roads under construction, have your engineer go out on the job site and teach your street department personnel so they do know. Training is one of the most important and neglected areas of personnel management in the public sector. (I've already been on that soap box in the chapter of the same name.) Find out what that developer is doing in street construction. What you don't know can hurt you. See Appendices G and H for information and diagrams on curb and utility cuts.

A good technique I have seen used to protect the new surface of new streets in a new subdivision while the builders are still bringing heavy equipment in and out of a development is to only put down the subcourse of the asphalt. After all the building is completed, or almost all of the building, then the developer can come back in and put down the final course of asphalt. I am quite certain the developer will not be too wild about this idea; but if you can get your engineer to concur and then your commission to back your demands, the developer will see it your way, or he won't develop. Do you get the picture? Your city should have the final say! You may want to specify this requirement in your subdivision development regulations.

Budgeting has already been addressed in another chapter; but while we are on the subject of the street department, we need to discuss gasoline taxes. In the wake of a lot of crumbling infrastructure (that means all of your streets, drainage systems, and old water and sewer pipes that are falling apart primarily due to age and lack of proper maintenance), several states have enacted special gasoline taxes that are then revenue shared back to local governments. In almost every state, the enabling legislation for this particular source of revenue mandates that the funds be used for the repair and general maintenance of streets and drainage systems only. Do not get into the spot of letting your commission put this money in the bank, or use it to pay the new secretary's salary, or anything like that. And for heaven's sake, don't you recommend any such thing. This money should be totally offset by expenses in the street department budget only. If you just don't know what to do with all of this money, you can probably even use it to pay salaries within your street department without getting into trouble; check with your city attorney or the state office of local government assistance or revenue sharing and ask for their opinion. Ideally, it should be used for capital expenditures in the maintenance of streets and drainage systems, such as your annual resurfacing program. See Chapter XXVI on vehicles, radios, and organization for additional information about the street department's vehicles.

Chapter XVII

WATER DEPARTMENT

Your city may, or may not, have its own water department. If you do have one, many of the same guidelines I stated in the previous chapter, on the street department, apply here.

Your water department personnel serve two primary functions; they are to read the meters monthly, quarterly, or whatever you have established in your city as the standard period; and they are to maintain the water plants, lines, equipment, etc. They are not trained nor equipped to perform new construction. When your commission/council members get that gleam in their eye indicating how much money can be 'saved' by having the water department install that new line that the engineer says should be upsized to better serve the citizenry, your job is to do everything within your power, to include falling on your sword and bleeding on the commission chamber's nice carpet, to get the commission to contract the job out to the private sector.

The maintenance of the potable water plants is a rather complex operation. In most states, you have to have at least one state certified operator 'in charge of' the water plant maintenance. In some states, these operators are divided into different 'classes' or levels. You are required to have a certain level of operator on staff to ensure the plant is running properly, based on how much water the plant(s) produce daily. In some smaller cities, your water superintendent may be the only certified operator on your staff. You should encourage your superintendent to get all of his staff certified; it can only enhance the capabilities of your department, and thereby the quality of service you deliver to the citizens. Accordingly, if you are going to ask your people to become certified as a part of their job, you (the city) should pay for the classes and the testing. Likewise, once they become certified, you should try to work it out that they get a pay raise to reflect their certification, and set them apart from the noncertified persons monetarily; a 5% raise is a commonly accepted figure [more about that in Appendix C, Section XX, Sample Ordinance A, Article III (Pay Plan)].

What is complex about operating a water plant? I am glad you asked, otherwise, I'd have to leave out this part. At a minimum, your city is most probably injecting chlorine into the water supply. Do you realize that chlorine is a deadly gas? I knew you did. When handled properly and with caution, there is nothing to be afraid of; but the chlorine certainly needs to be 'respected' by those who handle it. Aside from the chlorine, your plant(s) must have complex automatic charting equipment that keeps records on the 'ebbs and tides' of the water pressure in your water lines. It may also have a charting system for the levels of water maintained in your storage tanks, or when your pumps turn off and on. Your city may also inject fluorides into the water system. If you recall from your last visit to your friendly dentist, fluorides are important in keeping our teeth and bones strong. It is so important in fact, that some state health departments have a grant program available, whereby the state will assist the city to get a fluoride injection program initiated for their city water supply.

In addition to all of this, your water superintendent must have a detailed understanding of how ground storage tanks interface with high service pumps, to keep the water pressure adequate in the lines for your citizens to draw upon that water and use it. You may have some elevated water storage tanks that work in conjunction with the ground tanks and the high service pumps to keep your water system operative. If there is a power failure, how does your water system continue to deliver water to your customers/citizens? There is probably an emergency generator system that provides the necessary electricity to keep the service pumps operational. Your water superintendent, however, must know all of these workings, and perhaps more importantly, what to do when they don't work properly, in order to keep your water plant 'on-line.'

Another key function of your water department, is the inspection of the installation of new water lines in new subdivisions by the developer, and his subcontractors. Likewise, if you are doing some upgrading work in the city and you were successful in getting your commission to contract the work out, the upsized lines going in the already established part of town also need to be inspected as they are constructed. You are going to have that water line in the ground for a long time, hopefully; so you want to ensure the work is done properly.

You need to talk with your water superintendent and ensure that he knows what is necessary about such new line inspection. If he doesn't know, it is not a big deal to have your city's consulting engineer teach what he and his men/women should know about new line installation and inspection. You can find out if your water department personnel know about this by asking a few key questions; When should the water lines be installed in a new subdivision under construction? Before, or after the grade elevation has been done? [Answer: after.] How should the 'bed' the water line is going to lay in be prepared? [A: The water line should be laid on gravel, not bare dirt.] Are you (the water department) making the subcontractor walk in all of the lines before back filling? [A: Yes.] What provisions are being made to keep the lines sanitary and free from mud and other infiltration? [A: The ends of the pipes should be capped off until they are connected to another pipe. No open pipe ends should be exposed to loose dirt in open trenches, nor to gravel.] What quality of service lines are being utilized? [A: Cheap plastic black hose is the wrong answer especially if it is being stored in the direct sunlight. This type of storage causes this pipe/hose to deteriorate even more quickly; it becomes brittle.] If meters are being installed, what is their quality? [A: Cheap is not good. This does not mean the meters need to be the top of the line, but they should be serviceable.]

One test is to see if the valves within the meters can be easily turned off and on, once the meter is hooked into the water supply. Some cheaper meters can be turned on once, and anything else causes a malfunction.] Does the city have 'specs' on the meters to be used? [A: Yes, at least the meters should meet specifications dictated by the city.] Are the valves being installed of sufficient quality that they can be used without malfunctioning the first time they are under stress? [A: The turning off and on test mentioned above is a good test here, too.] Who is doing the mapping of the new lines? [A: Someone should be mapping the lines as they are installed. Assuming the water line piping contractor can read and comply with the subdivision's engineering plans, the mapping is already accomplished. Inevitably, however, for many different practical reasons, there will be some minor changes in the original plans. Consequently, after the lines have been laid, the developer's engineer should supply the city with a set of "as built" plans. These will serve nicely as the maps of the water lines. I would encourage your water superintendent to reduce the relative details off of the "as builts" into a detailed water line map location book.]

If your water department does not have a set of maps of where all the water lines in the city are, then that should be the number one priority that you give to them. The maps should indicate where the lines run in relation to the streets, what size the lines are, where the valves are, where the hydrants and stand pipes are, where service taps are located on the lines, and so forth. This information should be maintained in a notebook format, copied, and allocated in each water technician's truck, as well as a copy for the fire department and one for the city manager's office. These books are invaluable in controlling damages from water line breaks and the related loss of service to the customers in the area. By knowing which valves to turn off, many customers' water supply will be uninterrupted while the actual break location is isolated.

Another key job of your water department personnel is to monitor, record, report and bill your citizen/customers for the amount of water used. Each customer/home will have a water meter somewhere at that address. Some are in the front yard, some in the back yard if there is an alleyway or easement running through there, and some meters are even located inside the house. The traditional method of reading meters is for a man/woman from your department to go to each water meter, physically read the numbers thereon and record them into a book. See Appendix B (Meter Reader Job Description). After all the meters in a particular book have been recorded, the meter-reader takes the book to a clerk in your utility billing office. The clerk compares the current reading to the last reading, takes the difference which indicates the amount of water used, and calculates a bill from those numbers, using an ordinance-adopted price schedule. Hopefully, a good deal of this process is computerized, thus reducing the labor time and thereby the production costs.

Once the clerk has calculated the bill due the city, she/he must produce a bill and mail it to the customer/citizen in order for the city to get paid. Regardless of how this process works in your city, and I am going to discuss that further in just a minute, there are some key factors that should be going on as a part of this billing process in every city.

As the manager, it is your job to ensure these steps are being properly accomplished. You must look at the water department as a business. Although you are a city and it is a city's job to deliver services to the citizens, there are some services that should be paid for with tax dollars; and there are some services that should be offset by 'user fees'. Traditional city services are those that should be provided with tax dollars: police protection, fire protection, general administration of the city, and street maintenance. Services that are not equally utilized, however, should be paid for with user's fees, according to how much of that service is used by each user. Water service is an excellent example. If I use 26,000 gallons in a month, than I should pay more than you who only used 15,000 gallons in that month. Some other examples of services that should be delivered from the revenues of user's fees are sewerage service, electricity, maybe garbage, and maybe recreation.

If you are delivering a service out of the revenues of user's fees, then that department should be financially managed as an 'enterprise fund.' Recall, I discussed this in the budget chapter. The point is, you need to collect enough revenue for the service delivery to totally offset the running of that department's expenses, like a business. The local hardware store does not operate at a loss just because they want their customers to like them, and neither should you. If your commission/council on the other hand, wants to keep fees down for some reason, then they must understand that the loss of revenue must be made up from some other means, like regular tax dollars. I don't recommend this approach. I have always found that politicians find it more palatable to raise the fees for a service that is operating at a loss rather than raise taxes. When you are setting these fees by ordinance, ensure that you have done your homework and present a true and accurate picture to your elected body. You should not only be generating enough revenue through your rates to meet the operating expenses, but you are also allowing for some capital improvements, like the replacement of one of your departmental vehicles each year or one every two years, something along those lines. Also, consider capital improvements for the replacement of antiquated water lines, pumping equipment, upgrading of water plants and upsizing of lines as they may be needed.

Another key issue in the administration of your water department is the 'connection charge' or 'tap fee' as it is more commonly called. I discussed this issue in the budget chapter, also. This is the fee you charge for all new service. Ideally, this fee should go directly to a capital fund to provide for the long term capital projects within your department, like the construction of new water plants, drilling of new wells, closing of wells no longer used, etc. This fee needs to be calculated by the engineer periodically, to ensure that the tap fee being charged is fair and reasonable. The fee should be calculated such that the tap fee charged is equal to, or slightly less than (yes, I said less than and not more than) the actual cost of producing water and delivering that water to a new connection. (It must be equal to, or less than the cost incurred by the governmental entity to provide that service, because of several court decisions that basically state that governments can not provide services to make a profit.) A new connection is defined as a totally new meter installation at an address previously unserviced by your water department - a new house, for example. This would not be a house that has been empty and is now occupied by a new citizen.

In dealing with citizens/customers and collecting their money for the delivery of water service to their home, you are going to run into a disgruntled or otherwise unhappy citizen/customer every now and then. Generally the reason they get upset is because they feel they are being over-charged for water used; they do not believe they could have used that much water this billing cycle when they never used that much water before. Chances are, they have developed a leak somewhere between the water meter, located on the edge of their property, and the faucets within their home. A 'running' toilet can account for the waste of as much as 18,500 gallons of water in a three month period. A leak from a quarter inch hole in a service line can cost 1,181,500 gallons of wasted water in the same three month period. So, when your citizens get upset about what they believe to be an excessive water bill, have one of your water technicians go to their home and do a little investigation to see if they can determine the source of the problem. Be very cautious not to get into the business of repairing leaks on the citizen/customer's side of the meter. This is like the traditional separation of church and state. If a plumber, or worse the whole local plumbers' union, even thinks that the city water crews are repairing private citizens' water leaks, you are likely to encounter something tantamount to a battle.

As part of your own general education, you should have an understanding of where your water comes from initially and how it gets into your citizens' homes. Most public water supplies come from the underground water systems. There are lakes, pools and streams, all underground. This water is generally more pure than the water we normally see, surface water, in the aboveground lakes, streams, etc. The reason the underground water is more pure is because the earth has acted as a natural filter process and purified the water as it seeped down through the different levels of earth, rock and other materials to get into the underground water system. This underground water system is generally referred to as the 'aquifer.' Technically, there are several layers or elevations of the aquifer, and so there are several levels of underground lakes and streams. Again, the lower you go, the more pure the water is likely to be. On the other hand, the deeper you drill in order to get water, the more expensive the drilling is. If you are fortunate enough to be getting your water from the second or third aquifer, your well depth is probably between 800 and 1,400 feet below the surface. Do not let someone convince you that a two hundred foot deep well will work just fine! It will work just fine for an irrigation well, but not for potable water. (Potable water is a technical term that means water that is suitable for drinking. Nonpotable water is either water that has some impurities in it that make it unfit for human consumption and/or water that has not been tested and therefore may not be fit for human consumption.)

Depending on where your city is located and how much artificial irrigation is needed to keep yards green, etc., you may want to become an expert on shallow wells for the purposes of providing water supply for irrigation purposes, for car washes, etc. If you are in an area where multiple water supplies are utilized routinely, make sure you have a rapport with the local health department such that you can mutually ensure that nonpotable water is not being used for potable purposes. Although, generally, it is not good to use treated water (chlorinated) for irrigation purposes and it is certainly more expensive, it is not practical, more often than not, to have separate water supplies at each customer's house. In areas where a lot of artificial irrigation is needed, it is common for the residents to have a shallow well in their back yard for irrigation purposes and a water meter in their front yard for potable purposes. If they do not have this arrangement, they may have a second water meter on their property that measures water used strictly for irrigation. This is because some sewer companies charge the customers based upon the amount of water the customer puts into the wastewater treatment system to be treated. The water used for irrigation goes into the ground and not the sewer pipes, so the customer should not be charged for irrigation water utilized.

Chapter XVIII

SEWER DEPARTMENT

Many of the comments that I have made on the water department in the previous chapter apply to the sewer department as well: user fees, maintenance versus new construction by your city crews, etc.

Your city may have its own sewer department. If you do not have one, chances are the wastewater sewers are operated by some private agency and/or the developer of one or more of the subdivisions within your city. Remember that we discussed the storm water sewers in chapter fifteen, Drainage? Do not confuse these two different types of sewers. In some locales, the storm water sewage system may be combined with the sanitary sewage system. When this is the case, this type of sewage system is called a "combined sewage system." Imagine that! Combined systems are less prevalent today than many years ago.

It is possible that your city may have septic tanks on individual homes in addition to sewer plants servicing other parts of the city. There are people who philosophize that wastewater sewer capacity should only be utilized for commercial and industrial customers as well as multifamily residential customers. These advocates contend that all single family residential customers should be on their own septic tanks. All that is fine, if that is what your city 'fathers' (council members) want. You must also bear in mind that you are probably going to be saddled with whatever was established by your predecessors and the council members' predecessors.

If septic tanks are prevalent in your city, there are some things you need to know about this type of wastewater disposal. A septic tank is merely a tank buried in the ground in the front or back yard of the house. The wastewater sewer lines from the house run into the septic tank. The septic tank acts as a settling device; the larger solids remain in the tank. There are bleeder lines off the septic tank where most of the liquid runs out of the septic tank into the earth. It is common for septic tanks to require cleaning out, after several years of use. The intervals between pumping out septic tanks vary with the type of soil in which the septic tank, and more particularly the bleeder lines are located. In some older parts of a city, you may find homes that have abandoned their septic tanks and hooked on to the city's sewer system when the collection lines crossed in front of the house.

Septic tanks built today are closely monitored by the health departments and environmental agencies in the area. If a developer is going to install septic tanks, as opposed to hooking new homes onto a sewer system, the minimum size of the lot the home can be built on may be a quarter of an acre. In other locales, one full acre may be required in order to allow the installation of a septic tank. Although this does not concern you directly, you should have a working knowledge of the standards enforced in your area. The belief is that if septic tanks are used more densely than a specified quantity per acre, health problems may result. Another concern involving septic tanks is the proximity of any tank to a potable water well. If you suspect this may be a problem in your area, check with the local health department to see what the policy is on this matter.

Anyway, if you have a sewer plant, you have a professional obligation to learn how it works and to get it fixed if/when it ceases to work. Sewage is the liquid conveyed by the sewer. The sewer is a pipe or a conduit, generally a closed system, that does not flow at a full level. Sewerage is defined as the art of collecting, treating and disposing of sewage. For all intents and purposes, sewerage and sewage are interchangeable terms. Sewers carry human excreta, industrial waste (waste by-products from industrial processing: dyeing, brewing, paper making, etc), dish water, bath water, and storm sewage. Storm sewage, you should recall, is the liquid that runs off the surface of the ground, particularly the roads, during and following a rainfall. Ideally, storm water sewage will be handled separately from wastewater sewage. (See Figure 5.)

If your city operates a combined sewage system, i.e. one that does not separate wastewater from surface water, the treatment of this sewerage is of paramount importance. There are some older systems that dump sewerage directly into surface bodies of water in the event the volume of water from a major storm would overload the treatment system. It doesn't take a rocket scientist to figure out that such a configuration results in pollution of the streams and lakes. You, as the manager, need to guard against such a problem. A combined sewerage system must meet the same rigorous treatment as a separate wastewater system, since the wastewater is the most contaminated form of sewerage being processed. Conversely, however, it doesn't matter if the storm water sewerage is treated like wastewater sewerage. If wastewater sewerage is treated like storm water sewerage, it is simply insufficient treatment.

Figure 5. Sewerage Treatment Plant drawings

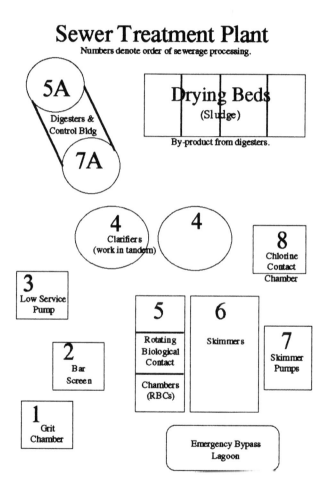

Sewer Treatment Plant
Numbers denote order of sewerage processing.

If your city operates separated systems, infiltration is the term used to identify storm water (surface water) sewage that somehow leaks into the sanitary sewerage system. Infiltration can also be identified as wastewater sewage that leaks into the storm water system, although this is a less likely occurrence. Infiltration of surface water into the sanitary sewers can cause tremendous problems usually stemming from the designed maximum volumes that the sanitary sewer system(s) is/are designed to carry and process. When surface water enters into the sanitary sewer system, the volume of liquid increases, often to the point of causing the system to malfunction from overload.

Perhaps the most common manifestation of this problem is a lift station overflow or back up into residents' basements because the excess volume of water is too great for the lift station pump to move. The solution to this problem is to seal the leaks in the sewer pipes and/or the top and sides of the lift station to prevent this surface water from entering into the sanitary sewer system. This is easy to say; but without the use of highly technical television camera viewing of the insides of the sewers or extensive excavation, it is virtually impossible. If you believe you have a lift station that is repeatedly failing to function properly, discuss the problem with your engineer. Also bear in mind, not everyone can be an expert on everything! It may be necessary for your city's consulting engineering firm to subcontract another engineering firm that specializes in wastewater management; i.e. sewer systems.

What's a lift station? I am glad you are paying attention. A lift station is a big man-made hole in the ground. It is an integral part of a gravity feed sewer collection system. The wastewater enters this hole at some particular low spot, from an underground pipe slightly slanted downward from the previous lift station, thus a gravity fed pipe. The lift station motor then picks up, or 'lifts' the wastewater to another pipe that is markedly elevated from the entrance (lower) pipe. This second pipe is also slightly canted down hill. The point where this pipe exits the lift station is the highest point of the pipe. The wastewater then begins another downhill (gravity feed) journey to the next lift station, or to the wastewater [sewer] treatment plant, which ever comes first. See Appendix B (Job Description of Lift Station Operator.) See Figure 6.

Figure 6. Lift Station drawings

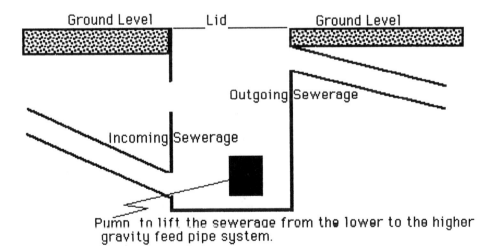

Pump to lift the sewerage from the lower to the higher
gravity feed pipe system.

As big as problem as the above described situation is, the reverse of this problem is more ecologically and legally dangerous. If sanitary sewerage infiltrates into the storm water system, then this means raw sewage is being introduced into the environment without proper processing. This problem is more difficult to discern, unless a tell-tale odor is noticed. It is, however, easier to diagnose through the use of dyes. This is another technical problem that needs to be discussed with your engineer.

Needless to say, it is paramount that the sanitary sewage systems work properly. Most sewer plants and lift stations have a red light and/or a bell, siren, or other audible alarm on them. When they malfunction, for whatever reason, this light should come on and the alarm should sound. That should be your first indication that something is wrong. The neighbors will probably call the city offices or the police department and report the noise. If not, your police should notice the light and noise as a part of their normal patrol. (You may need to prompt the police by telling them this is something to watch for if the city has had a problem with notification that the alarm is sounding and the light has turned itself on.) Depending upon how sophisticated the system is, especially if it is a plant that has malfunctioned as opposed to a lift station, the plant may have the capability of initiating an emergency automatic telephone dialer, with a prerecorded announcement of the malfunction. If you do not have such an automatic dialer installed, you may want to look into the cost and/or feasibility of this.

A sewer treatment plant (sometimes referred to as an STP) is an exceptionally complex operation that is very expensive to manage and difficult to operate properly. See Appendix B (Job Description of Treatment Plant Operators I thru IV.) Periodic inspection by an outside agency is a true help to the city. Daily testing by the sewer department is a must to ensure adequate treatment of the water. Basically, very basically, the sewer treatment plant is a large tank, or a series of tanks, with divided chambers. The wastewater enters into the sewer plant in an initial chamber. In that chamber there is already 'sludge'. This sludge contains living and growing bacteria, commonly referred to as 'bugs.' The big bugs then 'eat' the little bugs, or so the saying goes; and that is how the wastewater treatment process begins. The solids in the wastewater (you know what the solids are; use your imagination), settle out in separated tanks within the STP, and become a part of the bacterial sludge. The wastewater fluid is then injected with liquid chlorine and piped to a settling pond. As this water leaves the STP, it is now known as effluent, that is treated sewerage. Although not a commonly used phrase, you should know that the wastewater coming into the sewer plant for treatment is sometimes called 'influent' or nontreated sewerage. Technically, influent is the name assigned to any liquid as it enters into some receptacle. Effluent refers to that liquid as it leaves a receptacle. So it is possible that effluent may not be 'treated sewage' if the receptacle the effluent is leaving is not a treatment facility. For example, every lift station has influent and effluent associated with it; but no chemical treatment has transpired within the lift station.

Sewage treatment is defined as any artificial process to which sewage is subjected to remove or change its objectionable contents, thus rendering the sewage less dangerous and no longer offensive. Sewage disposal is the act of disposing of sewage by any one of several means. These terms, treatment and disposal are independent; i.e. sewage may be disposed of without having been treated.

The treatment of the effluent can be accomplished by one of several different methods or some combination thereof. The water may go to settling ponds and nowhere else. Once in the settling ponds, the water will percolate back into the soil and ultimately into the aquifer. Some percentage of this water will evaporate into the air, depending on how sunny the days are, etc. If your settling ponds, also referred to as percolation ponds, will not percolate, then obviously, you need some additional form of treatment for the effluent. One such method is to set up a 'spray field.' A spray field takes effluent from the percolation pond and pumps the water through a series of pipes to a system of sprinklers on some vacant ground. The water is then pumped through the sprinkler system where it is distributed on the ground throughout an area. The water then percolates ('percs') back into the soil and ultimately into the aquifer. Your percolation/settling pond may have an aeration system in it to aid in the treatment of the effluent.

It is possible that your perc ponds and/or spray field may be located several thousands of feet away from your treatment facility. When this is the case, your effluent is merely piped and/or pumped, probably through a series of lift stations, to this remote location.

If you have any questions about your particular facility, I would recommend that you ask your sewer department superintendent/ supervisor. As a check on him/her and for the furthering of your own education, then ask your consulting engineer the same questions when the opportunity presents itself. If the answers don't jibe, your city has a problem; and that's one of the things you're getting paid to figure out.

Sometimes, people will refer to primary, secondary and tertiary sewer treatment. The primary treatment of the wastewater is that which occurs in the sewer treatment plant. The secondary treatment, in the example, is the percolation, or settling pond. The tertiary treatment, if your city utilizes same, is what happens to the effluent next - perhaps the spray field treatment or something else. Obviously, the more stages of treatment the water is processed through, the purer the water becomes.

Chapter XIX

SANITATION DEPARTMENT

The sanitation department is another department, like the water department, where your citizens are customers. The most economically feasible method of financially administering the sanitation department, again, is to set up an enterprise fund. We already discussed this quite extensively in the budget chapter. The point is that this is a service being delivered to the customer/citizen that, in my opinion, should be paid for with user fees.

Unlike water, it is not too easy to determine that customer 'A' used, or had, this much garbage this week and customer 'B' had that much garbage this week, and then adjust their garbage rates accordingly. I guess it is easy to state the above, but it requires a tremendous amount of financial gymnastics to take any action about the problem; most probably it is more trouble than it is worth to establish variable rates for residential garbage collection. I would advocate a flat rate fee for single family residential garbage collection, based upon how much it costs the city to collect the garbage.

Garbage is very expensive to get rid of safely and legally. In addition to your obvious expenses of labor, specialized vehicles, fuel to run the vehicles, etc., you also have the expense of the 'dump fees' or 'tip fees' to consider. A dump fee is the amount you pay to the owner of the local landfill in which you dump your city's garbage. A tip fee, similarly, is what you pay if you dump your city's garbage at a transfer point, relying upon the operator of the transfer point to actually take the garbage to the landfill. Obviously, the tip fee is going to be higher than the dump fee, since you are receiving more services if you pay for tipping your 'packer truck' at the transfer point as opposed to driving on to the landfill.

You must make calculations to determine which is a better expenditure of the taxpayer dollar: to pay extra for the tip fee or to have your city's packers driven to the landfill. When making these calculations, do not forget to include labor time for the driver, fuel, time out of the city (and therefore not picking up garbage which is what these employees are being paid for, not driving down the road), etc. While I am thinking about it, find out from your sanitation department supervisor what his/her policy is on the full garbage packer going to the landfill/transfer station. The right answer is for that truck's driver to drop off his collector(s) at another driver's truck, while the first driver goes to the landfill/transfer point alone. There is no reason to waste labor dollars by allowing collectors to ride to the transfer station with the driver.

Another method of disposing of solid waste is through incineration. Some groups of governments are forming a co-op or other joint venture to build an incineration facility. Some of these incinerators are not only used for burning, and thereby disposing of solid waste; but they are also designed so that they create a by-product which is sold, creating income for the incineration facility. This by-product is generally steam which is sold to area nurserymen for use in greenhouses, etc. When you consider this issue of disposing of garbage, most people realize that it is becoming a greater problem daily. There is only so much land available to use for landfills. If you have the opportunity, check into incineration.

A related money saver is recycling. Most people think of it as a pain in the neck and extra work. But recycling newspapers, aluminum, and glass products saves space in landfills, money in dump fees, and is better for the environment. Consider a city-wide recycling program. Check with salvage dealers in your area; see how they might help you with such a program. There are several options available to a city in initiating a recycling program. You may want to create several collection points around the city where citizens can bring in their recyclable materials, placing them in specific dumpsters, according to each material being recycled. You may decide to ask your citizens to separate the recyclable materials at their home; then the garbage collectors sort it and store it separately on the packer truck.

Short of utilizing a separate collection vehicle, however, this latter option of having your garbage collectors pick up and maintain the sorted recyclable materials, is not too feasible; there is very little storage space on a packer truck, other than the garbage compartment that compacts the materials placed therein.

It will, however, become increasingly profitable for cities to coordinate and actively encourage recycling programs. The profits will come from reduced volume of garbage to dump (and, therefore, reduced dump fees) and the sale of the raw materials to recycling corporations. There is a reticence to embark on recycling programs; they require more thought and work on everyone's part: the citizens who create the garbage, the collectors, the management personnel who must supervise the program, and the elected officials who must decide to create the program on a city-wide basis.

I have already alluded to the terms of driver and collector as being different positions. Your city may have different names for them, but the point is that every sanitation truck must have a boss and a worker or workers. Generally, the driver is considered the boss of the truck, while the worker(s) is/are the collector(s). That is not to say that the driver sits up in the cab and never gets out to assist in picking up garbage. Most drivers will drive and that is all, unless someone makes them get out as the need arises to help the collectors. That is your department supervisor's job, to see that the drivers are helping the collectors when necessary. There is nothing I know of that will demoralize collectors more quickly than working with a driver that never gets out of the cab.

The sanitation department is one of the departments with the largest exposure to dangers for your employees. Consequently, it is one of the departments most likely to generate claims against your workmen's compensation insurance company. Therefore, you need to stress job safety to your sanitation supervisor and, more importantly, be sure that he stresses safety to his employees. You should demand that every collector, and driver when they are performing a collecting function, wear heavy work gloves the entire time they are collecting refuse. You should have a set of published rules and regulations about the maximum weight garbage can/receptacle allowed, in order for it to be picked up by your collectors. See Appendix C, Section XVI (Safety and Workmens' Compensation). (I recommend a 35 pound maximum.)

Additionally, these rules should include the policies on picking up grass clippings, shrub greenery trimmings, tree branches (cut to length and bundled), etc. This published list of rules and regulations should then be communicated to the citizenry. Tell new people moving into the city, too. If you do not do this, you will have one or both of two problems. Either your sanitation department employees will have lots of back injuries from picking up too heavy objects, and/or your citizens will call in complaining because their big/heavy garbage can was not picked up. Another important way to avoid workmen's compensation claims for back injuries is to have your department supervisors (not just the sanitation supervisor) conduct training classes and spot inspections on the proper way for a person to lift items -- with the legs, keeping the back straight.

Because garbage, sometimes referred to as solid waste, is so expensive to get rid of, this department is one that you should look at very closely, check how it is administered, and be sure that the user fees are being stretched to their limit. You need to know, for instance, how many households one garbage truck with one driver and one collector can pick up in a day. This is a good indicator of the point when a garbage truck needs to be added to your fleet. This is not to be confused with buying a replacement truck for the one that wears out. My experience is that one truck, with a driver and a collector, can pick up between 600-700 homes in one, eight- hour day.

Although I have no personal experience with this next item, I know that some manufacturers are now marketing a 'one-man garbage truck.' This truck is designed so that it can be operated by a driver only. He drives the truck and picks up the garbage all by himself. It is my understanding that some of these trucks require specialized 'garbage cans' in order to work. If this is the case, then you must ask if the city is going to buy these cans for all of the citizens, or are the citizens going to be required to purchase them? Anyway, if one man can operate a garbage truck, that would be a tremendous savings in labor. And, as you should know from your personnel and budgeting classes, labor is an ever increasing and ongoing expense. If you can save labor money by cutting your work force in half, over a period of time this is certainly something to consider when you purchase a new garbage truck.

Chapter XX

PUBLIC WORKS DEPARTMENT

If your city has a public works department, then the four departments discussed in the preceding chapters are probably included therein, as the street division of the public works department, etc.

If you have a city engineer on your in-house staff, he/she could perform the duties of the public works director or department head. The position of the director of public works is really an assistant city manager for the specific area of public works. If you do have such a department, then the superintendents/supervisors of each of your public works areas, (water, streets, sewers, and sanitation) actually work for the public works director; the director in turn works for you, the city manager, hopefully. Let me put it this way: If you are the city manager and you are not in a city administrator position, then everyone on the city payrolls, except the elected officials should be working for you. (Technically, a City Administrative Officer [CAO] works for the elected officials body; but so do each of the department superintendents/supervisors. A CAO is only a coordinator of the other department heads, while the elected officials are actually everyone's "boss.") Anyway, if you have the luxury of having a director of public works or any other midlevel manager, do not usurp his duties by going directly to a division superintendent; go through the director of the department and let him/her deal with the division superintendent. Do not jump the chain of command. See Appendix B (Job Descriptions of Administrative Assistant, Building Maintenance Supervisor and Personnel Director.)

You may want to establish the position of acting public works director. The idea here is to have each of your public works-type department supervisors get some midlevel management experience, while simultaneously allowing their assistant supervisors to get some departmental supervisory experience. What I am suggesting is that you create this position, administratively, and then have each of your public works-type supervisors assume the position for 30 days at a time, rotating back to their respective department at the end of their 30 day period of special duty. This would be an administrative action you could make to allow the supervisory hands-on experience to grow and to give yourself some assistance in managing the city. Just an idea! Although I always encourage keeping the elected officials informed on what you, as the manager, are doing in the city, the creation of this position would not need to come through the legislative body; you are not paying anyone any more money to assume the duties, and it is not a permanent position occupied by one individual.

Another idea that I will address here, that could fall under any one of several categories, is aesthetics within your city. Once thought of as an expense only affordable by the rich, aesthetics are becoming recognized as an investment in the city, as well as in the property values of the private landowners within the city. What I am referring to are trees, shrubs, flowers, and the general maintenance of city-owned property. The city-owned property in your city may only consist of that property where your city hall building sits. Or, it may mean several parks within the city, several city-owned buildings throughout the city, a city cemetery and/or medians upon the streets, to name a few areas. You need to provide landscaping of your city properties that makes you proud to show your city off to other people. If you are proud, your citizens will be proud; and this attitude will become infectious. Whole neighborhoods and subdivisions will take on major landscaping programs just to keep up with what the city is doing. Who wins in the end? Everyone!

When designing and deciding what kind of things you are going to do to add to the aesthetics of your city, you need to keep in mind that whatever you design, build, or plant, must be maintained by city employees with city equipment. Don't go overboard. Make certain you involve your elected officials in the design and conception process. The elected officials may want to appoint a citizen committee to be in charge of the designing and planting of landscaping on all city properties. You may have to prioritize your landscaping desires and bite off a little each budget year. But in ten years, just think of what an aesthetically improved city you will have.

Although an added expense, I would highly recommend at least consulting with a landscape architect when considering aesthetic improvements to the city. You might hire a registered landscape architect outright. A landscape architect will be able to advise you about which plants do well in the urban environment and which do not. Which flowers like sunlight, which like shade? What plants require lots of water, and which ones do well in periods of drought? Part of the problem, unique to city properties, is that some of these properties become very arid. For example, any earth in a street median is going to absorb a good deal of heat off the adjacent pavement. Consequently, this particular earth does not retain the moistness of a private lawn. Planting a tree, or shrub that requires a lot of water on a median is probably a futile effort. Consult with an expert; it will save you money in the long run. His/her expertise is actually an investment in your city's future. If you and the committee involved do not know any landscape architects, talk with your city's engineer for suggestions.

The types of plants that should be utilized vary with the climate of your particular city. Talk with your local county extension agent for ideas as well as local nurserymen and citizens with 'green thumbs.' Be sure you, and/or the committee, keeps traffic sightability in mind, as well as the climatological considerations.

Once the city decides what and where it wants landscaping, then you need to consider whether your city employees can do the work or whether to bid out the whole project. An interesting alternative would be to try to involve local civic groups in landscaping specific areas of the city as a regular project, to plant and maintain the medians on Main Street, for example.

You may want to tie in a renovation/ restoration of your downtown area with a new aesthetics program. "Make the old better than the new." Promote the historic aspects and significance of your community; capitalize upon the "Roots" phenomenon.

Chapter XXI

BUILDING DEPARTMENT
AND CODE ENFORCEMENT

The building department can be one of the biggest headaches you have as a city manager. If you have a good building official, a large part of this 'headache' will take care of itself; but there are still problems that only manager or the commission can resolve.

The building department is going to be made up of several different types of employees, according to how much growth your city is experiencing, how big your city is to start with, and your city's history of size and growth. I hope, for your sake, you have a building official.

The building official is the administrator of the building department. Depending upon your city charter and the size of your city government, he may also be the zoning administrator and the code enforcement officer. In all probability, the building official started out in the building industry as a subcontractor in some specific area of expertise or as a general contractor. It is of paramount importance that the building official has a broad knowledge of the many facets of building contracting and construction. It is even more important, however, that the building official remembers that he is now on the other side of the fence; that is to say, his job now is to protect the consumer and not building contractors or subcontractors.

Some people say that when the building official is doing his job, you will get all kinds of complaints about him: he is too difficult in enforcing the standards, he is generally hard to get along with, etc. There is some element of truth to this. I have seen a building official be tough as nails but very equitable. I have had developers and contractors tell me that one particular building official was the most difficult but the fairest man with whom they had ever worked. A great deal depends on how the building official carries out his business. If you get no complaints about a building official at all, however, you may need to be a little concerned. You will have to look into the situation and use your own judgment.

The building official is primarily an administrator; however, the building official still should do some periodic inspection to assist, and simultaneously check up on, the quality of inspection being performed by his inspection staff.

Another member of the building department team is the building inspector. You may have more than one inspector. You may have inspectors that have different areas of expertise as opposed to one who inspects all the different areas. In large measure, my comments on complaints apply to the building inspector as well as the building official. Do not confuse a building inspector with the building official. To quote a friend of mine, "There is as much difference between a building official's position and the building inspector's position as there is between the city manager's job and that of a deputy city clerk."

The building inspector's job is just what the title implies; he is the person that goes onto the job site and checks compliance with the building codes in the construction of each building. Obviously, the nature of his job versus the amount of building going on within your particular city may demand that he only performs spot inspections or spot checks. The key, however, is that the building inspector should never let the contractor know what he is going to check nor when. This is the most likely method to ensure quality construction and no corner cutting. If the building inspector is properly performing his job, chances are he is out of the office seven or more hours each day. Clearly, this allows the building inspectors to have a great opportunity to goof-off or otherwise steal time from the taxpayers, if he is of a mind to do so. It is the building official's job, and your job, to be sure that the taxpayers are getting their money's worth from the inspectors. See Appendix B (Job Description of Building Inspector I.)

The last member of the building department team may be a clerk or administrative assistant to the building official. Your building department may be responsible for a large amount of city revenues from the issuance and sale of building permits. Due to the nature of their jobs, the building official and the building inspector will probably spend a great deal of their time out of the office. Consequently, it is important to have someone available to answer their telephone, arrange for sequential inspections, and physically issue permits that have already been processed by the building official and are awaiting pickup by the permittee.

You may be able to have a secretary, or deputy city clerk assist the building department on an as needed basis, or you may need to have a full time clerical person within the building department. You will have to make this judgment based on experience and on the number of permit applications and requests. If you have a full-time person clerically assisting the building department and you observe that person reading books, knitting, or otherwise not working for the taxpayer when he/she is being paid to do so, you must either get more work to do from other areas, reduce the job to a part-time status, or even terminate the position. This clerical person should fall under the purview of the city clerk when the building official is not in the office. One of your key jobs as the city manager is to ensure that taxpayers are getting their money's worth; I can not over stress this fact.

No matter who receives the money for building permit fees, that person should be bonded. Anyone who has a job in handling money should be bonded for his/her personal protection and the protection of the city.

The work of the building department and the standards for the inspection of construction work within your city are going to be based upon some building code. There are several different building codes that may be adopted by a city as a standard for inspections within that city. The Southern Building Code is a popular code, for instance. The most revered code, however, is the one published by BOCA. BOCA stands for Building Officials and Code Administrators International, Inc. If your city does not currently have such a code adopted by reference through the ordinance process, I highly recommend you adopt one. I would also recommend that you ask your elected officials, the people that are actually going to adopt this standard, to strongly consider adopting the BOCA code. Some will argue it is very complex and difficult to read with many cross-references. These facts, however, make it more totally inclusive.

As a matter of process, you should know that these codes are periodically updated by the drafting organization. It is common for a city to adopt a specific code "in its current form, and as amended in the future by the BOCA Organization" (or which ever group wrote the code you are adopting).

I mentioned sequential inspections above. I am referring to the inspections required as part of the building process for example: site preparation inspection, footer inspection, electric rough-in, plumbing rough-in, etc. For these types of inspection, the contractor or subcontractor calls the building department and informs them that some particular item is ready to be inspected on a particular job site. Ideally, the building inspector will make these required inspections and check for other things while on the same job site. Furthermore, the building inspector hopefully will make unannounced inspections over and above those that I refer to as the required sequential inspections.

Earlier, I also mentioned building permits. Building permits are a means for a city to control the building going on within its corporate limits while simultaneously ensuring that this ongoing building is in compliance with the adopted building codes, policies, etc. Additionally, building permits cost a fee and therefore are a source of revenue to a city. The argument can be made that the building department could be set up with an enterprise fund, just like the water department or the sanitation department. Whether you choose to do this or not, your building permit fees should be sufficient to offset the salaries being paid to your building department personnel. If you are in a high growth area, your permit fees sometimes may even exceed your salary expenses for a year. You must monitor this type of situation very closely to determine if you need to hire additional inspection personnel to keep pace with the demand for inspections, or whether your current staff can handle the work load.

Building permits should be required for virtually any building that goes on within your city limits, to include, but not limited to: new home construction, new office or other commercial construction, 'substantial' renovation of an existing structure, construction of any additional buildings on property with construction already present (out buildings), construction of any fence on a property, erection of antennas (to include satellite dish television antennas) on a property, and other related types of construction. It is important to understand that building permits are required to enable the city to monitor, control, and enforce compliance with codes of construction within the city.

Building permits are not designed to make money for the city, but rather fees are charged to support the cost of hiring and training inspection personnel.

I also briefly mentioned zoning administration earlier. Your city should have a zoning ordinance adopted which dictates different classes of zoning the city recognizes and sets forth the requirements for each of these zoning districts. Zoning is another exceptionally complex subject that intertwines completely with planning as a multidisciplined field of study. I am discussing zoning here rather than the planning chapter because I have found that most smaller cities do not have an in-house planner. If you have a planner, you should consider the work load of the planner versus the building official to determine who can best do the job of the city's zoning administrator. Anyway, in addition to the zoning ordinance, your city should have an official zoning map. This zoning map also may serve as the official map of the city, indicating current city boundaries thereon with updating after the official adoption of each annexation. Generally, a city will have several different major classifications of zoning with subcategories in each of these classifications. Your major classifications are probably residential, commercial, industrial, and perhaps agricultural.

Residential zoning probably will be divided into smaller single-family homes, average sized single-family homes, larger-size single-family homes, duplex family homes (which may be allowed in the same zoning district as the smaller-size single family homes), and multifamily homes. Multifamily homes may have several categories in and of itself. These categories most probably will be identified by a set of letters and numbers. For example, your residential zoning categories may be identified as R-1, R-2, R-3, and so forth. You may even have an R-E zoning category, for residential estate. Other zoning categories will probably be similarly identified; for example C-1, C-2, I-1, and so forth.

The commercial classification will probably have a category for neighborhood commercial districts, 'strip center' commercial districts, and heavy commercial districts. A strip center is a small shopping center that may be in close proximity to a residential neighborhood. Strip centers are generally considered not to be a very intense form of commercial use of the property. Neighborhood commercial districts are characterized by a single convenience-type food market in a generally residential area. Heavy commercial districts are characterized by large shopping centers, malls, restaurant areas, etc. The industrial classification may have several different categories or may have only one or two; the sophistication and intensity of industry in your city will mandate the number of categories.

Some general rules of thumb regarding zoning follow. If you have specific questions on zoning, discuss it with your building official or city planner. If you want information beyond that, see if your city is in the area of a regional planning agency, an area development district, or a council of governments; they should have a planner on staff that can assist you.

It is generally a bad idea to have intense use of any one zoning classification adjacent to a not so intense use of another classification. For example, if you allow a mall to be built adjacent to a single family area, you will probably be handling complaints from the single family homeowners forever. Instead, try to adjust the zoning of areas so that there is transition from more dense use into less intense use. If you inherit a situation where the zoning and the construction of buildings thereon already exists, you have no choice but to make the best of the situation. The city, or actually your city commission, can change the zoning in an area; but you can not force the new zoning on the use already in existence on any particular parcel of property. That use has been 'grandfathered' on that specific piece of property in that particular rezoned district.

If that use thereon ever ceases to be and said cessation lasts for the specified period required in your zoning ordinance (maybe 90 days or six months), then the new zoning classification comes into effect on that property. The grandfathering which allowed the previous use expires. Likewise, if the grandfathered use is stopped and a different use is initiated, the grandfathered use is no longer allowed; and the new zoning comes into effect.

When one general classification of zoning is immediately adjacent to another classification, there should be a buffer area in-between those two types of uses. For example, if a residential area is next to a commercial office building, there should be some dense landscaping, perhaps 50 feet in depth, on the commercially zoned property before the property line of the residentially zoned property. Buffer strips vary in size and materials. Their purpose is, as the name implies, to provide a buffer between the two different types of land-use.

Some cities have problems with 'spot zoning.' Spot zoning is a buzz word used to describe an area that has a zoning out of character with the area immediately surrounding it. An example of this might be an old factory in the middle of town that now has residential areas all around it. If that factory's property has an industrial zoning classification in the midst of residential classifications all around it, the factory property could be referred to as spot zoned. It may be that the factory property has been rezoned to a residential classification and the existence of the factory on the property is a grandfathered situation. This would not be spot zoning.

Spot zoning is generally considered poor planning, although some cities thrive on spot zoning; in fact, it is commonly accepted in those cities. One in the middle of the Texas oil region comes to mind. To have or not have spot zoning is a decision your legislative body must make consciously, for then the city will have to live and deal with the existing situation. It may be that your city will have to make some broad rezoning legislation and grandfather the preexisting uses until those uses cease to function. Then, as explained above, the new zoning will take effect. If you believe you have a spot zoning problem, discuss it with a trained planner and form a course of action for your legislative body to consider.

Another hat your building official might wear is that of the city's code enforcement officer. Exactly what code enforcement means in your city depends on whether your state has passed the enabling legislation to allow your city to have a code enforcement process. Code enforcement can take on many different faces. Your police department is involved in code enforcement, as well as your building and fire departments. When someone refers to code enforcement as an entity, however, it is usually tied directly to the enforcement of zoning regulations.

Basically, code enforcement legislation, if it exists, allows your city to enforce certain standards of living within your city limits. What types of things do code enforcement officials and code enforcement boards deal with? Anything from prohibiting grass/weeds becoming too high on a property within a given city, or county and/or zoning district; "junk" cars on a residentially zoned property; construction of a house or other structure too close to a property or set-back line. What the board and officials get involved in will be based largely on your city's zoning and other code regulations.

The enabling legislation probably will call for administration and process serving by the city staff, with a citizen board serving as the governing body for penalties for noncompliance. Your city commission may very well have the position of an appellate board. Some code enforcement legislation provides for the city's code enforcement (citizen) board to have the authority to fine a citizen found to be in noncompliance up to and including $250 a day for every day he/she remains in violation.

As I alluded to earlier, you may have a person whose sole job is code enforcement. Or, this may be an additional job for your building official, and/or fire inspector, and/or the city manager. Yes, the city manager may very well have to assume many of the duties of code enforcement officer in smaller towns.

The most important thing relative to code enforcement matters is to be absolutely certain that you know exactly what the regulations state and exactly what the violations are. Dates and times of observation, notification of property owners and the proof thereof is paramount. When a board of volunteer citizens appointed by the local elected officials is considering leveling fines against another citizen, the decision needs to be based upon black and white facts; there can be no gray areas.

If the framework for the code enforcement process exists within your city and yet has not been utilized or not utilized lately, a lot of problems can be solved and still more problems avoided by getting the code enforcement system back on track. If the code enforcement process has not been practiced and your city is experiencing a lot of violations and related code enforcement problems, it may only take one or two strong cases decided by the board for the message to get around town that violations will not be tolerated.

The best advice I can give regarding code enforcement actions is: Make certain all of your information, supporting documentation, and evidence of violations, as well as that of your subordinates, are completely accurate and in order. In short, prior to taking anything to the code enforcement board, make sure your 'ducks are lined up in a row.'

The building official, at a minimum and perhaps the building inspectors, need to have a good working rapport with the local health department which may be at the county level of government. Regardless of the code enforcement situation within your state, health department officers can enforce standards of living to be met, for example, running water, functioning sewers, adequate heat, etc. Furthermore, the health department may be the controlling authority for the digging of wells, some levels of plumbing inspections and related items to building a home. Consequently, your building department personnel should know and be able to work with the health department personnel.

You, as the manager, should find out how these matters are handled within your particular locale, what the law states and how it is enforced. This knowledge will aid you in ensuring there is decent housing within your city. Bear in mind, however, that over regulation can be a problem, too. Over regulation may mean that people with limited income cannot find an adequate place to live. If you believe this is a problem in your city, you may want to check with the closest office of the federal government's Housing and Urban Development Department (HUD). They may be able to assist you in providing acceptable housing for the poor. If your city is rather sizable, it may even have a HUD project within its boundaries.

Chapter XXII

PLANNING DEPARTMENT

The size of your city, and how much development is going on in your city will determine if your city has a planning department. If you have such a department, it is most probably a one person department, unless your city has a population of 20,000 people or more. If you do not have a city planner, chances are you, the city manager, will have to perform the majority of the work the planner would otherwise do. So pay attention to this chapter!

Whether or not you have a planner, your city most probably will have a planning commission of some kind. A planning commission is usually a group of volunteer citizens who have been appointed by the legislative body. This planning board usually makes recommendations to the legislative body regarding zoning changes, variances, permitted uses, etc. If your city does not have a planner, the city manager will have to serve as the primary staff adviser to the planning commission. This means the manager will need to be intimately familiar with zoning law in general and the zoning within the city specifically.

In smaller cities where a planning commission is the closest entity the city has to a building official and/or a building department, the planning commission may have to perform many of those functions addressed in the previous chapter. Similarly, the city manager, yes I'm talking to you, must be even more familiar with planning and building department functions if you do not have those respective professionals upon which to rely. If you do not have all the luxuries of a large staff, you may want to consider having your planning commission act as the Development Review Committee (DRC).

The city planner practices urban planning, generally defined as those activities associated with, and incidental to, land use and land-use regulations. See Appendix B (Planner's Job Description.) An often overlooked problem in local government is confining planning to the subject area of land-use. In actuality, of course, local government's financial activities need to be planned; certainly the budgetary process is a planning process. Street resurfacing, street cleaning, demands upon the water and sewerage systems, police and fire departments - all of these are areas that you as the manager need to keep in mind in the planning process. Your city planner can probably give you a good deal of insight into the basic techniques of planning. It's your job to implement these techniques across the board and to disallow the exercise of planning to be restricted to the planning department and land-use activities.

The city planner is the person who reviews all of the proposed development plans within your city and coordinates each of those plans with what is already in place, other proposed developments still in the planning stages, the zoning and related regulations within the city, and perhaps most importantly, commonly accepted planning principles. If your city is experiencing a tremendous amount of development, a planner can easily earn his/her keep by looking out for the best interests of the city and forcing the developer to comply with those interests. Technically, the city council/commission is the only one that can force the developer to comply; but if the planner has a good past record of success with his recommendations to the commission, often times the developer will comply with the planner's requests without trying to fight the issue. The importance that good planning and quality development has in your city will dictate whether your commission may want to adopt the policy that a developer either complies with the city's policies and requests or goes to another city to develop; i.e. the city is not making any deals with developers.

Recall my previous discussion of the development review committee(DRC). Depending on the personalities involved, the planner can act as the chairperson of that committee and take a lot of worry off of the city manager's shoulders. It is most important that you, as the manager, and the planner have a very good working relationship; even more importantly, both of you should know the commission's desires and feelings on developmental issues. If these relationships exist, it then becomes a very methodical process for development plans to be reviewed and recommendations made to the commission for their approval and/or enforcement.

In addition to reviewing proposed subdivision plans, etc., the planner should also be the keeper of the official city map. The planner should post all annexations/de-annexations, once they are official, as well as all zoning districts and changes. If you have a planner, you may want to have him/her serve as the city's zoning administrator. Recall my discussion in the building department chapter.

In addition to cooperating with you, the planner also needs to have an excellent working relationship with the building official and the engineer for the city. This is important to the planner's getting input to properly review proposed development plans. Ideally, your planner will have a good working relationship with the water superintendent, street superintendent and fire inspector as well, because all need to have input for the review of proposed development plans.

The planning department should be entirely familiar with different mapping techniques and understand how to write legal descriptions of property. It is, therefore, imperative that the planner, or you as the manager without a planner, understand metes and bounds, townships, ranges, sections, quarter sections, north, south, east, west, and the ability to read backwards. If you are laughing, you don't understand! Furthermore, it is important to understand how a subdivision is platted with blocks and lots.

The planner needs to understand and be able to differentiate between arterial, collector and other streets and to understand the setbacks needed from these streets and the requiring of additional setbacks in certain areas/streets to facilitate the widening of those streets in the future. The planner also needs to understand, practice and facilitate the generally accepted principles of annexation, de-annexation, development patterns (strip, cluster, buffer zones, etc.), and land-use zoning.

In some states, every city is required to have a comprehensive land-use plan (CLUP) on file, both in the city and at the state agency which monitors these plans. A CLUP is a master plan for the development of the city and any future land that may be annexed into the city. A CLUP is generally written and/or undergoes a major revision once every five years and is supposed to project the plan for the use of the land within the specified boundaries for the next five years. The CLUP may need to be written to provide for the minor amendment thereof periodically, probably no more than twice annually. The need for this flexibility will be dictated by the state mandate. The state may not allow any amendment, other than the five-year revision. Many times, when a CLUP is required by the state, it is written by the city (or more likely by a consultant) and placed in the file and forgotten until time to turn in a revision to the state. This is not good. If a CLUP is properly researched and written, it can be an invaluable tool for managing and planning the growth of a city. If you have a CLUP, read and study it. Then review it with your planner and/or the regional planning agency. Use it to manage your city. Make the system work as it is intended to work.

I would stay away from CLUPs written by a consultant. I know this is going to cause consultants to be unhappy with me, but my problem with these documents is that they are largely 'boiler plate.' In order to be uniquely applicable to the city for which it is written, I believe a CLUP must necessarily be written by people within the city with input from citizens. It should not be something thrown together with a word processor inserting the name of one city for another.

Another concept your planner, and you as the manager, should be familiar with is crime prevention through environmental design (CPTED). CPTED affords criteria for the review of subdivision design plans that can pay a city large law enforcement dividends in the future. If you are not familiar with CPTED, you may want to contact the National Crime Prevention Institute at the University of Louisville, Shelby Campus, Louisville, KY, 40222.

If you have questions about any of these concepts and you don't have an on-staff planner, check with your regional planning agency, local university supporting a planning or engineering school/department, or state municipal organization. Some of these concepts can mean the difference between excellent and marginal quality of life for your citizens.

I want to share some observations on land-use regulations from Professor Robert Taylor, of the Earth Science Department of Montana State University in Bozeman, MT. I believe they are absolutely on target and provide an insight for the new city manager.

"If the idea of zoning and land-use regulations is to avoid conflict between property owners and land-uses, then a project that creates conflict during its planning stage should probably not be approved.

"A municipality does not exist to guarantee economic success to individuals, but to provide for the common good of its citizens. It is a privilege for an entity to join the city; and if there is no benefit to those already in the city, then that privilege should not be extended.

"Public comment from those residents who will be directly affected by a land-use decision should be the primary determining factor in the approval or disapproval of a subdivision or other land-use decision."

One last point we as city managers need to bear in mind: It matters not how illogical an approval is. If the elected officials of the city decide to overlook your staff/management objections to an annexation or development, then it is simply a policy decision with which you must live. You cannot get emotionally involved. (This is much easier to say than to do, but knowing is a part of the battle.)

Chapter XXIII

DEVELOPMENT AND
THE DEVELOPMENT DEPARTMENT

Chances are, unless your city is experiencing massive development, you will not have this department. If you were to have one, however, your building and planning departments would probably be downgraded to 'divisions' and come under this department. If you have an in-house city engineer and he/she does not serve as the public works director, he/she would be a likely candidate for this department-head spot.

Since you probably won't have this department, you're possibly asking, why I brought it up. You need to know that there are several areas of concern in dealing with developers.

First and foremost, you should understand that developers develop to make money. That sounds simple enough, but I think all of us forget that issue sometimes. Your job, and that of the city staff, is to make sure that they comply with all of the rules, regulations and policies of your city for the safety and welfare of your citizens. If the developer can comply with all that and still develop, fine. He/she may claim he "I'm not going to make any money if I do everything the city wants done." Then, depending on your commission's feelings, I would tell him/her to go develop in some other city!

It is the city's job to provide quality development, not just development for the sake of development. You should also be aware of the fact that some developers have paid bribes to both elected and appointed city officials in order to get by a regulation or policy. I am not condemning all developers; I just want to make sure you have your eyes open to what may happen. Accepting a bribe is unethical, lest there be any doubt; furthermore, the bribing of a public official is against the law in every state with which I am familiar. So beware.

Your city should have subdivision regulations or development regulations that control the development within the city. Such a document may be adopted by ordinance but should be specified as an appendix to your city's charter. Your city should have specific policies set forth, amendable only in exceptional cases and only by informed action of the city commission/council. The idea of negotiating every issue separately for each developer does not work.

Some areas that should be addressed by your subdivision/development regulations are delineated below:

Developers should post a surety or performance bond to ensure completion of their work as required and specified by the city.

Is an estimated cost of improvements included and certified by your city engineer? Perhaps your city will want to consider a law enforcement impact fee (or other impact fees). See Appendix A.

Let me stop right here and make a point. The city engineer and/or the city's consulting engineer should not, for professional and ethical reasons, be allowed to work for any developer that is developing within the city. If this situation exists, one of the built-in checks has been eliminated; that is, the developer's engineer would be submitting his plans to the city engineer for approval. He would be approving his own plans.

A surety/performance bond is not the same as a maintenance guarantee. A maintenance guarantee should also be required by the city's regulations. This guarantee is designed to protect the city for the first year, two years, or whatever is specified in the regulations, after the city accepts dedication of the public streets and related infrastructure. Theoretically, if there are major shortcomings in workmanship, they will appear in the first year and be repaired by the developer not with tax dollars from the city.

Is there a maintenance bond included with the plans? Is the bond for 110% of the estimated cost of the improvements? A maintenance bond ensures that the publicly dedicated portions of the subdivision will be maintained for a specified period.

Do all improvements that are to be dedicated show on the plat, and are easements and rights of way identified in writing on page one of the plat? Water systems, wells, treatment facilities, lines, pump stations, storage facilities? Sewer systems, treatment plants, gravity collection lines, lift stations, and/or force mains? Are easements, with dimensions, clearly shown along with rights of way? Are all utility easements a minimum of ten feet wide with 15 feet being the desired width?

Subdivisions, including but not limited to residential development, commercial development, industrial development, and variations of any of these, should be approved by the city commission in phases. First, the commission should approve a preliminary plat of the subdivision, based on staff research and recommendations for actions and changes from the staff, as the commission sees fit. The final plat approval should include every item that the commission wants the developer to do and changes with which the developer must comply. After the subdivision is built out, generally accepted at about 80% occupancy, the city should then accept the dedication of public streets, easements, and related infrastructure.

Are specifications for the development included on the plans, or are they a separate document? If separate, are they referenced on the plat/plans?

Are the water lines of sufficient size to provide for extension and growth? Are the service lines and all hardware of specified quality to prevent unnecessary early repair? Are these specifications a part of the development regulations?

Are your fire hydrants properly located and of sufficient spacing? Is the spacing part of the regulations? Talk with your fire chief, find out what his hose capabilities are. In a residential subdivision, 300 to 350 feet between hydrants is fairly common. 750 feet between hydrants is the maximum distance of which I am aware. The key issue here is how much hose capability your fire department possesses. If the hydrants are 750 feet apart, this means the fire department has to have a supply line (hose) that is at least 375 feet long; the radius between hydrants. A greater distance between hydrants means that the fire department can not hook onto a hydrant and have sufficient hose to go from the hydrant to the area in front of the house fire where the pumper truck should be located to fight the fire.

How is wastewater sewerage going to be handled? Is there to be a city-owned sewer plant or a private company? Does the existing plant have capacity? Should you charge the developer for improving the plant? Are they going to use septic tanks? Has the county health department approved the plans?

Are you going to limit the size of the lots and/or the size of the buildings on the lots?

What provisions are there for storm water drainage? How much is going to have to be retained on site, for how long? How large a storm event will the subdivision handle? Are there any flood plains in the subdivision? What are your requirements for setbacks from bodies of water? Are bulkheads or headwalls addressed? Are first floor/basement elevations shown on the plans?

Are sidewalks required? How wide? Whose ownership? Are they to be placed on the road right of way or on the private property side?

When are the sidewalks going to be installed? (It is best, in my experience, if they are installed immediately prior to the final inspection on each house. This will result in far less damage to the sidewalks during the construction of the house.)

When is the final street surface going to be paved? Bulldozers, backhoes, and related construction equipment are very hard on asphalt, especially new asphalt. Make the developer wait to install the final surface course until the 60 - 80% occupancy level has been attained. Is the street properly designed? How thick is the base? Is it properly compacted/tamped? How thick is the asphalt? Subcourse? Final course? Does the drainage system work with the streets, or are there low spots that lack positive outfall?

Have the street names been approved by your city? There is nothing worse than having two streets with the same or a similar name in your city. When firefighters or police officers are rushing to the scene of an emergency, they love to guess which street is the correct one. Wouldn't you? What if your house was the one on fire? Don't allow a developer to repeat the street name already given to other streets in your city, if at all possible. You don't need to have streets named, for example, "Bobway" and "Barbway." Just think of how confusing that might be coming over the radio in time of emergency. "Which street did the dispatcher really say?"

Are driveways properly designed? Is the concrete specified at sufficient pounds per square inch (PSI) so as not to break down in two years? If that happens in a whole neighborhood, the neighbors will be coming after the city, asking why the city did not protect them from these 'evil developers.'

Do the clearing, grubbing and grading plans show the original and final contours? Do all of the lot sizes meet frontage and depth requirements for the zoning ordinance?

Is a composite plan included showing ALL utilities? Can all the lots be served by the utilities?

Are you going to have underground utilities within your subdivisions? Although the utility companies will scream that these are more expensive to install, they do seem to have a better record of service. And, they are much more aesthetically pleasing than overhead power lines.

Has there been a traffic impact study? Are the daily trips in any intersection in the proximity affected to the point that the developer should bear the cost of upgrading the intersection? Are there sufficient stacking lanes? Deacceleration lanes? Is ingress/egress sufficiently limited and channeled so as to not adversely affect the overall flow of traffic in the area?

Are you going to require at least dual ingress/egress to every subdivision? This will allow emergency vehicles to have more than one access to an area.

Have the impacts of this new development upon area schools, police services, fire services, and sanitation services been studied, allowed for, and generally addressed?

Is there a required landscaping plan? What about buffer areas between differently zoned parcels?

Off-street parking requirements?

What about the widths of roads, intersections, etc.?

Your engineer and building official can help educate you on all these questions. You should know enough about it, however, to ensure that the best interests of the city are being provided for and taken care of in any development. You should have a developer's agreement, mutually specifying every nonstandard element of subdivision approval for every development the commission/council has approved.

When you lack personal expertise in an area, do not be afraid to bring someone into the discussion/project who has this expertise. If you are dealing with sewer systems, get an engineer who is a wastewater expert. Not every civil engineer has experience with wastewater systems; in fact, most have not had any such experience. It's much cheaper to hire a consultant and have the work performed correctly from the beginning, as opposed to to going back and fixing it later. Retrofitting always cost more than it would to do it right the first time. Certainly, if you must retrofit something, though, the same recommendation goes: hire an expert and get the job done correctly. Look to the correct long-range solution. The quick fix only gets you in trouble tomorrow.

Chapter XXIV

PARKS AND RECREATION DEPARTMENT

The parks and recreation department is another area where you can make your citizens very happy or very irate, based on how good a job you do in this area. You should also know that parks in general, and playgrounds specifically, are a key source of liability claims and therefore a source of high insurance premiums. Many cities have had to take playground equipment out of service or close a park down completely. Hopefully, this is not the case in your city. You should be cognizant of these problems, however, so that you can guide your city away from such trouble.

Activities such as skateboard tracks/courses are the kinds of things that are generally considered a liability nightmare by insurance carriers/underwriters. If you are considering implementing a new activity within your parks/recreation department, call your city's insurance agent and see what he/she has to say about the prospects. If the insurance company threatens to raise your rates or discontinue your coverage if you implement such a program, those are the kind of things your elected officials need to know before they make a decision on a matter.

Most city recreation departments are responsible for establishing and coordinating a little league baseball program and other related phenomena, i.e. industrial softball leagues for adults, soccer leagues, perhaps gymnastics classes or other indoor/bad weather activities. These activities do not, however, necessarily need to cost your city a lot of money. Most such programs can be administered through your recreation department director with the help of parental organizations. Team equipment will usually be sponsored by local businesses in exchange for having their business name appear on the shirt/hat of the team they are sponsoring. See Appendix B (Job Description of Recreation Supervisor.)

Your parks department can do a great deal to improve the general attitudes of your citizenry by cultivating and maintaining attractive green space. You do not need to spend a fortune to have city properties looking attractive and neat. If you have the opportunity, I would strongly encourage considering hiring a landscape architect to design plantings and grade-levels for a certain area within a park, or at city hall, or whatever. Recall the similar discussion in the public works department chapter. If you hire a good landscape architect, you will never be sorry. Aesthetics, after all, are a symbol of civilization. There are people who argue that buildings and grounds mean nothing if they are not aesthetically maintained. You would be absolutely amazed at how pleasant a few spring and summer flowers can look, strategically placed. Your citizens will love you for it.

The key function of most of this department's employees is the maintenance of the buildings and grounds that belong to this department. The parks/recreation director needs to be an expert at working with volunteers; most of the administration of leagues and similar activities will be performed by volunteers as opposed to paid city staffers.

As this book is being written, physical fitness is all the rage. Consequently, many cities have built "fitness trails" in one or more of their parks. You probably have seen some of these; they are a series of exercise stations with directions posted at each one. The participant runs from one station to another, performing specific exercises at each station. When considering such a project, you may want to try to get one or more local civic clubs involved. They may want to 'adopt' some of the stations as a service project. This may mean the club would pay for stations and/or install and maintain them. You should also consider making certain fitness trails or portions thereof for the handicapped citizens of your community.

Recreation equipment is very expensive. Sometimes, too, the green space available for parks is at a premium. If you can foster the opportunity, you may want to consider a joint venture between your city's parks department and the local school board. The purpose of this joint venture would be to provide access to the school board's playgrounds within your city for your citizens after regular school hours and particularly in the summer months. Your bargaining chit for this venture is the offer to have city employees maintain the school playgrounds in exchange for this improved accessibility. If a school board doesn't have to load up lawn mowers and move them from a central location to cut the grass in the school yard within your city, they may be interested in allowing you access to their recreation equipment.

Chapter XXV

MAINTENANCE DEPARTMENT

Your city may have its own maintenance or shop department if the city owns enough vehicles to warrant it. This department will be very small, consisting of a few mechanics and a supervisory mechanic. In spite of its size, this department can save your city literally thousands of dollars annually in repair costs, not to mention preventing the frustration of having to wait on some garage to fix vehicles you need NOW.

The key to having your own maintenance department is having one in which all of the departmental personnel are trained professionals. They know their job and perform it properly and quickly the first time. See Appendix B (Job Description of Auto Mechanic I.) If you have a maintenance crew that merely shuttles police cars back and forth between the city and the local dealership, get rid of them.

This is not to say, however, that some jobs can not better be done outside of your city shop at a specialty repair place. For example, if you do not own your own wheel alignment machine, no amount of work by your shop personnel will be able to get the wheels aligned on your vehicles without taking them elsewhere. If your city does not own its own paint booth, vehicles will have to be taken to a local body shop to be painted. This, however, does not mean that your maintenance employees should take a wrecked/damaged vehicle to the body shop for everything. Most mechanics know about body work. If yours do not, send some of them to a short school or arrange with a local body shop to teach one of your mechanics how to do general body work. Then when one of your city employees has an accident with a city vehicle, your shop people can do all the repair work short of painting the vehicle.

Your maintenance department should assist you, the city manager, in performing routine and periodic inspections of the city-owned vehicles to ensure they are in safe operating order. Once these inspections are conducted, your shop people should get the needed repairs made as soon as is feasible. Sometimes, the only repairs that need to be made are for a shop mechanic to teach the boom mower operator how to use a grease gun everyday, if you get my drift.

Sometimes the maintenance department building becomes a hang out for other employees who have broken down equipment. It is your job and the job of each department supervisor, especially the shop supervisor, to see that this does not occur!

Chapter XXVI

VEHICLES, RADIOS and ORGANIZATION

Needless to say, in order to deliver most city-rendered services, the city needs to have some vehicles. Some of these vehicles required are highly specialized and consequently very expensive. Some of these vehicles are not required for every city. You have to justify the expense in your own mind, before you can go and justify the expense to your decision-making/legislative body.

Regardless of what vehicles you inherit, or what vehicles your city buys, you need to have methods of controlling and maintaining those vehicles. I recommend establishing a 'bumper number' system for every vehicle, including trailers and other vehicles that may not have bumpers; such as tractors and mowers.

Further, I suggest that you have your maintenance/shop department maintain copious records on services rendered to each of these vehicles, by their bumper number. This will help everyone ensure that the scheduled services are being performed in a timely manner, and it will help you discern if/when one particular vehicle begins costing too much money to maintain. When a vehicle begins to cost too much to maintain, you need to make a cognitive decision as to whether it is worth keeping; or can it be more economically replaced? I am certain that you do not want a 'lemon' in your garage at home. So, you shouldn't want a 'lemon' in your city's 'garage' either.

I also suggest that you assign these 'bumper numbers' by departmental blocks. For example, you may want to use the numbers from 101 through 110 for your general government department. In order to make the 'bumper numbers' a viable system, you must have these numbers painted on the vehicles. Yes, every vehicle your city owns, except those covert surveillance vehicles utilized in the police department, needs a number. I do not recommend trying to 'change the world' in one fell swoop. Chances are, even if your city does not generally use vehicle numbers, your fire, and perhaps police departments will have some numbers on at least some of their vehicles. Try to merge those numbers already being used into the system of vehicle number assignment that you devise. For instance, perhaps your police department is already using numbers 20 through 28. Maybe the 20 series numbers can be issued to the police, or maybe you can assign them the block of numbers from 220 through 239. When assigning blocks of numbers, provide for additional vehicles that may be purchased in the future.

What kind of vehicles and how many vehicles your city should have is primarily a function of the services your city delivers, coupled with how many employees your city has. Do not be foolish enough to think that you need one vehicle for every employee in the city. This is true, or at least should be a goal in some departments; but generally this is overkill.

There have been a number of studies regarding vehicle use and the pooling thereof that have proven that vehicles receive better care when they arc the sole responsibility of one individual.

So... regardless of how many vehicles you have, I strongly recommend that you have your department supervisors assign vehicles such that each one has a primary driver who is responsible for the care, maintenance and cleaning of that vehicle.

Although some people, including employees, may accuse you of trying to run a military unit, I also strongly recommend that you establish a series of periodic inspections of the city vehicles. The easiest way I have found to do this is to just select a day and schedule vehicle inspections by department. When I first began this program, I had monthly inspections until the vehicles were normally appearing as I wanted the city to be represented. Then I went to quarterly inspections. What did I look for? Safety items and cleanliness! Not only is periodic vehicle inspection a good method of making the drivers take care of their vehicles, but it also provides you a check on whether your shop department is doing their job in a timely manner. Verify that all the lights and turn signals work on vehicles. Look to see if they are clean, inside and out. A clean vehicle will last longer, get less rust, and generally improve the attitude and pride of those that need to work with that vehicle on a regular basis. Also, check the primary fluid levels on the vehicles. I usually took one of my shop department mechanics with me and let him check the oil, radiator level, and general condition of the engine. Did you know a dirty engine operates much less efficiently than a clean one? As I have said before, perception is a very important aspect of your citizen relations. Do you think a citizen likes to see a city vehicle driving down the street that has dirt and mud all over it? What happens after a couple of years of this, when the dirt and mud changes to holes and rust? Does this present a professional image? Does this make your citizens think their tax dollars are being well spent? Think about it!

The police department is one of those that it would be very helpful to have one vehicle per sworn officer. If you have that capability, or can ultimately achieve same, I highly recommend that you allow those officers that live within the city to take the vehicles home with them. This concept is referred to as the 'Indianapolis Plan.' It improves the 'presence' of the police department which has far reaching effects in and of itself. Suppose you were a thief considering breaking into homes in your city. As you drove through the city you observed police cars parked in driveways and on the streets here and there. What would you (the thief) do? Probably go where there are less cops. Additionally, it improves the response time of the individual officers, especially in time of emergency. They don't have to come to the station, get a set of keys, and get a patrol car. They can respond from their home. Likewise, the individual officer will take better care of his/her car, if he/she is the only one to use it. If you get an officer that is the exception to the rule, and that officer's car is not up to standards, there is only one person that can possibly be responsible for this problem. Right?

While I am on the subject of the police department, I recommend you utilize a little innovation and creative thinking, when it comes to providing sufficient vehicles for your police. Regardless of whether you employ the Indianapolis Plan, you need to have individually assigned cars for certain personnel. Due to the nature of their positions, these certain people need to be able to take their cars home, and to have the cars with them at all times that these individuals are on call. That does not mean, however, contrary to what they would have you believe, that each of these people needs a full-size traditional police car! We are not talking of patrol lieutenants nor patrol sergeants. These officers literally live in their cars eight hours a day, and for many reasons patrol units do need to be full-size vehicles. Detective cars, administrator's cars (operations commander, services commander, even the chief), and perhaps some others, do not need to have a full-size car and all the related expense of same. In fact, I can easily make the argument for detectives, relative to covert operations, that a midsize type of car blends in with the majority of cars on the street much better than does a full-size vehicle.

And, while I am speaking of detective cars.... The size of your city and the amount of crime that goes on therein will dictate how important it is to protect the identity of 'unmarked'/covert surveillance cars. You need to discuss this with your chief and see if it is a problem in your city. Ask for his input of what you, as the manager, can do to solve this problem or alleviate it. Should you have a garage or privacy fence around the police station parking lot? Can you work out a deal with a local used-car lot owner to lease detective cars from him for 60 +/- days at a time, and then rotate the cars back onto his lot? Certainly you should ensure that your unmarked units are utilizing covert license plates, available through coordination with your state police and/or division/department of motor vehicles. Be creative. Encourage your chief to be creative!

What types of vehicles do you need in your city? This is going to be something you will have to answer for yourself. A lot depends on what you inherit, what types of services you deliver, and what the commission/council, and the citizens expect of the city employees. I do, however, have some suggestions of types of vehicles you might consider, fuel for thought, as it were. These suggestions are in no particular order.

Street Department You should have some pickup trucks/utility type vehicles. You will definitely need at least one dump truck. A street sweeper: If you have any input on this, try to go with the new technology of a vacuuming unit. Stay away from the older tricycle-wheeled, elevator mechanism; they are a maintenance nightmare. You may need a wood chipper mounted on a trailer and pulled by a dump truck. This vehicle may be a part of the sanitation department instead of the street department. (The point is, there are trees on city right-of-way, even if you don't have any parks, etc. They need to be cared for and maintained. Sometimes it is easier to chip citizens' tree trimmings than it is to compact the trimmings into garbage trucks.) You may need one or more utility trailers to haul tractors, equipment, and other things. You probably will need a trailer mounted sprayer tank to assist in killing weeds in drainage ditches, etc. You may need a 'grade-all' type of ditch excavator; see my discussion on this matter in the street department chapter. You most probably will need some big mowers: a bush hog, perhaps a bat-wing mower, and a boom-mower if you have very many ditches. Recall, I discussed many of these specifics in the street department chapter, too. Your street department will probably need a backhoe.

Water Department You will need some pickup/utility type trucks. If your city is experiencing any new development to speak of, I strongly recommend at least one of your public works-type departments have a four-wheel drive pickup. With this type of vehicle, your department personnel can get into the hard to reach locations early in the development stage and inspect to ensure the proper laying of main water and sewer lines, the proper preparation of road base, and other preliminary but exceedingly important early processes that otherwise would probably go uninspected. I also strongly recommend that you purchase utility bodies for your pickups, as opposed to regular pickup beds, as you purchase new and replacement vehicles. This will allow your people to carry a quantity of equipment in their vehicles at all times and to keep this equipment secured and protected from the weather. For those pickups your city already owns, purchase the locking tool boxes that mount in the bed of the truck next to the cab; at least your people will have some tools with them that can be secured and will not have to spend 30 minutes or more a day loading and unloading tools. The water department will probably need at least one dump truck or stake truck (the ability to dump may not be important), a backhoe, a utility trailer and a trencher. Using a little innovation, I recommend that your water department use an electric car-type vehicle for the meter readers. Most every city allows their meter reader(s) to use a pickup truck when, in fact, all that reader needs is some form of transportation and a very small space to keep meter books. Therefore, the majority of the space of the pickup is wasted. The pickup costs about $0.57 per mile to operate. An electric car-type of vehicle costs about $0.17 per mile. I do not recommend a golf cart-type vehicle, as they have problems on hills as well as length of viable battery charge. I am sure you have seen, or at least heard of these electric-type cars. They look like a cross between a toy and a car and have a top speed of 35 miles an hour or so. They're designed for people to commute when they do not have to travel on high-speed roadways.

Sewer Department This department will need basically the same equipment as the water department, except for the meter reader vehicle. It may be possible to share equipment from one department to another, but this may also become a maintenance problem as well as a time utilization problem. I do not generally recommend it. This is not to say that when one department's backhoe is in the shop, another department's backhoe can not be borrowed and used.

Sanitation Department The majority of the vehicles in this department will be big trucks with sanitation compactors or 'packers' mounted on the chassis. As the trucks wear out, it is very possible that the compactor body will still be functional and can be moved from one chassis to another, saving the city money. Your supervisor should have a pickup truck. This will enable him to spot check his personnel, as well as pick up an occasional 'miss' without dispatching a '2-mile-to-the-gallon' packer truck to pick up one can of garbage. You may want to consider getting an hydraulic arm to place upon a flat bed truck to pick up limbs, tree trimmings, and related trash. Some landfills will take greenery trash and will not accept garbage. Often times such a landfill will charge a markedly lower rate per ton than does the traditional garbage landfill that must comply with many additional environmental agencies' regulations. Furthermore, many workmen's compensation claims have arisen out of picking up cut up trees and branches. These could be avoided if a mechanical arm was picking up this type of trash.

If your sanitation department is in the dumpster business, they will need some type of trailer for delivering same. I recommend a tandem-wheeled trailer.

Building Department This department also needs at least one four-wheel drive vehicle, assuming your city is experiencing some development. The reason is to provide your inspector with the ability to get into the development area before the roads exist, in order to make those all important preliminary inspections that otherwise may go undone. In this department, however, I recommend a car-type vehicle. Building inspectors and officials need to carry plans and other documents that the enclosed space of a pickup truck does not facilitate. Not every building inspector, however, needs a four-wheel drive car. I suggest only one such vehicle for the department. The other inspectors and the official can use traditional midsize or smaller sedans.

Planning Department Your planning department should have a car at its disposal to do site inspections.

Police Department We have largely discussed the vehicular needs of this department. You may want to provide the police with a retired ambulance (or similar vehicle) if you have one available, to use as a crime scene vehicle. The police have equipment that is needed at different scenes. Without a centralized vehicle as a depository, this equipment becomes scattered in many patrol cars, as well as the station. The net result is loss, abuse, and general diminishing of function. Remember, not every car in this department needs to be a full-size traditional police car.

In this department, you may need to add vehicle numbers to the roofs of the marked patrol cars, such that these cars can be seen and identified from the air. If your city is in a metro area where the county police and/or county sheriff owns one or more helicopters, police cars identifiable by police 'chopper' pilots can be very beneficial to interdepartmental cooperation.

Fire Department This department, without a doubt, has the most specialized and unique equipment and vehicular requirements in your city. Talk with your chief and learn about the equipment your city has and what he feels your city needs. Consider rescue vehicles, a 'mini-pumper', a tanker truck, a woods/brush truck, and a boat - depending upon the natural surroundings of your city. Your fire department should probably have a pickup truck or similar vehicle to run departmental errands. The chief and/or duty charge officer may want to have a station wagon or pickup truck to use to carry the extra equipment needed to command and control the department.

Parks/Recreation Department At the least, this department will need a pickup/utility truck, some mowers, and a utility trailer. Additional equipment may be needed, based on the facilities of this department as well as the variables identified above.

Maintenance/Shop Department This department will need a small pickup/utility truck to 'run parts' in at least. You may want to consider having your own wrecker in this department, especially if your city owns a relatively large number of vehicles. It does not take too many towing bills to justify a wrecker. Police cars often get stuck patrolling out of the way areas, areas that are likely hiding places for illegal activities and/or activists. City vehicles are notorious for needing jump starts periodically, or is that because the city employees abuse their vehicles?

General Government Department Depending on the size of your city, your car (and the city manager should have a city provided car, complete with at least a public works frequency radio) may be the only vehicle in this department. You may also want to consider having a small economy car in the general government department for making courier runs and general administrative errands. Without such a vehicle, you may find that you graciously give up your car during the day for such errands. That's OK, until there is an emergency to which you need to respond; and then where is your car? An additional, routine errand to be considered is the trip to the bank to deposit the city's revenues.

The uniformity of the paint job, or lack thereof, on city vehicles can be a very positive or negative factor on the attitudes of the employees and the citizens. Your police cars probably already have a uniform paint job. If you and your chief are happy with that, leave it alone. Your fire department may have a uniform paint job on their vehicles. If they do not, talk with the chief and figure out which color you want to be on all of the vehicles; and then start a program, as time and money permits, to accomplish this uniformity. Fire department vehicle paint has to be especially heat resistant, due to the nature of their function. You might look into the 'imron' process, or something similar.

The real uniformity problem, however, is most likely with all of your other city vehicles. Talk with your shop/maintenance superintendent about creating a uniform paint job. Work into this paint job the application of a city decal on the side of each vehicle. Traditionally this decal goes on the doors of the vehicles and should be the city crest or some adaptation. The sharper the decal makes the vehicles look, the more pride everyone is going to take in those vehicles. I recommend a simple white paint job for all of your vehicles, if your city has not already established a color of their own. With white, you can order new and replacement vehicles in this color, without having to pay extra for custom paint. As far as repainting the vehicles already in your city's inventory, it is not that difficult. If you have a reasonably good shop department, they can paint the vehicles themselves. If you have an excellent shop department, you will be totally amazed at how good the old vehicles look once the shop gets done with them. Talk with your fire inspector, however, and see if your state requires the use of a paint booth before you can paint vehicles. If this is the case, you may have to try to work out a program with a local body shop to allow your shop personnel to use their paint booth. I would not advocate paying hundreds of dollars per vehicle to get them repainted. I will guarantee you, however, that a city-wide uniform paint job will have positive effects.

Radios are one of the most important pieces of equipment in a city's inventory. Radios allow your personnel to talk with each other, request additional equipment at certain scenes, request assistance, call in emergencies, etc. Your police department probably has a radio frequency of its own. Likewise, your fire department probably has its own frequency, or one shared with other fire departments in the area. Your other departments within the city, however, will probably be sharing one frequency. This frequency is commonly called a public works radio frequency. In larger cities, different public works divisions/departments may have their own frequency, or the frequencies may be divided by areas of the city; but in smaller cities, everybody shares one. This has benefits. For one thing, the city administrative offices can monitor all of the public works calls and intercede as necessary.

Virtually every vehicle in your city should have a radio in that vehicle, with the exceptions of tractors, backhoes, street sweepers and those types of specialty vehicles. If you have sufficient radios, and if you can adequately secure them and protect them from the weather, there is nothing wrong with having radios on these exception-type vehicles; but I would not buy new radios just to put them on these vehicles. Being able to communicate with all of your people all the time is invaluable.

A related invaluable tool that should be on all or your cabbed-type vehicles, is an external speaker for the radio. This allows your personnel to monitor radio calls when they are working on a site, and consequently are out of their vehicle; hopefully, this will be most of the time. While they are monitoring the radio, they naturally will be able to respond when they hear a call for them. These external speakers also cut down on the requirements for portable radios (see discussion below); they do not, however, eliminate the need for portables.

There are different types of radios for different purposes. There are also different limitations on types of radios depending on the band in which your city's frequencies are located. Aside from traditional vehicle radios, there are portable radios, what you and I would probably call walkie-talkies. There are also, however, portable radios that plug into housings in the vehicle and serve both purposes. For people in and out of their vehicle, i.e. police officers, these are very handy. Firefighters, on the other hand, have to have several people working off of the same vehicle; so these plug in radios are not practical. Therefore, it's better to buy portable radios for the fire department officers and leave traditional radios in the fire vehicles, not trying to double up. Building inspectors, water technicians, and such lend themselves very well to using portable radios that plug in and out of housings in the vehicle and double as vehicle radios.

For key supervisory personnel, those that may need to talk to several departments about different things, I highly recommend utilizing scanning-transceiver radios. Scanning-transceivers monitor several different frequencies, depending on how it is set up. Using this type of radio, the public works director and/or the city manager can monitor the calls on the public works frequency, the police frequency, the fire frequency, etc. Furthermore, you can transmit over any of those frequencies to direct your personnel as necessary.

If you elect to purchase such a radio, do not abuse it. You are not the chief of police or the fire chief. If your police are involved in an incident, don't try to be John Wayne and take control over the radio just because you can monitor what is happening. That is not your job, nor do you have training in that area. If, on the other hand, your city is experiencing a natural or man-made type of disaster, being able to direct police and fire units to different locations can prove exceedingly valuable and useful.

Assuming you inherit at least some radios, it is important that your city employees know how to use those radios and use them professionally. Professional use of radios is efficient use of radios. Aside from that, you would be amazed at how many civilians have scanners and monitor your frequencies to see what is happening. Once you have assured yourself that your employees have a basic working knowledge of radios, you should verify they have some type of call sign system. Again, I recommend that call signs be assigned in accordance with departmental integrity. Your police may use badge numbers as their call signs. The fire department may also. Call signs should generally be assigned to people, as opposed to vehicles. For example, you may assign the numbers 20-29 to your water department. Allow your departmental supervisor to assign the individual numbers. Your employees may already have some type of call sign system that works very satisfactorily, or that can be modified to fit into the overall city picture. Don't forget to allow room for some expansion when assigning blocks of numbers.

If you have radios in use in your city, you also must have licenses from the Federal Communications Commission to have those radios operating on the specific frequencies. Don't panic if you can't find these licenses; there should be copies at the/a base station for each frequency you have operating in your city.

The dispatch room of the police station is a likely room to have your FCC license for the police frequency. Look in the dusty picture frame lying in the corner. If you can't locate such a license after a thorough search, merely contact the FCC and ask them to mail you a duplicate.

My point here is that these licenses are required by federal law and do expire, generally every five years. Find your licenses, check their expiration dates, and make certain your respective department heads keep them current by requesting license renewal when appropriate. If you find your licenses have not been renewed, contact the FCC, advise them of the problem you inherited, and ask their assistance in getting the license renewed without a break in use of your radio frequency or equipment.

We have already discussed uniformity of vehicle appearance. You also need to consider the uniformity of your employees' appearance, and how this appearance is perceived by the public. If your sanitation department employees collect the trash in dirty shorts and nothing else, you can rest assured that your citizens do not have a very high opinion of those city employees. Never forget, city employees are paid by tax dollars. It behooves you, as the manager, to create and promote professionalism by your employees. If your city employees do not have a uniform to wear, talk with all of your supervisors and design one. There are uniform companies that will lease uniforms to you, clean and service them for a monthly fee. Or you may decide that blue jeans and a specially designed, silk-screened t-shirt, with the city crest or something relative, is the uniform you want your people to wear. The city can usually buy six sets of such a uniform for permanent, non-probationary employees for about half of the annual rental cost for uniforms provided by a uniform company.

Once you have uniforms, then you must make your supervisors enforce the wearing of those uniforms! Nothing is more wasteful than paying for special uniforms and not having them worn.

Chapter XXVII

GENERAL COMMENTS

This is the 'catch-all' chapter; all the little areas that I want to address with you that don't really merit a chapter of their own are in this section of the book. I will also be repeating some information that I consider vital to the functioning of a city and its manager.

COMMUNICATIONS WITH YOUR COUNCIL/COMMISSION

It is important that you keep your commission/ council informed on what is going on, both at city hall and throughout the departments of the city. One convenient way that I have found to do this is to write a memorandum to the commission before each commission meeting.

Your city may have a specified time period by which the commission agenda must be prepared as well as a set notification period for said agenda to be delivered to the mayor and council members. Whether this set time period exists or not, you should provide the mayor and commissioners with an agenda for the council meeting a few days prior to the meeting so that they can properly prepare for it. Along with the agenda, you should provide the mayor and commissioners with supporting material: proposed ordinances, resolutions, reports, staff recommendations, etc. Not the least of this supporting information can be a memo that you write to the commission, apprising them of each item on the agenda, what its all about. Depending upon the item, you may want to recommend a course of action you would like to see the commission take on the particular subject at hand. This entire conglomeration of information may be included in an indexed, report folder format which will allow the commission to have everything at their fingertips.

In addition to the agendaed items, I recommend that you keep the commission informed of other major events occurring, or about to occur, at the end of this same memorandum. You will find, after a couple of months of presenting the materials in this fashion, the commission will come to rely heavily upon the information and the format, you provide to them.

Depending upon the urgency or sensitivity of a matter, you may want to telephone or otherwise speak to each member of the council personally. As I have said before, just as in a marriage, the council-manager relationship may sour due to miscommunication or a lack of communication.

By the same token, remember that you work for the council or commission as a body. Do not allow the mayor or one of the commissioners to try to force you into actions that you feel are questionable with regard to your authority to take action without having the required public discussion, consensus, and/or directive of the entire commission as a unit. Remember, if one of them asks you to take some such action, your canned response might be, "I'll be glad to put this on the next agenda for the council's/commission's consideration."

Every state has its own sunshine laws. Sunshine laws are the public meeting and open records laws that dictate when and how information can be discussed, transmitted, and action taken. It is of paramount importance that you know what those laws are and how they impact upon your council/commission and your city.

You must comply with them. Sometimes, the members of your commission may decide to try to circumvent these laws. You may or may not be aware of these actions when they transpire, but you have to decide what to do about them. Discuss any matter you are unsure of with your city attorney. I would caution against confronting an elected official with, "You violated the sunshine law by doing thus and so." My point is, don't you violate the law. You cannot control what elected officials will do, but you are responsible for your own actions. In some states, if the city manager acts as an information conduit from one elected official to another, the manager has violated the sunshine law.

LEGAL REQUIREMENT FOR APPEAL

Somewhere, on one page of every agenda of every public body or group you have meeting in your city, you should include the following words, or something similar. It should routinely appear in the same place on all your agendas.

NOTICE: Any person who desires to appeal any decision from this meeting will need a record of the proceedings, and for this purpose may need to ensure that a verbatim record of the proceedings is made which includes the testimony and evidence upon which the appeal is based.

I believe these words are self-explanatory. I realize I have already discussed this in the general government chapter. I cannot overemphasize the important role it can play in keeping your city out of trouble. This does not exempt your responsibility of having minutes maintained by some member of the city staff. It does, however, allow these minutes to be a summarial document as opposed to verbatim. Nor does this warning relieve you of the responsibility of having the minutes of the meeting tape recorded, if this is required in your state.

Consequently, if you get wind that one of the councilmembers or the mayor is going to try to fire you at some specific council meeting and you intend to fight this termination, it might be very wise for you to hire a court reporter to create a verbatim transcript of the meeting for you.

BOMB THREATS

Unfortunately, at some point in time your city hall, police station or other public building is likely to receive a bomb threat. Hopefully, it will in fact be a threat and not an actual bomb; but you can never count on that.

I have made it a practice to place a copy of this bomb threat information form (found below) adjacent to virtually every phone in public buildings. If you or your personnel ever receive such a call, the police will find the information included on this form useful in their investigation. You must, however, conduct a training session with your employees so they know the form exists. They should try to remain calm if they receive a threatening telephone call or other communication; and they should, in fact, try to fill in the form as the threat is being communicated to them.

Figure 7. Bomb Threat Information Form
(Be calm and courteous -
do not interrupt or intimidate the caller)
ASK:
1. Exact location of the bomb:_____
2. Time set for detonation:_____
3. What does the bomb look like?_____
4. What is the explosive?_____
5. Why was it placed?_____
    Obtain as much detail as possible about the bomb and its location.
A caller may wish to avoid injury or death of people, only desiring to
destroy property. Request more information expressing a desire to save
lives!
RECORD:
date:_____   Time call received:_____
Exact language (words) used:_____
Male ( ) Female ( ) caller Adult ( )   Child ( )
 Ethnic voice pattern?_____
Speech (check all that apply)
( ) accent-describe_____
( ) slow   ( ) high pitch   ( ) loud ( ) broken
( ) rapid   ( ) low pitch   ( ) soft ( ) slurred
( ) normal   ( ) excited ( ) distinguished ( ) sincere
Were there any background noises? _____
Did the caller sound: ( ) drunk?   ( ) angry?
         ( ) mentally imbalanced? Explain in detail: ____
Other information/comments/observations:_____
Name of person receiving call: _____
Call received on extension #:_____
    DO NOT DISCUSS THIS CALL WITH ANY OTHER CITY
EMPLOYEES! Report this incident to the City Manager, the Fire
Chief, or the Chief of Police with this form, immediately!

EMPLOYMENT CONTRACT

Appendix E has some sample employment contracts, or agreements, for you to review and/or utilize. Because of the nature of the employment as a city manager, I highly recommend that you attempt to secure an employment contract as a condition of your employment prior to ever accepting the position. This may be difficult in your first job, as you are an unknown quantity; but I still recommend you make an attempt to secure some form of contract for your own protection and peace of mind. After you develop a track record of accomplishments, it will probably be easier to get such an employment contract. If your council refuses your request, ask if you could bring it back to them for consideration in six months or a year.

The key issue is that without a contract, you are an at-will employee. It is most difficult to perform the already arduous task of managing a city if you are spending the majority of your time looking over your shoulder. If you are able to secure an employment agreement, you will have some comfort in knowing that when commission candidate 'x' runs for office promising his constituents that he is going to fire the 'no good' city manager, that you at least have some guaranteed source of income for a few months if candidate 'x' is successful. You should also bear in mind, however, that candidate 'x' may get elected and may see that you are doing a good job and decide not to pursue his campaign promises! Likewise, he may attempt to pursue those promises and find he has no support on the commission. The point is: Don't pack your bags prematurely just because someone is trying to fire you!

CITY ATTORNEY

You most probably will have an 'attorney for the city,' as opposed to a city attorney. The difference is, an attorney for the city is a lawyer in private practice who works for and represents the city on a retainer basis. It is most important that you and the attorney for your city have an exceptionally close relationship; you must be able to talk with him about anything at any time without fear of repercussions. If your city is large enough, you may have an attorney on staff who works for you; an attorney in this position is a 'city attorney.' If he is a consultant, he most probably will work for the commission, depending on what your city charter states. Regardless of who his/her boss is, in this litigious society it is important that you have free access to his/her consultation.

Ensure that you understand how your particular attorney bills the city. Many attorneys who represent a city in addition to their private practice will do most of or all of their work for the city for the retainer they receive from the city. Some law firms, however, charge their attendance at commission meetings against the retainer; and all other services are rendered on an hourly basis. A five minute phone call from you, consequently, may turn into a quarter of an hour billing for the city.

That doesn't mean you don't make the phone call; it only means you must spend the city's money wisely.

CONSULTING ENGINEER

Like the attorney, your city engineer may be on staff or may be in private practice on a retainer. Unlike the attorney, if the engineer is on a retainer at all, it is probably very small; and therefore all of the work performed, except perhaps presence at the commission meetings, is charged to the city on an hourly basis. That does not mean you won't utilize the engineer's invaluable expertise. It only means you should have the authority from your commission to confer with the engineer as needed. If your engineer is on staff, this person is an excellent candidate for the director of public works.

STAFF MEETINGS

It is important, in my opinion, that you schedule and hold regular meetings of your in-house supervisory staff. There probably will be some reluctance to hold and attend such meetings, especially if they have not been required in the past. These meetings are part of your team building. If not for weekly/biweekly staff meetings, some of your supervisors would literally never see other supervisors. How can you build a team when people don't even know each other?

Your meeting should consist of your briefly advising the members of your team what transpired at the commission meeting, and what, if any, new directives you might have received as a result. Then it is always a good idea to go around the room to each of your supervisors, see what is on their minds, what things they need help with from other departments, etc.

If your meetings do not have much substance to them, after the above is accomplished, you may consider combining these regular meetings with some supervisory training classes. Or, have each of your supervisors, one week at a time, teach a class on what is going on in their department at that immediate point in time, what the focus is of their work right now. When you get back to that department, eight, ten or more weeks from then, there will be some new projects on which to report. Aside from this obvious education that is being accomplished by making each department aware of what others are doing, it also allows your supervisors to get some public speaking and teaching experience in a nonthreatening environment.

THE 'SCANDAL SHEET'

I am not sure there is anything that will help to build a team spirit quite like having your own employee newspaper or newsletter. If you and your secretary can put together a newsletter once a month in which you note the employees who have birthdays that month, special events going on within the city departments, which employee's family just had a baby, employment anniversary dates recognizing longevity and so forth, you will be amazed at how interested the employees become in what they are doing, how well it is done, etc. If you will spend the postage necessary to mail them home, you'll find even more response.

EMPLOYEE OF THE MONTH AWARD

Similarly, if you institute an "Employee of the Month" recognition program, the pride in job performance that results will amaze you. For $50 or less, you can purchase a wall plaque with several nameplates on it. Each month, select and recognize an employee that has been performing in a particularly exemplary manner. If you have your in-house newsletter functioning, this is the ideal place to make the announcement of the recipient of this sought after recognition. Within a couple of months, if my experience is any indicator, you will have a tough time selecting just one employee of the month because everyone is striving to be so recognized. Who is the end benefactor? The citizens of your city. They are getting more work, quality work, performed by city employees for their tax dollar. See Appendix C, Section XV for more information on incentive plans.

SUPERVISOR OF THE MONTH

This award may not be necessary or profitable for you; although if you have any doubt, you probably should implement it. It will certainly not hurt your team building efforts in the city. The point here is that you do not want your supervisors detracting from the morale of their subordinates by supervisors being routinely selected as 'Employee of the Month.' The supervisory personnel are supposed to be doing more work and quality work than the other employees, or they shouldn't be supervisors. Consequently, you must look beyond your supervisory ranks to recognize your regular employees. I hope you understand the distinction between this award and the previous one.

CITY CREST/FLAG

Another item that will aid in your team building efforts and bring a sense of pride within your employees is a city crest and city flag that your employees can identify with and around which they can and will rally. You will also find, I believe, that your citizens will enjoy having a city crest with which they can identify. Your city may already have a crest and/or flag adopted. If it does, use it. Have a decal made for the side of each of your vehicles. Have small stickers made that you can use to mark your equipment, especially items like fire and police department equipment that may be spread all over on the scene of some problem. These little stickers make your city-owned equipment readily identifiable.

If the crest is properly designed, it will give your people a sense of pride and ownership as well. You might even consider having shoulder patches made for your employees to wear on their uniforms. Have hats made with the crest on them and award them to your "Employee of the Month". The ideas are limited only by your budget and your imagination. Most cities fly an American flag in front of their city hall and other public buildings; I hope yours does. Anyway, if you have a flag pole flying your American flag, add a couple of snap links under the American flag and fly your city flag as well. Your city flag also should be in the commission chambers with the American flag.

CITY-WIDE NEWSLETTER

Depending on the size of your city, its population, and the amount of exclusive press coverage you receive, you may want to consider publishing a quarterly, or some other time frame, newsletter. In this newsletter, you should inform the citizens how their tax dollars are currently being spent and what plans the commission has for major programs in the future. Although you probably will and should do most if not all of the work in formulating this newsletter, it should officially come from the elected officials. Therefore, it is important that you discuss the concept with them and learn what they want to have noted in the newsletter and what they do not. In general, you will find that citizens want to know what is going on in their local government. They are much more supportive of programs that they are made aware of prior to the program being initiated. They are more interested in seeing programs or projects succeed when they were in on the ground floor. They will consequently support, and even advocate, these programs and projects.

Delivery of such a city-wide newsletter can be financially prohibitive if you use the traditional mail for each one. Nothing against our friends at the post office, but if you are planning such a mass distribution, you may want to investigate paying the local newspaper carriers to make delivery with their newspapers for five cents per newsletter, or some other agreed upon price. You might also check with local service clubs: Kiwanis, Lions, Jaycees, Boy or Girl Scouts, Little League, etc. They may be interested in making the deliveries as a small fund raiser, especially if you are going to have the deliveries made on a periodic basis. If you choose to use a group with children/adolescents making the deliveries, it is important that proper adult supervision ensures that the deliveries are actually made. It would be a shame to spend four cents, or more, per newsletter to have them dumped in a garbage can after the first few were delivered. It is also important for all concerned to understand that if you do not pay the postal service to make this delivery for you, you can not leave the newsletter in the resident's mail box; you must use some other receptacle.

DICTATING EQUIPMENT SAVES TIME

I don't know if you have any experience in using a tape recorder for dictation, but I suggest that you teach yourself. It will save you mountains of time, and you need that time to do other things. Speaking your letters, memorandums, and other correspondence into a tape recorder is much faster than your typing the correspondence yourself. It is far and away faster than writing the material out longhand and then giving it to your secretary to type. If you have a word processing program on the city's computer (more about that later), it makes this project even easier for you and your secretary to learn to dictate and transcribe, respectively.

Just have your secretary type your dictation into the word processor, print out the draft, and return it to you for correction and other editing. If your secretary only has a typewriter to use, you should still use dictation, but it will not be quite as efficient as it might until you both have more experience in doing this. Believe me, the time you save will be well worth it.

COMPUTERS

I discussed computers in the chapter on general government. The point I want to make here is that you need to be computer literate. You need to know what projects a computer can do for you and those that are not feasible. You need to know the limits of your city's particular software and when it would be prudent to ask the commission to purchase more software that will perform labor-saving functions. You need to be able to operate a computer to get some information. I am not saying that you should be able to walk into the accounts receivable section and make the computer tell you who has and has not paid their bills, but you should learn how to perform some of the more primary functions on a computer. Next to dictating correspondence, one of the biggest time savers I have found is the word processing program. I use it to maintain routine ordinance formats, "mail merging" of 'Invitations to Bid', bid awards, etc.

ORDINANCE WRITING

Drafting ordinances is not that difficult, and it generally is a part of your job. You may share this job with the attorney for the city, and you certainly should have him approve anything that you prepare for enactment. But if you rely on the attorney to draft every legal document the city needs, your legal fees will be higher than they would be if you performed some of these draft functions yourself. You can do it! Here are some general guidelines on ordinance writing. You can look to the samples in Appendix A for form. You must, however, comply with the state statutes on this subject in the respective state where your city is located.

An ordinance should deal with only one subject, and the title should clearly state what that subject is. Generally, the title should contain a brief caption for each section of the ordinance. An ordinance should be introduced to the legislative body in a written form by a member of that body (not by you, the manager). I am not advocating that you not take action when you see the need for an ordinance, only that you ask the mayor or a commissioner to bring the subject up with his colleagues.

An ordinance can not be enacted unless it has undergone two or more readings on separate days. Some states have exceptions to this concept if an emergency exists. At some point in time in the ordinance process, the ordinance title or a summary of the whole ordinance or the entire ordinance must be published in a newspaper. Check your state's laws on this.

Your legislative body's vote on an ordinance may need to be a roll call vote, in order to comply with the state law. This means that each member must verbally cast a vote for or against the motion to enact the ordinance, when his/her name is called. Ordinances are a permanent record of the city. Like most, if not all other actions of the legislative body, they must be maintained in a central place, usually the office of the city clerk, and indexed.

TELEPHONE NUMBERS

There are many, many phone numbers that you should have at your fingertips, and you should have a rapport with the people that will answer at the other end of the line when you call. These people can help you do your job better and more efficiently.

PROBLEM	AGENCY (phone number needed)
abandoned car	city police
animal bite, stray or unleashed animal	animal control
public bus information	local transit authority (if any)
copies of ordinances, deeds & other documents	county clerk's office
dead animals in road	city street department
electric service	*local electric utility company
telephone service	*local telephone company
cable television service	*local cable TV company
natural gas service	*local gas pipeline company
public library	local public library
voter registration	city or county clerk's office; by mail
property valuation and assessment	#county clerk's office

* Indicates your city may, or should have some type of franchise agreement with these companies, allowing them to operate within your city and dictating some do's and don'ts for both the city and the franchisee.

# Indicates your city may perform this function itself without utilizing the county program. If not, the county clerk's office is a good place to start looking for who performs the property assessment function within your area.

For drivers' licenses and vehicle license plates, you're on your own! Each state does it differently. (Find out how it works in your state and make that info available in the list above.)

YOU ARE A PROFESSIONAL

Don't be afraid to admit you don't know when someone asks you a question about something with which you are not familiar or do not feel totally up to date. It is far better to say, "I don't know what the current situation is on that matter, but I will find out and let you know as soon as possible" than to give out incorrect information. You can not possibly know everything about everything at all times. Don't make up an answer to make yourself look good; ultimately it will catch up with you and make you look foolish and/or unprofessional.

THE LAST CAVEAT

Whatever you do, make sure that you do the best job you possibly can do with the time, materials and resources available to you. Be proud of what you do and willing to put your name on any project that you undertake.

You are a model of leadership, of management, of consultation, of technical expertise. You are a professional.

APPENDIX A

SAMPLE ORDINANCES

I. Budget Ordinance

Anycity, Anystate

Ordinance Number 89-8

**AN ORDINANCE
ADOPTING AN ANNUAL BUDGET FOR
THE CITY OF ANYCITY FOR THE
FISCAL YEAR JULY 1, 1989 THROUGH
JUNE 30, 1990; BY ESTIMATING REV-
ENUES AND RESOURCES AND APPROPRI-
ATING FUNDS FOR THE OPERATION OF
THE CITY GOVERNMENT**

WHEREAS, an annual budget proposal has been prepared and delivered to the City Council; and,

WHEREAS, the City Council has reviewed said budget proposal and made necessary modifications, in public session.

**NOW, THEREFORE, BE IT ORDAINED BY THE
CITY OF ANYCITY:**

Section 1: That the Annual Budget for the Fiscal Year beginning July 1, 1989 and ending June 30, 1990 is hereby adopted as follows:

	General Fund	Capital Fund	State Road Fund	TOTAL
RESOURCES AVAILABLE				
Fund Balance				
Brought Forward	$250,000	618,000	40,000	920,000
ESTIMATED NEW REVENUES				
Delinquent Taxes	5,000			5,000
Prop. Taxes CY '89	587,700	28,000		615,700
State Road Aid			48,000	48,000
Alcoholic Bev.				
Licenses		10,000		10,000
Interest	48,000	32,000		80,000
Total Resources	890,730	650,000	88,000	1,678,730

APPROPRIATIONS

	General Fund	Capital Fund	State Road Fund	TOTAL
General				
Government	157,650			157,650
Public Safety	58,650			58,650
Public Works	231,300		40,000	317,300
Sanitation	194,200			194,200

Total
Appropriations **641**,800 -0- 40,000 727,800

ESTIMATED YEAR END BALANCE/RESERVE ACCOUNTS

248,930 650,000 48,000 950,930

Section 2: This Ordinance shall take effect on July 1, 1989.

First Reading held on June 1, 1989.
Second Reading held on June 15, 1989.

Attest: _____
                                John Doe, MAYOR

_____
City Clerk

II. Law Enforcement Impact Fee Ordinance

Anycity, Anystate

Ordinance Number 87-3

**A N   O R D I N A N C E
OF THE CITY OF ANYCITY ESTABLISHING
A LAW ENFORCEMENT INPACT FEE TO BE
USED EXCLUSIVELY FOR THE UPGRADE OF
LAW ENFORCEMENT STRENGTH MANDATED
BY THE POPULATION GROWTH, PROVIDING
FOR THE IMPACT FEE; PROVIDING FOR THE LIMITATION OF
EXPENDITURES OF THE IMPACT
FEE; PROVIDING FOR AN APPEAL PROCESS; PROVIDING FOR
SEVERABILITY; PROVIDING
FOR AN EFFECTIVE DATE.**

WHEREAS, the City of Anycity is experiencing an extremely high growth rate; and,

WHEREAS, the City of Anycity wishes to continue to provide police protection to its growth and population; and,

WHEREAS, new construction resulting from population growth placed a strain on the coverage possible by the Police Department within the City; and,

WHEREAS, it is a City Policy that new growth pay for itself by providing for the additional police officers is in the best interests of the general public; and,

WHEREAS, the National Average, as cited in the 1984 Municipal Yearbook (Pub: ICMA) is 2.35 police officers per 1,000 people and the South Atlantic Regional Average is 2.72 per 1,000; therefore it is the desire objective of the City of Anycity to staff 2.0 police officers per 1,000 citizens of population for the City; and,

WHEREAS, the City of Anycity finds that the police officers required to service each residential, commercial or industrial unit is essentially the same; and,

WHEREAS, the University of Anystate's Bureau of Economic and Business Research states that the average number of persons per household figure for 1985 is 2.45 individuals; and,

WHEREAS, the City of Anycity thus finds that each 164.1 additional households require approximately one additional police officer; and,

WHEREAS, the current cost per police officer on the road, in the City of Anycity is $42,358.

NOW THEREFORE, be it ordained by the
Anycity Council in lawful session assembled the following:

Section 1: Definitions
For the purposes of this Ordinance, the following words shall mean:

(a) Residential Unit: A structure which is used for domestic dwelling purposes for the household, including but not limited to a single family home, each unit within a multi-family structure or each housing unit within a building which meets the criteria for location in a residential or planned unit development zoning district under the Code of Ordinances of the City of Anycity.

(b) Commercial Unit: A structure which is used for non-residential purposes which houses a business enterprise, including but not limited to a structure used for business purposes, a unit within a shopping center or each unit within a multi-purpose building and which meets the criteria for location in a commercial zoning district under the Code of Ordinances of the City of Anycity.

(c) Industrial Unit: A structure which is used for non-residential purposes and primarily for manufacturing plants, assembly plants and warehousing, including but not limited to each division with a structure of a multi-purpose building and which meets the criteria for location within a manufacturing and warehousing or industrial zoning district under the Code of Ordinances of Anycity.

(d) Police Officer: For the purpose of this Ordinance, a police officer is defined as a sergeant, corporal, and patrolman; not command, administrative, nor investigative personnel.

Section 2: Law Enforcement Impact Fee
There is hereby imposed a law enforcement impact fee for all new residential, commercial and industrial structures within the corporate limits of the City of Anycity for the purpose of providing financing for additional police protection of the City.

Section 3: Limitations on Issuance of Building Permits
No person shall issue or obtain a building permit for new residential dwelling units, new commercial, or new industrial structures within the corporate limits of Anycity, or issue or obtain construction plan approval for new mobile home developments within the City limits of Anycity until the owner/developer thereof shall have paid the applicable impact fee to the City.

Section 4: Fees
(a) The impact fee imposed by this Ordinance shall be determined by use of data indicated above. This status shall be reviewed regularly to insure that inflationary measures and other external influences have not changed the amount of impact fee. The City Council may review this Ordinance on an annual basis and decide that a change in the impact fee is necessary.

(b) The impact fee shall be $xxx.xx per each residential, commercial, or industrial unit.

Section 5: Limitation in Expenditure of Impact Fees

(a) The impact fees collected by the City pursuant to this Section shall be kept as a separate fund account restricted to the funding of capital expenditures and first year salaries for police patrol officers to provide extra protection on an annual basis in conjunction with the implementation of the new fiscal year budget. Funds may be disbursed from the separate account pursuant to the Charter of the City of Anycity. All proceeds from said impact fees may be pledged for borrowing purposes, the same as any other source of revenue, provided said borrowing is for the purpose of providing additional police protection.

(b) A detailed audit trail of all impact fee revenues and expenditures must be maintained. Any impact fee collected must be expended within six (6) years of the date of collection, or be refunded to the building owner currently owning the structure that the fee was collected upon.

Section 6: Right to Appeal

A builder/developer may appeal the staff's decision to collect impact fees from him/her under the provisions of this ordinance. Said appeal must be based upon certain facts that would indicate that said builder/developer may not owe the City the full impact fee due to extenuating circumstances; i.e., the builder/developer has donated land to the City to use in construction of a Police Station, or the builder/developer has made cash contributions to the City encumbered for the City to purchase specialized police equipment.

In the event the builder/developer does in fact make such an appeal to be alleviated from full payment of the impact fees, the City Council will instruct the staff to give a credit of some dollar figure to the builder/developer in respect to the impact fee payments due. In other words, the City Council will decide upon a dollar figure value that the builder/developer's contribution has offset his requirement to pay impact fees.

Section 7: Severability

All ordinances and parts of ordinances that conflict herewith to the extent of such conflicts are hereby repealed. If an phrase, clause, sentence, paragraph, section or subsection of the ordinance shall be declared unconstitutional or invalid by a court of competent jurisdiction, such unconstitutionality or invalidity shall not affect the remaining phrases, clauses, sentences, paragraphs, sections or subsections of the ordinance.

Section 8: Effective Date

This ordinance shall take effect immediately upon its adoption.

First Reading held on _____, 19xx.
Second Reading held on _____, 19xx.

ENACTED THIS _____ DAY OF _____, 19xx.

ATTEST: _____
                                 John Doe, Mayor

_____
City Clerk

III. Development Review Assessments Ordinance

Anycity, Anystate

Ordinance Number 88-19

**A N   O R D I N A N C E
OF THE CITY OF ANYCITY ESTABLISHING
DEVELOPMENT REVIEW FEE ASSESSMENTS
FOR REZONING, SPECIAL EXCEPTIONS,
COMPREHENSIVE PLAN AMENDMENTS,
APPLICATIONS FOR PLANNED UNIT
DEVELOPMENTS, AND APPLICATIONS
FOR DEVELOPMENT REVIEW/APPROVAL
FOR ALL PROPOSED SUBDIVISIONS AND
COMMERCIAL SITE PLANS; PROVIDING
FOR ADMINSTRATIVE PROCEDURES;
PROVIDING FOR EXEMPTOINS; PROVIDING
FOR SEVERABILITY; PROVIDING
FOR AN EFFECTIVE DATE.**

WHEREAS, it is the policy of the City Council that whenever and wherever possible and equitable, the costs of development shall be incurred by the developer, i.e. the one(s) that will benefit most, and not by the taxpayers in general; and,

WHEREAS, The City Council believes the most practical and consistently accurate method of defraying the costs of development review functions is through a system of fees based upon the actual time spent by the City staff and those directly associated expenses including advertising, legal and engineering fees; and,

WHEREAS, the administrative procedures set forth below are an accurate method of assessing the costs of development review functions.

NOW THEREFORE, BE IT ORDAINED BY THE
CITY COUNCIL OF ANYCITY

Section 1: Establishment of Administrative Procedures
The following administrative procedures shall be utilized when collecting and processing all development review fees paid to the City of Anycity:

(a) Fees: Fees will be collected from the petitioner by the City Clerk at the time of filing every petition for rezoning, special exceptions, comprehensive plan amendments, applications for proposed subdivision plan review, and commercial site plan reviews. No action of any kind shall be taken until the fee is paid in full, except that the City Council may, prior to or at the time of application, establish an alternate method of payment of the applicable fees and charges. Upon payment of the required fee, a project account will be established.

(b) Project Account: Once the project fee is credited to the project account, the account will be maintained throughout the entire review process until final action by the City Council or until no further involvement of the City staff is required to process the project, whichever is the later occurrence. City staff time expended and directly related expenses, including advertising, legal and engineering expenses will be charged to the account. At no time will the account reflect a deficit balance.

(c) Supplemental Fees: The project account will be monitored on a weekly basis. If the account balance is reduced to 25% of the initial fee, a supplemental fee will be required before any further processing continues. Petitioners will be notified in writing by the Finance Director, or his designee, when the balance is reduced to 25% of the initial fee. The amount of supplemental fee will be 50% of the initial fee amount. Several supplemental fees may be necessary depending upon the complexity of an individual project. Upon closing the project account, any remaining fee balance will be returned to the petitioner.

NOTE: This process will incorporate the provisions for payment of fees incurred as addressed in Appendix _____ of the City Charter, Articles _____.

(d) City Staff Time Accounting: City staff members, both "in house" and consultants, involved in the review and processing of the aforementioned petitions shall maintain weekly records of their time expended upon specific projects. Said records will be submitted to the City's Finance Director for processing. "In-house" staff hourly rates will be determined by the City of Anycity's Wage and Salary Plan (in accordance with the Dunedin [Florida] Court decisions) and consultant's time will be billed to the petitioner at the same rate charged to the City. A debit based upon the time expended and the applicable hourly rate shall be charged against the project account.

Section 2: Application and Filing Fees

Applications with required supporting data and applicable filing fee shall be filed with the City Clerk of Anycity. The City Clerk will establish the Project Account in cooperation and coordination with the Finance Director. The City Clerk will also forward the application and all supporting documents to the City Planner.

The City Council hereby establishes the schedule of fees enumerated below for matters pertaining to land development.

The following initial fees shall be collected and processed for review of development within the City of Anycity, Anystate:

Petition for Rezoning to all districts except PUD. This fee is in addition to the standard $100 application fee.	$200.00
Total Fee =	$300.00
Petition for Rezoning to PUD Plus standard application fee.	$650.00
Total Fee =	$750.00
Petition for Special Exception This is in addition to the application fee cited in the Zoning Ordinance.	$150.00
Total Fee =	$250.00
Petition for an Amendment to the Comprehensive Land Use Plan	$500.00
Petition for Review of a Proposed Subdivision	$1,000.00
Petition for Review of a Commercial Site Plan	$750.00

This schedule of fees and charges shall be posted in the offices of the City Planner and the Building Official. The charges listed in this Section may be changed by the City Council via an Ordinance amending this Ordinance. This process would afford any interested persons at least fourteen (14) days notice under the present administrative requirements.

Applications or petitions initiated officially by the City through its duly authorized agencies or offices are exempt from the payment of these fees.

Section 3: Severability

All ordinances and parts of ordinances that conflict herewith to the extent of such conflicts are hereby repealed. If an phrase, clause, sentence, paragraph, section or subsection of the ordinance shall be declared unconstitutional or invalid by a court of competent jurisdiction, such unconstitutionality or invalidity shall not affect the remaining phrases, clauses, sentences, paragraphs, sections or subsections of the ordinance.

Section 8: Effective Date
This ordinance shall take effect immediately upon its adoption.

First Reading held on _____, 19xx.
Second Reading held on _____, 19xx.

ENACTED THIS _____ DAY OF _____, 19xx.

ATTEST: John Doe, Mayor

_____
City Clerk

APPENDIX B

SAMPLE JOB DESCRIPTIONS

NOTE: The Americans with Disabilities Act (ADA) enacted by Congress in 1990 requires that job descriptions specifically state the physical and mobility requirements for each job. To satisfy this new requirement, you will have to talk with your department heads and determine these requirements for each job in your city.

GROUP I
Building Maintenance Superintendent

MAJOR FUNCTION: Responsible for administrative and supervisory work in coordinating the maintenance and repair of public municipal buildings and facilities. Construction, renovation or maintenance work being performed by outside firms under contract is also the administrative responsibility of this position. Work is performed under supervision of the Public Works Director with wide latitude for independent judgment.

DUTIES: Organizes, plans and directs maintenance and repair activities. Assigns, supervises and reviews the work of personnel involved in trades-work - carpentry, painting, roofing, masonry, plumbing, and locksmith work. Estimates costs, materials and time. Procures and controls use of supplies and equipment. Consults and advises appropriate departments regarding building and maintenance plans.

KNOWLEDGE, SKILLS AND ABILITIES (KSAs): Thorough knowledge of the techniques, tools and materials used in the skilled trades and building maintenance and repair. Ability to lay out work, instruct and direct trades-workers; interpret blueprints, sketches, estimate costs; keep records and prepare reports; effectively deal with city employees and the general public.

EDUCATION: High school or vocational school; five (5) years experience in building maintenance and two (2) years relevant supervisory experience in general maintenance of large buildings and facilities. (Contractor's license may be required.)

GROUP II
Account Clerk I

MAJOR FUNCTION: Entry level bookkeeping , cashiering, payroll, inventory, and related tasks within clearly defined limits and established procedures without close supervision. Work is reviewed by a supervisor primarily through verification of financial records and statements and through periodic audits.

DUTIES: Posts to accounts payable, accounts receivable, and cash journals; computes and prepares agency billings; processes and verifies requisitions, purchase orders, billings, invoices, work orders; prepares and/or orders data for computer input and verifies computer printouts; prepares summaries and routine reports; maintains inventory records; operates ten-key machines, calculator, bookkeeping and posting machines and related equipment.

KSAs: Knowledge of the fundamentals of bookkeeping; office practices, procedures, and equipment; and standard clerical techniques. Ability to learn laws, rules and regulations relative to financial records; understand oral and written instructions; establish and maintain effective working relationships with other employees and the general public.

EDUCATION: Graduation from high school; one (1) year experience in clerical work involving financial records and accounts.

Accountant

MAJOR FUNCTION: Beginning level professional accounting work exercising initiative and independent judgment in organizing, maintaining and systematically reviewing financial transaction records under general supervision. Prepares financial statements and reports, participates in the design and revision of accounting systems, and may supervise clerical personnel. Work is reviewed through conferences, reports and internal audits.

DUTIES: Maintains records for the receipt and disbursement of municipal and federal funds; verifies trial balances, detail appropriations and expenditures; reviews reports, vouchers, requisitions and invoices for conformance with accepted procedures; interprets financial records and prepares monthly and year-end reports; compiles data for the preparation of budgets; maintains and balances journals; supervises and trains sub-professional and clerical personnel.

KSAs: Knowledge of the principles and practices of accounting; knowledge of the laws, rules, guidelines, and regulations applicable to governmental accounting and data processing applications in business management. Ability to maintain, analyze and interpret fiscal records and to prepare clear, concise, and accurate reports both orally and in writing. Ability to work effectively with others.

EDUCATION: Graduation from college with major in accounting or related discipline or equivalent training and experience.

Administrative Assistant

MAJOR FUNCTION: Responsible administrative staff work in assisting a department official or in the city manager's office. Regular exercise of initiative and independent judgment is required. May supervise other employees in department. Work is reviewed through conferences, observation and reports submitted.

DUTIES: Studies, analyzes and evaluates segments of the organization, develops recommendations; identifies and solves administrative and management problems which hinder effective and efficient operations; reviews and updates policies and manuals; coordinates inter-departmental and special projects. Usually participates heavily in budget preparation. Provides technical assistance to other personnel in implementing new or modified systems.

KSAs: Knowledge of the department's purpose, goals and procedures. Ability to plan, research and present written and oral reports. Ability to deal effectively with employees and the general public.

EDUCATION: Graduation from a four year university with one to two years responsible experience in public administration.

Clerk Typist I

MAJOR FUNCTION: typing and clerical work which follows established policies and procedures requiring limited judgment. Detailed instructions are given for new assignments, however, tasks are performed more independently as experience is gained. Work is reviewed in process or upon completion for accuracy and completeness. May be deputized to give effect to legal procedures.

DUTIES: Types articles, letters, memoranda, reports, statements, tabulations, etc., from copy, rough draft, or dictaphone; cuts and proofs stencils, operates mimeograph and copy machines; sorts and files correspondence, reports, vouchers or other materials numerically, alphabetically or by other established classifications; receives visitors, answers phones, distributes mail, and gives non-technical information; makes arithmetic calculations in preparation and coding of billings, cashier tapes, etc., and issues receipts for payments.

KSAs: Knowledge of business English, spelling, and arithmetic, office practices and procedures. Ability to understand and follow oral and written instructions; make arithmetic computations and tabulations accurately and with reasonable speed; learn clerical tasks and adhere to prescribed routine; meet and deal courteously with the general public. Skill in the operation of a typewriter.

EDUCATION: Graduation from high school or equivalent certification.

Computer Operator

MAJOR FUNCTION: Entry-level technical work in operation and care of electronic data processing equipment. Monitors and operates computer console and peripheral equipment. Work is performed under supervision of technical supervisor. Shift work may be required.

DUITES: Operates on-line and support hardware equipment; loads, compiles, replaces and updates programs; gathers data; maintains operating records. Monitors equipment to correct and detect error conditions; cleans, does minor maintenance and adjustments on same.

KSAs: Knowledge of operation, adjustment and care of standard EDP equipment. Skill in use of computer equipment. Ability to understand and carry out oral and written instructions.

EDUCATION: High school or GED and limited experience in data processing.

Personnel Officer

MAJOR FUNCTION: Professional public personnel work in areas such as recruitment, classification, training, employee benefits and special projects. Extent of review, by personnel director, is dependent upon nature of assignment. Supervision may be exercised over technicians and clerical employees. Work is performed according to established procedures but can involve independent judgment in formulating recommendations to supervisors in applying guidelines.

DUTIES: May include all of some of the following: Conducts position audits; prepares classification specifications, revisions, abolishment, consolidation; collects, compiles, analyzes salary and fringe benefit data; qualifies applicants; validates and prepares exams; does position evaluations; organizes and develops recruitment or in-service training programs; maintains and updates records on employees' status and employment history; interviews and screens applicants.

KSAs: Knowledge of theory and procedures of public personnel administration; research methods and objectives. Ability to express oneself effectively orally and in writing; to deal effectively with city employees and the general public.

EDUCATION: Four year college degree with two (2) years related experience or graduate work in the field.

Planner

MAJOR FUNCTION: Entry level professional planning work involving research and development. Conducts studies under general supervision; collects and analyzes data for use in city's comprehensive plan; supervises employees engaged in preparation of detailed graphic and written presentations. Work is reviewed by consultation and analysis of reports prepared.

DUTIES: Assists higher level planner in preparing reports and recommendations; evaluates ongoing programs for effectiveness; conducts feasibility studies; supervises updating of zoning and land-use maps; conducts field surveys; prepares project outlines; selects data sources; details plan specifications for capital improvements, master plan, major zoning changes or business projects.

KSAs: Thorough knowledge of principles and practices of city planning as relates to design and development of urban and regional plans. Knowledge of techniques required in map preparation, charts, sketches and complex graphics. Ability to prepare studies on and investigate urban properties and physical conditions; to supervise a small group of technical and clerical personnel.

EDUCATION: Four year college degree with major course work in planning or related field.

Recreation Supervisor

MAJOR FUNCTION: Responsible for administrative work developing and supervising recreation activities, usually for one center or division or the department. Involves responsibility for coordinating and integrating activities with general program of city. Assignments cover general procedure and policies, but wide latitude is given for working out details. Work is reviewed through observations and conferences.

DUTIES: Plans, organizes, implements and supervises recreational activities and programs of a specialized nature. Manages and coordinates a facility which could include a building, indoor center, playground, athletic center, or swimming pool. Trains and assists staff in the development and implementation of recreational programs. Assists in preparation of budget, prepares estimates and reports, performs required administrative tasks such as registration, scheduling, supply requisitions, building rental and equipment maintenance.

KSAs: Knowledge of principles, practices and techniques of public programs and needs of age group levels; of a variety of recreational programs and activities. Ability to develop community participation and interest in recreation activities, including utilizing a public relations program; to prepare clear reports and maintain records.

EDUCATION: Two (2) years of college and one (1) year of experience in physical education or recreation capacity.

Secretary I

MAJOR FUNCTION: Entry level secretarial work providing support services to a section. Applies independent judgment, initiative, and discretion in handling generally routine matters regarding office policy and procedures. Work is performed under general supervision and reviewed through observation and inspection of work products.

DUTIES: Takes and transcribes dictation; types correspondence, minutes, charts and reports; receives, screens and routes calls, visitors and mail; maintains fiscal, operating, personnel and activity records; takes and prepares minutes of meetings and public hearings; maintains appointment calendar; prepares requisitions for personnel and/or office supplies and equipment; may assist with payroll and posting.

KSAs: Knowledge of business English, punctuation, spelling and arithmetic; modern office practices, procedures and equipment. Ability to acquire knowledge of rules, regulations, functions, administrative procedures and policies of the assigned section; maintain complex files and related records; and establish and maintain effective working relationships. Skill in the operation of typewriters, calculating and duplicating machines and other office machinery.

EDUCATION: Graduation from high school; clerical experience preferred.

Executive Secretary

MAJOR FUNCTION: Executive secretarial work in the operation of the office of a department director, coordinator of several departments or city manager. Relieves the supervisor of operational and administrative details, screening controversial topics for the supervisor's attention. Supervises secretarial and clerical staff. Works independently, conferring with the supervisor on unusual administrative and legal problems.

DUTIES: Interprets, explains, and implements administrative policy and decisions; transmits orders and instructions with the authority of the supervisor; performs public relations function with the public, department heads, officials, personnel, and visitors; receives, screens and routes calls and mail; takes and transcribes minutes of specific Boards; coordinates meetings, conferences and appointments; processes all materials for meetings; maintains official records; supervises secretarial and clerical staff; and briefs supervisor on pertinent information and scheduling of priority matters.

KSAs: Thorough knowledge of business English, spelling, punctuation and arithmetic; modern office practices, procedures and equipment; agency rules, regulations, procedures, functions and personnel; office management and supervision. Ability to compose effective and accurate correspondence; keep records, assemble and organize data, and prepare reports; meet and deal with the public and personnel in an effective and courteous manner; plan and coordinate work of subordinates. Skill in the operation of office machinery including typewriters and dictaphones.

EDUCATION: Graduation from high school; four (4) years experience in responsible secretarial work.

GROUP III
Auto Mechanic I

MAJOR FUNCTION: Skilled work at sub-journey level in maintenance and repair of gasoline or diesel driven motors and related auto equipment. May assist mechanic of higher grade; work is performed under direct supervision.

DUTIES: Services and repairs brake systems; tests and repairs electrical systems; tunes and adjusts engines; removes, repairs and replaces component parts or assembles automotive systems. Welds metals, inspects vehicles for safety conformance, keeps records of work completed.

KSAs: Working knowledge of methods, materials, tools and equipment of automotive mechanical trade; of principles of internal combustion engines; of related occupational hazards and safety precautions. Skill in use and care of equipment. Ability to understand and follow oral and written instructions; to locate and repair defects in motor equipment; to complete time cards and work records legibly.

EDUCATION: Completion of high school, or equivalent and one year experience in automotive work.

Building Inspector I

MAJOR FUNCTION: Technical inspection work of building construction, alteration or repair for compliance with codes, laws and regulations for building, zoning, and licensing. Work requires regular use of technical judgment and discretion in applying standard trade practices. Review by Building Official is through oral and written reports and analysis or inspections.

DUTIES: Examines structures for soundness, safety and condition for human habitation and adherence to plans, codes, and standards of constructions. Inspects foundations, framing, roofs, lots and may also inspect electrical and plumbing systems. Advises property owners of needed repairs/alterations. Keeps records, issues orders and explains requirements to public and contractors, gives technical assistance in construction matters.

KSAs: Thorough knowledge of materials and methods used in building construction, alteration and repair trade techniques; minimum housing standards, national and local building codes. Ability to recognize faulty construction, substandard materials, conditions of hazard; to interpret plans and specifications to prepare reports and communicate clearly orally and in writing.

EDUCATION: High school diploma supplemented by completion of selected specialized training courses. Three years supervisory experience as a master craftsperson, contractor, or builder. Certification usually required.

Equipment Operators

MAJOR FUNCTION: Semiskilled (I) and skilled (II and III) work in the operation and basic maintenance of simple, complex and heavy trucks and automotive equipment. Involves responsibility for safe and efficient operation of equipment and safety of passengers and helpers. Variety of units may be operated; may load and unload, do manual tasks and/or supervise other employees assigned to equipment. Work is reviewed through personal inspection and observation of compliance with established work schedules.

DUTIES: Level I - Operates simple to moderately complex mechanical equipment such as flat beds, dump trucks, modified trucks, tractor-mowers, tillers, rollers and hoes, cement mixers, pumping equipment, air hammers and compressors.

Level II - Operates complex to heavy automotive and maintenance equipment such as large trucks, tractor-trailers, construction equipment, graders, pay loaders, and draglines.

Level III - Operates heavy automotive and related equipment such as diesel powered machines, bulldozers, draglines, cranes, excavation machines, graders, trailers, and street sweepers.

KSAs: Knowledge of operational characteristics of assigned equipment and of safe driving techniques and related occupational hazards. Skill in the operation of assigned equipment. Ability to work under adverse weather conditions; read and follow oral and written instructions; and operate assigned vehicle in the prescribed manner. Ability to detect improper functioning of mechanical systems and make minor adjustments.

EDUCATION: Valid state chauffeur's license. Experience in the operation of trucks, tractors, and other equipment. High school diploma or equivalent required.

Leadworker

MAJOR FUNCTION: Limited supervisory work assisting in and directing the activities of manual semi-skilled laborers. May assist foreperson of large groups of employees or act as working foreperson in charge of a small number of employees. Work is reviewed in progress under general supervision and upon completion.

DUTIES: Supervises personnel involved in construction, maintenance and repair tasks; inspects work in progress; modifies or adjusts work methods, assignments, crew sizes; keeps time and material records; determines need for equipment repair; trains and instructs subordinates.

KSAs: Knowledge of related methods, materials, tools and supplies in construction, maintenance and repair work; of safety precautions and hazards. Skill in care and use of pertinent tools, equipment and facilities. Ability to carry out written and oral instructions and plans; to plan, assign and supervise the work of several laborers.

EDUCATION: High school diploma, or equivalent with two years experience in road or grounds maintenance.

Lift Station Operator

MAJOR FUNCTION: Skilled technical and limited mechanical work in the operation and maintenance of a lift station within the wastewater division. Routine work is performed independently, but complex tasks may be closely supervised.

DUTIES: Conducts preventive maintenance program by inspecting pumps, motors, compressors, valves and float control systems. Does minor mechanical repairs, maintains equipment and facilities. Operates pumps, valves, motors, controls and switches.

KSAs: Knowledge of operation of heavy pumping equipment; principles and practices of hydraulic equipment. Ability to keep complete and accurate records; read and understand gauges and meters. Good physical condition and manual dexterity. May require shift schedules.

EDUCATION: High school diploma or GED with one year experience in wastewater systems.

Meter Reader

MAJOR FUNCTION: Routine field work in reading and recording readings of utility meters. Under general direction of supervisor.

DUTIES: Records readings, explains rates and rules to customers, reports meters in need of repair, and reports irregularities. May be required to do any of the following: connect and disconnect meters; operate small truck; and perform maintenance on meters.

KSAs: Knowledge of geography of city and meter reading practices. Ability to deal with the public, walk for long periods, and operate small truck under varying weather conditions.

EDUCATION: High school diploma, or equivalent, and possession of a valid state driver's licence.

Sanitation Collector

MAJOR FUNCTION: Performs routine, but heavy manual labor in the collection and disposal of all types of garbage and related refuse. May operate special sanitation equipment. Works under the direct supervision of the crew leader (usually sanitation truck driver) and the general supervision of the Sanitation Department Supervisor. May drive truck on an occasional basis in the absence of the driver.

DUTIES: Picks up garbage, trash and related refuse at residential and/or commercial premises; empties into large container; assists in lifting refuse into truck; uses pitchforks, shovels and similar hand tools to pick up general refuse and trash from curbs and other areas; assists truck operator in vehicle maintenance; washes and cleans truck; reports violations of refuse ordinances to supervisor.

KSAs: Ability and willingness to work constantly with unpleasant materials in all kinds of weather. Sufficient physical strength, stamina and agility to lift, move, load and carry heavy objects. Ability to understand and follow simple and specific instructions; and operate special equipment with on-the-job training.

EDUCATION: High school diploma, or equivalent. May require a chauffeur's license.

Treatment Plant Operators I-IV

MAJOR FUNCTION: Routine skilled work in the operation and maintenance of water or wastewater treatment plant facilities on an assigned shift. Responsible for safe and efficient operation of equipment used in purification of water. Work is performed in accordance with established procedures under general supervision and is reviewed through observation and analyses of plant records and reports.

DUTIES: Regulates flow and processing of wastewater, sludge and effluent. Cleans and operates water filters, valves, gates, pumps, engines and generators. Checks substations, monitors gauges, meters and control panels; maintains shift logs interprets and records meter and gauge readings; extracts samples and performs routine, complex and special chemical tests of water samples. Operates testing and chlorinating equipment. Does mechanical maintenance work and performs minor repairs.

KSAs: Knowledge of procedures, functions and servicing requirements of water plant mechanical equipment and machinery; of procedures involved in the purification of water. Knowledge of basic chemistry. Ability to understand and follow oral and written instructions; to inspect machinery and mechanical equipment for flaws or defects; to read meters and charts accurately; maintain records of shift operations.

EDUCATION: High school diploma or vocational school supplemented by courses in chemistry or mathematics. Driver's license required. Level I - Trainee position requiring some mechanical experience. Level II - Lowest level of state certification. Level III - Second level of state certificate. Level IV - Third level of state certification.

Originally published by the Florida City-County Managers' Association, Tallahassee, FL, 1983-84. Reprinted in part, with the FCCMA permission.

APPENDIX C

SAMPLE MERIT PLAN

This document can serve as a basis for your city's personnel policies. I drafted this document while working at a city. Read Chapter III, Personnel, of this book to more fully understand the nuances of this Merit Plan. At the end of this appendix is the enacting legislation for a Merit Plan; this plan can be adopted by reference.

Adopting by reference means that the ordinance to enact and adopt this plan merely has to reference this plan. This plan does not need to be reprinted into the body of the ordinance.

Table of Contents

SECTION 1: EXAMINATIONS:

A. General
Appointments, promotions and other personnel actions shall be based on evaluations, tests and/or examinations applying the merit principle.

B. Examination Types
There shall be three general types of examinations.

1. Open competitive (original employment)
2. Promotional
3. Noncompetitive (original employment)

C. Character of Open Competitive Examination
The administration may use any combination of selection techniques, as follows:

1. Written examination; which shall include written demonstration of each competitor's knowledge and skill in the field for which the test is being held and which may include standard tests of mental alertness and of ability in the use of English and mathematics, or of general educational attainments

2. Oral examination which may be used in lieu of or to supplement the written examination, or to obtain information regarding the abilities of the competitors that is not readily obtained in a written examination. Such oral examination may include tests or demonstrations of skills or leadership.

3. Performance tests which shall include such tests of performance as shall determine the ability, manual skills, and leadership of each competitor to perform the work involved and which may be either competitive or qualifying

4. Physical tests which may be either competitive or qualifying, and which shall consist of tests of bodily condition, muscular strength, ability and physical coordination

5. Interview which shall appraise each competitor's personal fitness for the position, such as the ability to get along with people, and other personal and temperamental qualifications

6. Rating of education, training and experience, which shall be based upon information in the application form, and such other data as may be secured through the interview or from other sources, and which shall be subject to investigation as to truth and completeness

7. The administration shall determine a final score for each competitor's examination, computed in accordance with the value for the several parts as established. The failure of any part of an examination shall disqualify the competitor in the entire examination and shall disqualify the competitor from participation in subsequent parts of the examination. All applicants for the same position shall be accorded uniform and equal treatment in all phases of the examination procedure.

D. Notice of Examination

1. The City Manager shall give public notice of any examination. Such notice shall be in a newspaper that has general circulation in the City of Anycity, and shall be posted on the bulletin board at the City Hall and the Anycity Post Office.

2. Copies thereof may be posted in other public buildings and distributed among public officials and other individuals and organizations as the City Manager may in each instance decide.

3. Public notices shall specify the title and compensation of the position(s), the minimum qualifications required, and any other pertinent information consistent with the provisions of these Rules, such as, value for each part of the examination, the closing date for and place and date of examination.

4. Notices of intention to give an examination may be announced on radio or television stations; may be mailed to schools or Universities, or to organizations where qualified persons may read them.

5. Notices of intention to give an examination may be published in magazines or other periodicals, or in the help-wanted columns of daily and/or weekly newspapers, as may be necessary to secure qualified applicants.

E. Eligibility

1. To be considered eligible to compete in an examination an applicant must meet the specifications for the class, including minimum and maximum age, be a citizen of the United States, and complete and file the application form prescribed on or before the closing date specified.

2. To be considered eligible to compete in an open competitive or open non-competitive examination an applicant shall be fingerprinted.

3. All applications shall be time stamped when received by the administration and assigned a serial number.

4. The City Manager shall determine if applicants meet the requirements for eligibility to take an examination and shall so notify the applicants.

5. It is the policy of the City of Anycity to adhere to all applicable statutes and regulations in the employment of minors.
    a. No person will be employed who has not reached his/her eighteenth (18) birthday.
    b. The City of Anycity will avoid the practice of Nepotism; no relatives of persons already employed shall be considered for employment.

6. Employment of job applicants with physical handicaps shall be considered on the basis of their capability for a particular position provided such handicap(s) do not constitute a hazard to themselves or others.

F. Disqualification of Applicants

1. The City Manager may refuse to examine an applicant, or after examination may disqualify an applicant, or may remove his/her name from any list, or may refuse to certify as eligible on a list, if the applicant.
    a. Is found to lack any of the preliminary requirements established for the position
    b. Is so physically disabled as to be rendered unfit for the performance of the duties of the class of position
    c. Is addicted to the use of any narcotic, or the habitual use of intoxicating iquor(s) to excess
    d. Has been found guilty of infamous or notoriously disgraceful conduct
    e. Has committed any other act which in the opinion of the City Manager would bring discredit to the City of Anycity
    f. Has been dismissed from the public service for delinquency, misconduct, or other similar cause

184

g. Has used, or attempted to use, political pressure or bribery to secure any advantage in the examination or appointment
h. Has made a false statement of material fact in his/her application
i. Has directly or indirectly obtained information regarding the examination to which, as an applicant, he/she is not entitled
j. Has taken part in the administration, or correction of the examination
k. Has violated any of the provisions of these rules

2. A disqualified applicant shall be promptly notified and given the reason or reasons for such disqualification.

G. Conduct of Examination

1. The City Manager shall make all reasonable effort to preserve the anonymity of candidates.

2. When a list is established, each candidate shall be notified of his/her relative place on the list, or of his/her failure to attain a place on the list.

3. If the City Manager finds that the conditions under which an examination was held were not such as to be fair to the candidates, he may order that the completed examination, or any part thereof, be cancelled, and that a new examination be held.

4. The candidate with the highest final earned rating shall rank first and the other candidates shall be ranked below in the order of the relative earned rating attained.

5. Whenever two (2) or more candidates have equal final earned ratings, their names shall be arranged on employment or promotional eligibility lists in the serial order in which their applications were received by the City Manager, unless only one of them is a citizen of Anycity. In this event, that is equally qualified candidates, preference shall be given to the citizen of Anycity.

6. A manifest error in any examination, if called to the attention of the City Manager within ten (10) working days after the establishment of an employment or promotional eligibility list resulting from such examination, shall be corrected and candidates affected by such correction shall be notified.

H. Review of Examination
Any examinee, or his/her authorized representative, shall be permitted to review the test papers of said examinee and the score assigned thereto under the following conditions:

1. All phases of the examination must have been completed and the eligibility list or lists established therefrom.

2. Written request for such review must be made to the City Manager by the examinee, or by his/her authorized representative, within five (5) working days after notification.
3. Such review shall be permitted only in the office of the City Manager during business hours. The City Manager shall safe guard all official records from addition, deletion, removal, or other alteration, or copying.

4. Any error found to exist shall be corrected, but such change shall not, per se, invalidate any list, certification, or appointment.

I. Promotional Examination

1. A promotional examination shall be conducted in the same manner as open competitive examination and under the same general requirements as to selection techniques, subject to the following additional requirements:

2. A person is eligible for promotional examination if he/she satisfies all of the following requirements on the closing date for filing applications given in the official announcement of the examination.
   a. Such person must be a qualified employee of the City of Anycity.
   b. Such person must meet the minimum requirements established for the examination.
   c. His/her current Employee Service Report rating must be satisfactory, or better.

3. Notices of promotional competitive examinations need only be circulated in those departments where there are employees eligible to compete.

J. Noncompetitive Eligibility
When the City Manager shall find that there are not enough applicants to justify a formal test, he may in that particular case and instance direct that the selection for an eligibility list for the position or positions open be non-competitive, and be based upon consideration of qualifications, experience, training, interviews, and reference checks.

SECTION II   ESTABLISHMENT & USE OF ELIGIBILITY LISTS

A. General
The four kinds of eligibility lists for a class of positions, each to consist of an active and an inactive sections are:
   1. Reemploymentlist
   2. Transfer list
   3. Promotion list
   4. Original employment list

B. Eligibility Lists
The City Manager may, subject to these Rules and Regulations, establish for a class of positions lists of these eligible for consideration for appointment from: lay-off notices, approved transfer requests, and from the results of promotional and original employment examinations.

C. Time Limit
No name shall remain on an eligibility list for more than one (1) calendar year.

D. Duration
The names of those eligible shall remain on an eligibility list for the duration of the list unless removed for cause, as covered in these Rules and Regulations, or unless by reason of receiving a permanent appointment.

E. Temporary Appointment
When an eligible, whose name appears on an eligibility list, is appointed to fill a temporary positions, for which no eligibility list exists, his/her name shall continue to be certified on such eligibility list as a candidate for permanent appointment.

F. Mandatory Removal
The name of an eligible shall be removed from a promotional list or lists if he/she is demoted, or if he/she resigns.

G. Amendment of Lists

The City Manager may amend an eligibility list by addition or removal:

1. Addition: An existing list of eligibles may be merged with a list of eligibles who have qualified in subsequent examinations, the lists to be merged in the order of the relative earned ratings.

2. Removal: An eligible who has been considered for appointment a total of three (3) times, by two or more department heads, without receiving appointment, or who has declined an appointment, may be removed from an eligibility list.

H. Restoration to Lists after Removal

The City Manager may restore the name of an eligible to an eligibility list upon receipt of acceptable written information showing that the cause for removal no longer exists, or that an error was made in making the removal.

I. Cancellation of Eligibility List

The City Manager may cancel an eligibility list at such time as the list becomes unsatisfactory because of a high percentage of unavailable or inactive eligibles on such list, changes in qualification standards, or for such other reasons as may be in the best interests of the System.

J. Inspection of Lists

Eligibility lists shall be available for inspection during the regular office hours of the City Hall. The items used in determining an eligible's final rating shall be open to inspection only by the individual candidate concerned, or his/her authorized representative, as covered in these Rules and Regulations.

K. Reinstatement

There shall be no reinstatement of any employee to an eligibility list except in connection with a finding in favor of the employee at any step in the Employee Review procedures, Section XIV.

The Rules and Regulations in Sections III, IV, & V shall apply in all other instances.

SECTION III   CERTIFICATION - APPOINTMENT FROM
ELIGIBILITY LISTS

A. General

1. The department head, subject to approval by the City Manager, shall fill position vacancies by appointment of eligibles, subject to his/her satisfactory completion of the probationary period.

2. Positions shall be grouped into two (2) types for the purpose of appointment: competitive and noncompetitive positions.

B. Requisitions

1. When a vacancy occurs in any position, or if a new position or positions are duly authorized, a requisition shall be submitted by the department head to the City Manager for each such vacancy.

2. Prior to budget preparation each department head shall advise the City Manager of any new personnel needs anticipated for the next fiscal year.

C. Administration of Competitive Positions

1. To fill vacancies, the City Manager shall certify to the department head those persons standing highest on the appropriate list.

2. The following employment eligibility lists shall be used by the City Manager in the sequence indicated:

1st: reemployment list (those former employees who were laid off through no fault of the employee)
2nd: promotion list
3rd: transfer list
4th: original employment list

D. Reemployment List
1. When a permanent employee is separated from the System by lay-off, his/her name shall be placed on a reemployment list, for consideration for re-employment, should a vacancy occur for which he/she meets the requirements. The names of available eligibles, up to three (3) shall be certified to the requisitioning department head.
2. Any reemployment shall be probationary unless it is to a position of the classification from which the appointee was laid off.
3. The order of recall, if there is more than one (1) person on an employment list, shall be in order of length of service prior to layoff, other considerations being equal.

E. Transfer List
1. The City manager may, without holding tests or examinations, certify on a Transfer List the names of available eligibles, up to three (3), for consideration for transfer from one position to another in the same class.
2. The administration shall maintain suitable lists of those employees who have given notice in writing of his/her desire to be transferred to a position of the same class in another department.
3. If it is found that a person with the requirements to fill a position is not available on the Reemployment Lists, then the City Manager shall survey the Transfer Lists.
4. No person shall be transferred without prior notice to his current department head and approval of the City Manager.
5. No employee shall be transferred to a position for which they do not possess the qualifications and if their services are not currently rated as satisfactory or better.

F. Promotion List
1. If it is found that a person with the qualifications to fill a position vacancy is not available on the Reemployment Lists, nor on the Transfer Lists, then the City Manager shall determine if there is a current Promotion List of eligibles for the position.
2. If there is such a Promotion List, up to three (3) eligibles thereon shall be certified to the requisitioning department head.
3. If there is no such promotion list, the City Manager shall review the merit qualifications of employees who are receiving salaries lower than the minimum of the class requisitioned.

G. Original Employment List
1. If a vacancy cannot be filled through the use of reemployment, transfer, or promotion lists, the City Manager shall certify persons from an original employment eligible list, appropriate for filling the position.
2. If such an original employment list of eligibles is not available, or if it does not suffice to fill the requisition, then a temporary appointment may be made as provided for in these Rules and Regulations.

H. Appointment
If, after interview and consideration, the department head shall make a probationary appointment from among those certified on any list, the department head shall, no later thank the next business day, so notify the City Manager in writing.

I. Temporary Appointments
1. When the department head finds it necessary to fill a vacancy and the City Manager is unable to certify eligibles for such vacancy, because there is no existing

188

appropriate list, or because no certified eligibles are acceptable, the City Manager may authorize the department head to fill the vacancy by means of a temporary appointment.

2. No temporary appointment shall be made without the prior approval in writing of the City Manager. No commitment shall be made for services rendered by any temporary appointee prior to the date and time of such approval.

3. A temporary appointment to a position shall expire two (2) calendar weeks after a list of certifiable eligibles has been prepared for such position. A temporary appointment shall automatically expire three (3) calendar months from the date of such appointment and shall not be subject to renewal, except as provided hereinafter.

4. If the City Manager is unable, within two (2) calendar weeks prior to the ending of the three (,) calendar month life of a temporary appointment to certify an acceptable eligible for the vacancy in the class of position to which the temporary appointment was made, the department head may recommend to the City Manager at least one (1) calendar week prior to the expiration date of such temporary appointment, that the temporary appointment be continued for a further period, not to exceed three (3) months.

5. With the City Manager's approval, the temporary appointment shall be extended for such period.

6. During the life of any extension of a temporary appointment, the City Manager shall continue his efforts to prepare an eligibility list for such class of position, provided, that during any extension of a temporary appointment an eligibility list may consist of one (1) or more certifiable eligibles for such class or position.

J. Full-time or Part-time Positions

1. Each position shall be designated as either full-time or part-time, as defined in these Rules and Regulations. Such designation shall be used in any requisition or communication to the City Manager regarding any position.

2. A permanent employee may be assigned to fill a vacancy on a temporary basis where such assignment involves neither a promotion nor a demotion. Any permanent employee so assigned shall return to his/her former position when the term of the temporary position ends.

3. The following positions may be designated part-time.
    a. Relief Dispatchers
    b. Part-time certified Police Officers and Firemen
    c. Building Inspector
    d. Others - as approved by the City Manager

K. Administration of Noncompetitive Positions

1. Appointments to positions being filled on a non-competitive basis shall be made by the department head from certified re-employment, promotion, transfer, or original employment lists of eligibles, furnished in that order by the City Manager as available.

2. All such appointments shall, as with competitive positions, be subject to the satisfactory completion of a six (6) month probationary period, prior to the appointment being made permanent.

SECTION IV   HOURS OF WORK - WORK WEEK

A. General

1. The normal work week for city employees shall consist of forty (40) hours of duty, computed on the basis of eight (8) hours per day, five (5) days per week. With the approval of the City Manager, department heads may schedule personnel for ten (10) hour duty days, four (4) days per week. Duty in excess of these amounts may be performed when deemed necessary by the department head or City Manager, and shall be compensated for in accordance with the following policies:

B Allocation

1.   The hours during which the departments, offices and activities shall be open for business or in operation shall be determined by the City Manager and shall be subject to change by the department head, with the prior approval of the City Manager.

2.   The assignment of an employee or employees to shifts or to hours within those during which the department, office or activity is open for business shall be at the discretion of the department head and approval by the City Manager.

3.   It is likely that a work load in excess of that which can be accomplished under the hours and/or days of an established category will exist from time to time. All employees are required to work the additional hours when called upon to do so It is also possible that part-time work schedules may become necessary, as covered below.

C. Part-time

1.   The work week and/or the daily hours of work of a given position may be changed to a scheduled part-time work week and/or daily hours of work when full-time service is no longer required by reason of shortage of work or of funds, material change in departmental organization or for other related reasons. Such changes may be made only with the prior approval of the City Manager.

2.   Before the work week and/or the daily hours of work of a permanent employee shall be changed to a part-time work schedule, all temporary and probationary employees in the same class of position in that department shall have been dismissed in that order.

3.   The change of permanent employees to a part-time work schedule shall be made in inverse order of length of service, other considerations being equal, in the class in the department.

4.   Part-time personnel employed by the City of Anycity shall be entitled to Social Security benefits (FICA) and Workmen's Compensation Insurance in addition to the rate of pay.

5.   If the City has the occasion to employ "casual labor", they shall only be subject to Social Security benefits.

SECTION V · ATTENDANCE REGULATIONS

1.   An employee shall be at his/her place of work in accordance with these Rules and Regulations and departmental regulations.

2.   No employee shall be paid for other than time worked unless, in accordance with the Rules and Regulations, he/she is authorized to be absent.

3.   Each department in maintaining attendance records shall enter thereon information as to days absent or tardy for each employee and in each instance, whether such absence or tardiness was authorized. A copy of such record shall be forwarded to the payroll clerk each payroll period the information to be recorded in the personnel record of the employee concerned.

4.   Additionally, each department head shall report any personnel absent within his department to the Finance Director, daily. Said report shall indicate whether employee is sick, receiving compensatory time, missing without the department head's knowledge or other nature of the absence.

5.   Each employee shall be responsible for notifying his/her department head of his/her inability to report for work, and of the reason for each such absence or tardiness. Calls to other than his/her department head or the City Manager shall not be considered proper notification.

6.   Failure by an employee to conform to the requirements of attendance such as unauthorized absence and/or tardiness, shall subject the employee to disciplinary action.

SECTION VI   HOLIDAY REGULATIONS

A. Holidays
1.   The eight official paid holidays for employees of the City of Anycity shall be:

New Years Day	Memorial Day
Independence Day (July 4th)	Labor Day
Thanksgiving Day	Christmas Eve
Christmas Day	

Floating Holiday (to be scheduled by the City Manager each year, to fall either on the day following Thanksgiving or the day after Christmas.)

B. Holiday Compensation
1.   When paid holidays fall on a Saturday, the preceding Friday shall be observed as the holiday. When a paid holiday falls on a Sunday, the following Monday shall be observed as the holiday. If an employee is required to work on a holiday, he/she shall be compensated by time off.
2.   Employees working on a shift basis who are required to work on an official holiday, or for whom a holiday falls on a scheduled day off, will be granted an additional day off or be paid an extra day's pay, at the straight wage rate, as the employee chooses. Affected employees shall submit their preference as to compensatory time or pay to their department head prior to the official holiday.
3.   The following listed categories of employees specifically do not qualify to receive compensation or compensatory time for the day on which a holiday falls.
   a.   An employee who is absent without the specific approval of his/her department head for such absence on his/her scheduled working day immediately preceding and/or following the day on which an official holiday falls.
   b.   Temporary employees
   c.   Part-time employees without regularly scheduled hours and/or days of work.
   d.   Employees on authorized leave except vacation leave.
   e.   Employees on Workmen's Compensation or other disability compensation.

4.   Nothing set forth herein shall be construed as relieving the heads of the various departments, offices and activities of their responsibilities for the performance of required functions. Heads of departments shall determine what persons may be spared to observe holidays.

SECTION VII   POSITION CLASSIFICATION

A. General
1.   The Classification Plan shall consist of the approved class specifications adopted for each class of positions in the System of the City of Anycity.
2.   The Administration shall prepare and maintain a list of class titles and class specifications for all positions in the System and shall allocate by evaluation all positions to an appropriate class.

B.   Preparation
1.   The Administration shall review the proposed classification plan with affected department heads.
2.   After hearing such suggestions and recommendations as department heads and other interested persons may present, the Administration shall review such information and shall prepare a classification plan with such modifications as may be considered proper.

C.   Allocation of a Position to a Class
1.   In determining the class of positions to which any position should be allocated or reallocated, the specifications of each class shall be read as a whole.

2. Consideration shall be given to the general and specific duties, responsibilities, working conditions, qualifications required for appointment and relationships to other classes.

3. The use of particular expression or illustration as to duties and/or responsibilities shall not be held to exclude others not mentioned that are substantially similar as to kind and level of difficulty and responsibility.

D. New Positions and Changes to Existing Positions

Whenever new positions are authorized and created, whenever the duties and/or responsibilities of existing positions change, or whenever the classification plan is amended, the Administration shall allocate or reclassify the affected positions.

E. Class Title

1. The title of each class shall be the official title of every position allocated to the class for all purposes having to do with the position.

2. Such title shall be used to designate the position on all payrolls and on all reports of official personnel transactions.

3. No persons shall be appointed to or employed in a position under a class title which has not been approved by the Administration and which is not the official class title as adopted under the covering resolution.

F. Class Specifications

The class specification shall constitute the basis for the tests to be included in the examination procedure for the class and for the evaluation of the qualifications of applicants.

G. Administration of the Classification Plan

1. Classification of a New Position

a. The department head shall notify the City Manager in writing when a new position is to be created.

b. The City Manager shall study and evaluate the position and allocate the position to the appropriate class.

c. If no appropriate class exists, a new class shall be created and a new class title and specification shall be prepared.

2. Reclassification

a. The department head shall notify the City Manager in writing whenever a permanent material change is to be made in the duties and/or responsibilities of any position. Such notification shall clearly describe the proposed changes in detail.

b. The City Manager shall study and evaluate the proposed changes in relation to the total job content and shall allocate the position to the appropriate class.

c. If no appropriate class exists, a new class shall be created and a new class title and specification shall be prepared.

d. If the proposed changes are such that a reclassification or new classification are not necessary, the department head shall be so notified in writing.

3. Classification of a Vacant Position

a. When a position becomes vacant for any reason, the Administration shall reexamine the duties and/or responsibilities of such position to determine if the position is still properly classified.

b. If necessary the position shall be reallocated to the appropriate class.

c. If no appropriate class exists, a new class shall be created and a new class title and specification shall be prepared.

4. Classification Plan Review

a. The Administration shall review annually the duties and/or responsibilities of each position to determine whether or not the position: (1) is still necessary, (2) is properly allocated, and (3) is adequately defined as to duties and/or responsibilities.

b. Should it be determined as a result of this review that any position should be eliminated, reclassified, reallocated, or redefined, the Administration shall initiate procedures therefore in accordance with these Rules and Regulations.

H. Effect of Reclassification of a Position

1. A permanent employee occupying a position which is reclassified shall continue in such position only if he/she is eligible and is appointed to the reclassified position in accordance with the Rules and Regulations governing promotion, transfer, or demotion.

2. Any permanent employee whose position is reclassified may compete in any examination held to fill the reclassified position.

I. Employee Change

No employee, either by classification or reclassification, change of title or otherwise, shall be promoted, transferred, demoted, suspended, or re-instated, except in accordance with the Rules and Regulations.

SECTION VIII   POSITION COMPENSATION

A. General

1. The Compensation plan shall be based on the classification plan and directly related to the evaluation grades in order to maintain related rates of pay for the several classes of work.

2. The rates of pay shall be based on general rates of pay for comparable work in public and private employment in the area, cost of living data, maintenance and other benefits received by employees, and other economic considerations.

B. Administration of the Compensation Plan

1. No position shall be assigned compensation at other than an established step in the compensation plan; or that is more than the maximum step; or less than the minimum step; except that these provisions shall not apply to part time employment Part time employees may be paid on an hourly or daily basis.

2. Appointments to positions in the System shall be made at the minimum step applicable to the class of positions, except as provided hereinafter.

3. Appointments to positions in the System at other than the minimum step applicable to the class of positions will be considered only if the department head shall submit a written request to the City Manager and attain his prior approval.

4. The following shall be the basis for consideration for such approval:

a. In recognition of the exceptional qualifications of an eligible employee or applicant such rate shall not be in excess of the third step of the rate change applicable to the class of positions.

b. When economic or employment conditions make recruitment of applicants at the minimum rate for a class inadequate to meet requirements, approval may be granted by the City manager with the consent of the City Commission that the compensation of all employees in that class of positions shall be increased to the new rate.

5. Promotion- The rate of compensation of an employee who is paid less than the minimum of his/her new class of position shall be adjusted to the new minimum. Any promotion shall be at least a one step increase in the new range over the step in the lower range.

6. Transfer- An employee transferred to another position without promotion or demotion shall not have his/her rate of compensation reduced without his prior permission.

7. Demotion- The rate of compensation of a demoted employee shall be fixed at any step within the rate range for the new class of position from which he/she is being demoted, but not above the third step of such rate range.

8. Return from Military Leave- When an employee is restored to the Merit System, his/her rate of pay shall be fixed on the step within the range for the class of position which is nearest to, but not less that, the rate of compensation for the classification of position when he/she left the employ of the City for military service.

9. Step Increases

a. Step increases above the third step within the range approved for the class of positions shall not be automatic, but shall be based on merit.

b. Merit shall be based on the quality of work, conduct, attendance and potential as documented by Employee Performance Review ratings and other recorded measures of performance.

c. All proposed merit increases shall be submitted for the consideration and approval of the City Manager on the form provided.

d. When an employee has completed the probationary period, the department head shall complete an Employee Performance Review on the employee, and if he/she is rated to receive an increase, the department head shall complete the appropriate form. The department head has the option to grant the raise upon a satisfactory rating, extend the probationary period up to 1 year from the date of hire or terminate that employee.

e. Any proposed increase in pay shall require the consideration and approval of the City Manager. Above one step increases are reserved solely for employees who have demonstrated above average work performance, conduct, attendance, and potential and who are rated above satisfactory by their department heads.

1) The department head shall in each case document the reasons for their recommendation for such proposed pay increase in such form and manner as the City Manager may prescribe.

2) Such pay increases may be either at the end of a new employee's six month probationary period or upon completion of 80 classroom hours or performance reviews will be denied or approved in the month of April, and the raises will be effective upon the re- commendation of the Merit System Board and approval of the City Manager.

10. It shall be the responsibility of the City Manager to ensure that employee advancement above one step of a pay range shall be for merit only and not automatic.

11. General Adjustment - Adjustments given throughout the compensation plan because of cost of living or other economic considerations shall not be considered as step increases.

12. Certification of Payrolls- It shall be the responsibility of the City Manager to certify all payrolls. No wage, salary, or compensation for services rendered shall be paid to any person holding an appointment to a position in the System unless the payroll for such wage, salary, or compensation shall include the name of such person or shall bear the certification of the City Manager that the person named therein has been appointed and is performing service in accordance with the provisions of the System's Rules and Regulations.

C. Personnel Action Form

CITY OF ANYCITY
PERSONNEL ACTION FORM

TO: CITY MANAGER

SUBJECT: RECOMMENDATION FOR HIRE /
RATE INCREASE / PROMOTION
(Line out inapplicable ones)

INDIVIDUAL:

OLD POSITION TITLE:
NEW POSITION TITLE:
OLD POSITION CLASSIFICATION
NEW POSITION CLASSIFICATION

194

OLD RATE (HRLY, BI-WKLY)
    NEW RATE (HRLY, BI-WKLY)

EFFECTIVE DATE:

    DEPT HEAD APPRD:
        CITY MANAGER APPRD:

DEPARTMENT   DATE
(*) PLEASE ATTACH COPY OF COMPLETED APPLICATION ON NEW HIRES.

D.   Notice of Termination Form

DATE OF TERMINATION:
REASON FOR TERMINATION:

DEPT. HEAD APPRD:.
        CITY MANAGER APPRD:.
DEPARTMENT   DATE

CoA GG-PA-l Jan 84
City of Anycity

        SECTION IX   COMPENSATION PLAN
                    (not included)

        SECTION X   PROBATION

    A. General
    1.   All original employment shall be probationary. Also, if an employee who is on
probation transfers to another position, the probation period shall start from the date of
transfer.
    2.   The probation period is an integral part of the evaluating, testing and/or
examination process and shall be used by the department head for closely observing a
probationary employee. It shall be utilized for the most effective adjustments to the duties
of the probationary employee and for the elimination of any probationary employee
whose work performance, attendance and conduct does not meet the required standards.

    B. Duration
    The probation period shall begin immediately upon appointment and shall be for a
period of six calendar months worked, except that the department head, with written
approval of the City Manager, may extend the probation period up to one year from date
of employment if it is deemed to be in the best interest of the City.

    C. Evaluation of Performance.
    1.   At any time, but at least twice and not later than three months after their date of
probationary appointment, and not later than fifteen calendar days prior to the conclusion
of the probationary period, the department head shall appraise and evaluate the
employee's work performance, conduct, attendance, and potential in writing on the
Employee Performance Review provided, and shall rate such probationary employee as
satisfactory or unsatisfactory.
    2.   The final required Employee Performance Review Report shall be in the hands
of the City Manager at least ten calendar days prior to the terminal date of the employee's
probationary period.

D. Rejection

During the probationary period an unsatisfactory probationary employee may be rejected and dismissed at any time without the right of appeal or hearing in any manner.

E. Appointment

1. A probationary employee who has received a rating of not satisfactory on their final required Employee Performance Review Report shall not receive a permanent appointment.

2. In order to receive a permanent appointment the department head must notify the City Manager in writing on the Employee Performance review Report required at least ten calendar days prior to the expiration date of an employee's probationary period that the employee's rating is satisfactory and that he is to continue in the position.

3. Department heads shall notify the City Manager by a Performance Review Report submission. Should the report be an unsatisfactory one, a conference between the department head and City Manager shall be held to discuss the matter, prior to taking final action.

4. No probationary employee shall be paid for work performed after the concluding date of their probationary period unless the City Manager shall have been notified as in paragraph X-E-2 above, that the probationary employee had attained a rating of satisfactory.

F. Reinstatement

An employee rejected and dismissed during the probationary period from a position to which they were promoted or transferred shall not be returned to the position from which they were promoted or transferred unless it shall be the decision of the City Manager that such return is in the best interests of the System.

G. Service Date

Upon the satisfactory completion of a probationary period and upon receiving permanent appointment, an employee shall receive credit for service from the date of their probationary appointment.

SECTION XI   SUSPENSION , DEMOTION, DISMISSAL,
             LAYOFF AND RESIGNATIONS

A. General

1. The sequence of disciplinary actions will be:
   1st step - formal verbal warning
   2nd step - informal written warning (i.e. hand written memos)
   3rd step - formal written warning (i.e typewritten letter)
   4th step - suspension without pay
   5th step - dismissal; except that disciplinary action may start with the third or fourth step when it is the decision of the City Manager, that because of the seriousness of the offense or infraction such action is warranted.

B. Verbal Counseling

1. The department head may verbally counsel a permanent employee for disciplinary purposes or for other good and sufficient cause.

2. The department head may supply the City Manager with written reasons for, and notification of, such verbal counseling. The department head, however, is not required to notify the City Manager of only a verbal counseling. Whether the City Manager is advised or not, however, the department head will keep a written record of the verbal counseling for his department's records.

C. Written Warning

1. The department head may issue a written warning to a permanent employee for disciplinary purposes or for other good and sufficient cause.

2. The reason or reasons for such written warning shall be given in writing, one copy to be sent to the City Manager for review and inclusion in the employee's service record.

D. Suspension

1. The department head may initiate the suspension of a permanent employee without pay for disciplinary purposes, or for other good and sufficient cause. Emergency suspension by anyone other than a department head must be in writing to the City Manager prior to such suspension.

2. The reason or reasons for any proposed suspension and the proposed period of any such suspension shall be given in writing to the City Manager and shall require the prior approval of the City Manager to be valid a copy to be served upon the affected employee before the suspension shall become effective.

3. No employee shall be suspended for more than (30) calendar days in any calendar year, except that extensions may be made pending any investigation(s) and/or hearings(s).

E. Demotion

1. The department head may initiate the demotion of a permanent employee when such employee's work is unsatisfactory.

2. A permanent employee may be granted a demotion upon their request and such demotion shall be termed and recorded as voluntary.

3. The reason or reasons for any proposed demotion, involuntary or voluntary, shall be given in writing to the City Manager and shall require the prior approval of the City Manager to be valid; a copy of such form to be served upon the affected employee before the demotion shall become effective.

4. The rate of compensation of a demoted employee shall be fixed at any step within the rate range for the new class of position which does not exceed their current rate of pay in the position from which they are being demoted, but not above the third step of such range.

5. The demoted employee shall be required to serve a probationary period of six (6)months in the new position satisfactorily before again receiving permanent status; provided, that a permanent employee taking a demotion as an alternative to a layoff shall not be required to serve a probationary period in the new position.

F. Dismissal

1. The department head may initiate the dismissal of a permanent employee for cause or for the good of the System.

2. Dismissals are permanent terminations of employment. The reason or reasons for any proposed dismissal shall be given in writing to the City Manager and shall require the prior approval of the City Manager. A copy of such form shall be served on the affected employee before the dismissal shall become effective.

3. Temporary and probationary employees may be dismissed at any time by the department head without the right of appeal or hearing in any manner. The reason or reasons for the dismissal of a temporary or probationary employee shall be given in writing to the City Manager.

4. Causes for removal, whether on duty or off, shall be based on, but not restricted to:

Incompetency; wanting in adequate strength, capacity, or physical and/or mental qualifications Permanent or chronic physical or mental ailment(s) or defect(s) which incapacitate the employee for the performance of their duties
• Insubordination
• Inefficiency
• Neglect of duty

- Absence from duty without leave for five (5) consecutive working days
- Excessive absenteeism or tardiness, hindering the work of the department or activity
- Being found guilty of infamous or notoriously disgraceful conduct
- Having committed an act which would bring discredit to the City
- Violation of any law, rule or regulation pertaining to or affecting employment in the City
- Offensive, indecent, or abusive conduct
- Addiction or the use of any narcotic, drug, or the habitual use of intoxicating liquor(s) to excess
- Theft, or willful neglect, or misuse of City funds, property, equipment, material or supplies
- Discourteous treatment of the public
- Prohibited political activity
- Any other related activity or activities which would bring discredit on the City

G. Layoff

1. No layoff of an employee from the System shall be made as a disciplinary action.

2. The department head may recommend to the City Manager, the layoff of a permanent employee in the System when it is deemed necessary by reason of shortage of work or funds, the abolition of the position by the City Commission, material change in departmental organization, or for other related reasons which are outside of the employee's control and which do not reflect discredit upon the employee.

3. Before any permanent employee shall be laid off, all temporary and probationary employees in the same class in that department shall have been dismissed in that order.

4. The layoff of permanent employees shall be made in inverse order of length of service, other considerations being equal, in the class in the department.

5. The reason or reasons for any proposed layoff shall be given in writing to the City Manager and shall require the prior approval of the City Commission. To be valid, a copy must be served upon the affected employee sufficiently before the effective date of the layoff to give the employee seven (7) calendar days notice of such layoff; except under conditions beyond the control of the City government.

H. Resignation

1. To resign in good standing a permanent [Merit] System employee shall give their department head at least two (2) calendar weeks notice, unless the department head shall, because of extenuating circumstances, agree to permit a shorter period of notice.

2. A written resignation shall be supplied by the employee to the department head, giving the reason or reasons for their leaving.

3. Such resignation shall be forwarded to the City Manager by the department head, together with an Employee Performance Review Report on the required form, and official notice of the resignation, giving any pertinent information concerning the reason or reasons for the resignation.

4. The resignation of any employee who fails to give notice shall be reported to the City Manager immediately by the department head together with an Employee Performance Review Report.

5. Failure to comply with the notification requirement shall be entered on the service record of the employee and may be cause for denying future employment by the City or recommendation for employment by others.

6. To resign in good standing a department head shall give the City Manager at least (2) calendar weeks notice in writing, stating the reason(s) therefore, unless the City Manager shall, because of extenuating circumstances, agree to permit a shorter period of

notice. Failure to comply with the notification requirement shall be entered on the service record of the department head and may be cause for denying future employment by the City or recommendation for employment by others.

NOTE: It is important to bear in mind that sick leave is not the same as compensatory time, nor shall these two be considered interchangeable at the time of resignation.

SECTION XII: LEAVE POLICIES

A. Vacation Leave

1. Vacation leave (ordinary annual leave) is a benefit which may be earned, accumulated and used by City employees. The sole purpose of leave (or vacation) is to grant the employee time off with pay.

2. A qualified employee of the City of Anycity, upon application to and with the approval of their Department Head, and the City Manager, shall be granted vacation leave in compliance with and subject to the following provisions and conditions:

New employees shall satisfactorily complete a probationary period of six months from date of hire before earned leave may be credited to their respective leave accounts; provided however, that following satisfactory completion of the probationary period, earned leave shall be credited to the leave account retroactive to the date of employment.

The following table indicates vacation leave authorizations at the stated years of service.

YEARS COMPLETED SERVICE	WORKING DAYS AUTHORIZED
One year service (Upon satisfactory completion of the six month probation an employee is eligible to take one week vacation, and the other week upon his yearly anniversary.)	Two (2) weeks vacation
Two (2) to Ten (10) years	Two (2) weeks vacation
Ten(10) to Fifteen (15) years	Three (3) weeks vacation
Over fifteen years of service	Four (4) weeks vacation

3. A break in continuity of employment of 90 days or more, shall place the employee at the initial step in the accumulation of vacation time rate.

A break in service shall be defined as a voluntary severance on the part of the employee from employment with the City, and/or an involuntary termination on the part of the City; firing the employee. A layoff of the employee or a military leave of absence shall not be considered breaks in employment.

4. The scheduled time of vacation leave cannot be changed without the approval of the Department Head and the City Manager.

5. Earned vacation leave shall be scheduled by each Department Head for the ensuing calendar year in such a manner as to give preference to: first- supervisory personnel, and second-to those employees with greater seniority, without permitting under-staffing of his/her department at any time; said vacation schedule shall be completed by the department head, based on requests made by his employees, and approved by the City Manager. This process shall be complete by January 1st. After such schedules are completed and approved anyone wishing to change their scheduled week(s) must choose a week(s) when: it is convenient for that department; no other employees' vacations, including lower seniority persons, will be changed without their consent; and the administration will have at least one (l) week's notice of the change(s).

Vacations are intended to enhance the employee's well-being and morale by providing periodic relief from the pressures and tension of employment; however, virtually any employee may, upon request, forego the taking of leave and accept compensation in lieu thereof. Such request shall be submitted in writing through the Department Head to the City Manager for approval.

A qualified employee whose duties involve financial transactions for the City shall be required to take an annual vacation leave.

6. If the day on which an official holiday is observed, as designated in Section 6 of these rules and regulations, shall fall within the period of vacation leave being taken by an employee, it shall not be charged to their vacation leave. The employee may, at the discretion of his/her department head have their vacation leave extended one (1) day or be paid one (1) regular working day's wages in lieu of the day off.

7. A qualified employee who leaves the City through retirement or termination of employment shall be paid for any vacation leave, and sick leave accrued but not taken. Compensation shall be at wage rate as of the date of termination.

8. A qualified employee while suspended for disciplinary reasons shall not accumulate service time for vacation leave; should he/she be exonerated previous status shall be retained.

9. Upon retirement severance pay may be granted by the City Commission only.

10. A qualified employee while suspended pending investigation(s) and/or hearing(s) shall not accumulate service time for vacation leave or other purposes pending disposition of the matter(s) on which the suspension was based.

B. Sick Leave
1. Policy- Paid sick leave is a benefit extended to full-time employees to provide the security of continued pay within certain limitations.

2. Definition- Sick leave is defined as: 1. Illness, injury, incapacitation of the employee. 2. Sick leave may be charged when an employee is on maternity leave or disability sick leave, to supplement the disability pay for which the employee will receive.

3. Eligibility- Permanent full-time employees shall accrue sick leave on pay period basis. Probationary employees accrue from the original employment date, but shall not be eligible to receive paid sick leave until the probation period is satisfactorily completed and permanent status is approved.

Seasonal, temporary, part-time or emergency employees are not eligible for paid sick leave. Full-time employees who are on sick leave shall not loose their seniority, accrual of vacation time or sick leave time.

4. Benefits- Accrual of vacation and Sick Leave benefits will begin on the first Pay period after the employee is hired. Accrual of Vacation and Sick Leave benefits will terminate the pay period prior to termination of employment with the City of Anycity.

5. Maximum Accumulation- Each eligible employee shall be allowed to accumulate a maximum of 192 hours paid sick leave.

6. Incentive Conversion - Each employee who has earned and accrued in excess of 192 hours paid sick leave shall be paid for those hours over and above 192 hours at the end of the fiscal year. The ratio of payment shall be 8 hours sick leave to 8 hours pay at the rate which that employee is currently making at the end of the fiscal year.

7. Sick Leave Pay upon Termination/Resignation: An employee who is either terminated or resigned will be paid for all accumulated sick leave time at the ratio of pay that employee is making upon notice of termination or resignation.

8. Proof- An employee who takes three consecutive sick leave days will be required to present a physicians certification, stating the reason for the need of the three consecutive days. An employee who returns to work without the physician's certification shall be reported to the City Manager, and will dealt with accordingly. The City Manager shall decide whether the employee has a valid excuse for not having a physician's statement, or whether the days should be considered as personal days off and be deducted from compensation time or no pay due.

C. Compensatory Time and/or Overtime

Guidelines pertaining to Compensatory or Overtime will be provided at a later date - pending a final clarification of the Fair Labor Standards Act.

D. Disability Sick Leave

1. Definition- An employee who is disabled by illness or injury which incurred sometime other than normal working hours is entitled to Disability Sick Leave. The disability must not be a result from a self-inflicted injury or negligence. The employee must supply the City Manager with a physician's certification that the employee is unable to perform his/her duties.

2. Disability Sick Leave status shall continue during the period of actual disability to a maximum of ninety (90) calendar days.

Should a disabled employee be unable to return to work at the expiration of the ninety day period, the case shall be reviewed by the City's Merit System Board which shall then recommend that the City Manager approve or disapprove the continuation of disability sick leave status. If approved by the City Manager the leave status shall continue for the duration of actual disability, up to a maximum of an additional ninety days, after which it shall terminate.

If disapproved by the City Manager the disability leave status shall terminate immediately.

3. Accrual of Benefits During Disability Sick Leave: During the disability sick leave status time period an employee may use any accrued sick leave benefits, compensation time accrued, or vacation time accrued to supplement his/her disability sick leave benefits.

4. Termination of Disability Sick Leave: In addition to the time limitations set forth above, disability sick leave status may be terminated by: 1. The employee's physician's certification that the employee is physically able to return to work. 2. Termination of employment of the employee, for any reason. 3. Entry into employment of any kind by the employee, including self-employment.

5. Effect on Other Benefits: While on disability sick leave status an employee shall not accrue any regular sick leave benefits, or vacation benefits, but shall not lose his/her seniority of their job position.

E. Maternity Leave

Maternity leave is authorized absence from work without pay during and immediately after an employee's pregnancy.

The employee shall notify her department head by at least the beginning of the fifth month of her pregnancy as to when she desires maternity leave to begin and if she wishes to return to work after delivery.

She shall furnish a medical certificate showing the expected due date and may be allowed to work as long as her physician furnishes written approval.

Pregnancy disability benefits shall be those that comply with Public Law 95-555 and State Laws. The employee will be placed on a disability sick leave status, and will be eligible for those benefits. The employee may draw from her accrued sick leave, compensation time, or vacation benefits to supplement the disability benefits. The employee shall not accrue sick leave or vacation time while on disability sick leave.

F. Workmen's Compensation

1. Policy: It shall be the policy of the City of Anycity to provide benefits to any employee injured as a result of job duties.

2. Injury Reporting- All employee injuries, of any description of size shall be immediately reported to the supervisor by the injured employee. If the employee is injured to the point that he must have medical attention immediately, the supervisor will make those arrangements immediately. If the employee is capable of getting an accident report filed first, then he/she must do so, and then receive medical attention.

3. Benefits- An injured employee shall be paid regular salary for the first eight days of his/her injury. At this time, Workmen's Compensation insurance will take over. The employee may, if he/she chooses, charge his/her accumulated sick leave to supplement the Workmen's Compensation checks up to their regular salary rate. If the employee uses up all of the sick leave he/she has accrued, then he/she may draw benefits from compensation time accrued, or vacation time accrued.

4. Failure to Report- Should an employee not immediately report the injury to the department head, or assistant, both City and Workmen's Compensation may be withheld. An investigation and determination will be made as to the facts of the accident before benefits are approved.

5. Investigation- There will be a team of three department heads which will investigate each accident, talk to witnesses, and secure the circumstances which the accident occurred. After the initial investigation, a report will be forwarded to the City Manager, which states whether the accident was preventable or unpreventable, and the supporting reasons.

The City of Anycity is very interested in advancing our safety precautions to insure the well being of our employees. This investigation will provide the information necessary to find problem areas regarding safety in the normal performances of our employees.

G. Funeral Leave

1. In the event of the death of a member of the immediate family; child, parent, spouse, brother, sister, guardian, step-parents, step-children, grandparents (both sides), parents-in-law; the department head shall be notified and sufficient working days leave will be granted to an employee to allow for a total of three (3) days funeral leave.

2. If the funeral is at such distance that more than three (3) days funeral leave is desired, the funeral leave may be extended, upon application for such extension, at the discretion of the City Manager. Such extension of time shall be charged against: 1. Compensation Time accrued. 2. Sick Leave Time Accrued. 3. Accumulated Vacation Time. If deemed essential, the City Manager may grant leave without pay to facilitate a funeral some distance away from the city.

3. Only scheduled working days falling within the period of funeral leave will be compensated for.

H. Leave of Absence (Personal)
1. A leave of absence is authorized absence from work for a definite period of time without pay.

2. Only a qualified employee is eligible for a leave of absence.

3. Requests for Leave of Absence
a. A written request for leave of absence shall be supplied to the department head by the employee, giving the reason(s) for such request and the period of leave sought.
b. Such request shall be supplied at least ten (10) working days before the requested beginning date of such leave, unless the department head, shall, because of extenuating circumstances, agree to permit a shorter period of notice.
c. The department head shall forward the request to the City Manager together with the departments head's recommendation(s).

4. Granting of Leave of Absence
a. Any leave of absence shall require the favorable recommendation of the department head and the approval of the City Manager.
b. Approval of a leave of absence shall be at the discretion o, the City Manager for such reason(s) as he may find to be valid and for a period not to exceed sixty (60) days.
c. In considering a request for a leave of absence, employee's lengtn of service, service record, experience, and the requirements of the department for the period of requested leave will be taken into account.

5. Extension of Leave of Absence
Any extension of a leave of absence of over fifteen (15) calendar days shall be requested in writing at least one (l) calender week before the expiration date thereof and shall be filed with the department head. Thereafter the procedure for handling such requested extension shall be the same as for an original request.

6. Restrictions on Other Gainful Employment
Any employee while on leave of absence who shall engage in any other gainful employment shall be deemed to have resigned without notice and his employment with the City shall be terminated unless the City Manager shall determine that such other gainful employment shall be permitted due to extenuating circumstances.

7. Failure to Return to Work
Any employee who shall fail to return to work from a leave of absence on or before the expiration date thereof without notifying his dept. head and making satisfactory arrangements with him, or without reasons acceptable to the City Manager, shall be deemed to have resigned without notice and his employment with the City shall be terminated.

8. Restoration of Former Position
Upon the expiration of a leave of absence the employee shall be restored to the position he held at the time said leave was granted, or to a position equal thereto and at its established rate of pay.

I. Military Leave.
1. Granting of Leave
a. A qualified employee who is a member of any military reserve unit of the United States, or any National Guard Unit, will be granted Military Leave for such time as he is in the military service on field training or active duty for periods not to exceed 15 calendar days per calendar year. Employees of the City of Anycity shall not be denied the right to enlist or participate in the reserve programs of the armed services as a matter of policy.

b. It must also be recognized, however, that the City of Anycity has responsibilities to its citizenry, just as does the country. Those responsibilities, to provide for the health, safety, and welfare of the residents of the City, cannot be jeopardized by activities of City employees which conflict with their assigned City duties. For example, should several members of a City department join a reserve organization and be required to undergo an active-duty training period, their absence during that period would create an unacceptable hardship for the department, and severely curtail its effectiveness.

c. Such leave shall be granted by the City Manager on the basis of orders from proper military authority.

d. Notification of such military leave shall be made to the City Manager by the department head.

e. An employee whose membership in a reserve organization has been approved, and who is required to attend an active-duty training period, shall attend such training period up to 17 days with pay. (Florida Statutes 115.07. Other state laws may differ.)

2. Approval of Enlistment

An employee considering membership in a reserve organization shall advise the appropriate department head as to the identity of the organization and dates and hours of its activities, and shall have the approval of the department head before joining the organization.

3. A qualified employee ordered for preinduction physical examination shall be given up to two (2) scheduled working days off with pay for the purpose by their department head, upon seeing orders from proper authority.

4. Calls to Active Duty

a. A qualified employee who is called to active duty in the armed forces of the United States shall be granted Military Leave by his/her department head upon seeing orders from proper Military authority.

b. Notification of such military leave shall be made to the administration by the department head.

c. The employee shall be paid any vacation leave accrued but not taken, with his/her final pay check.

5. Returns from Active Duty

An employee returning from Military Leave who was discharged from the armed forces of the United States under honorable conditions shall be re-employed by the City in a position no lower than the grade and compensation level in which he/she was employed at the time of departure, upon condition that such employee is physically and mentally suited to perform the required duties; that the employee makes application for reemployment within ninety (90) days following his/her discharge from the armed forces of the United States; that such military service did not exceed four (4) years; that the employee reports for duty when so instructed.

6. An employee returning from Military Leave who was discharged from the armed forces of the United States under honorable conditions shall receive the same status as to benefits they would have had if they had not left for military duty.

7. Personnel actions with regard to employees and the armed forces of the United States shall be subject to and comply with Federal and Florida Statutes and the regulations relative thereto.

SECTION XIII   OUTSIDE EMPLOYMENT

1. Prior to engaging in any outside business or employment, City employees shall advise their department head, or the City Manager in case of department heads, of the organization and the position the employee is to be filling.

2. Any employment engaged in by any employee that may bring discredit upon the City, will not be approved by the City Administration.

SECTION XIV   EMPLOYEE SERVICE REPORTS

A. General
1. Each permanent employee shall have his/her work performance, conduct, attendance and potential appraised and evaluated semiannually, as of the anniversary date of his/her original appointment, promotion, which ever date is the most recent.

2. Other appraisals and evaluations of permanent employees may be made at other times at the discretion of the department head.

3. Appraisals and evaluations of an employee's work performance, conduct, attendance, and potential may be required at any time by the City Manager.

4. Appraisals and evaluations of a probationary employee's work performance conduct, attendance, and potential shall be made under Section 10.

B. Evaluation Procedures
1. Appraisal and evaluation of an employee's work performance, conduct, attendance and potential shall be made on the Employee Performance Review Report form provided for the purpose.

2. The preparation of the Employee Performance Review shall be the responsibility of the employee's department head.

3. All Employee Performance Review Reports shall be forwarded to the City Manager for final review before they are placed in the personnel file of the employee, there to become a permanent part of the employee's service record.

4. Employee Performance Review Report forms for all required appraisals and evaluations of employees shall be sent to the department head concerned fifteen (15) calendar days prior to the required date. Suspense calendar records and due dates will be maintained by the personnel clerk in the general government office.

5. All Employee Performance Review Report forms, other than the final required report on probationary employees, shall be completed, reviewed, and in the hands of the City Manager fifteen (15) calendar days after the required date for the appraisal and evaluation.

6. An Employee Performance Review Report that is unsatisfactory in any category shall be reviewed with the City Manager by the department head and shall be discussed with the employee by the department head after such review and approval by the City Manager. The employee shall initial each such category as evidence that the matter has been explained to and discussed with him/her. Such initialing by the employee is not to be interpreted as meaning that the employee is either satisfied or dissatisfied with the appraisal or evaluation.

7. Employee Performance Review Report ratings shall be considered in all matters concerning changes in the status of the employee.

8. All Employee Performance Review Reports shall be typed by a Deputy City Clerk prior to submission of a report for the City Manager's review. Copies of the completed report will not be made until after the City Manager has reviewed same.

C. Nonexempt Employee Performance Review Form

CITY OF ANYCITY
EMPLOYEE PERFORMANCE REVIEW

INSTRUCTIONS: Do not complete this form until you have read and understand the contents of the Employee Performance Review Section of the Merit Plan. (Section XIV)

Employee name: _____ Original Rating Employment _____Period FR:__ TO:__
Date
Position Title:_____ Department _____
Job Description: See Wage and Salary Plan available in the office of the City Manager.
Date of last Merit Increase_____ No. of days sick leave used during current rating period_____
List any commendation or disciplinary action since last review:____
_____.

****
EVALUATION:
Rate Each Factor   1= Excellent   2= Satisfactory
                     3= Improvement Needed 4= Unsatisfactory

I QUANTITY OF WORK: (1) (2) (3) (4) COMMENTS:_____

II QUALITY OF WORK: (1) (2) (3) (4) _____

III WORK HABITS:
a. Dependability   (1) (2) (3) (4)
b. Job Knowledge   (1) (2) (3) (4)
c. Punctuality   (1) (2) (3) (4)
d. Initiative .   (1) (2) (3) (4)
e. Attendance   (1) (2) (3) (4)
f. Appearance   (1) (2) (3) (4)
g. Safety   (1) (2) (3) (4)
h. Talkativeness   (1) (2) (3) (4)
III OVERALL (1) (2) (3) (4)   STRENGTHS:_____

IV INTERPERSONAL RELATIONS/COMMUNICATIONS SKILLS:
a. Attitude reflected in behavior.   (1) (2) (3) (4)
b. Interaction with employees   (1) (2) (3) (4)
c. Interactions with citizens   (1) (2) (3) (4)

IV OVERALL (1) (2) (3) (4) WEAKNESSES:_____

V FLEXIBILITY/ADAPTABILITY:
a. To job changes   (1) (2) (3) (4)
b. To changes in procedures   (1) (2) (3) (4)
c. To changes in personnel   (1) (2) (3) (4)

V OVERALL (1) (2) (3) (4)
(Use back if additional space is needed)

****

RANKING: Rank this employee's standing as opposed to all of the other employees in your dept.

1st ___2nd__3rd___ 4th___ 5th__ 6th __7th__ 8th __9th __10th__

NOTE: Only compare like job classifications

Rated By:_____ Title:_____Date:_____

Date Reviewed with employee:_____ Comments by the employee:_____

This report has been discussed with me and I have received a copy. I agree with my rating: ( ); I disagree ( ):
        or, I want to appeal this rating ( ).

I understand that my appeal of this rating must be made within seven (7) lays of today's date.

Signature of Employee_____Signature of Rater_____

CoA PA-EPR-l Oct 85

D. Exempt Employee Performance Review Form

CITY OF ANYCITY
EXEMPT EMPLOYEE PERFORMANCE REVIEW
Period Covered from_____to_____

Employee Name_____ Department_____
Position _____Range & Step_____
Date of Last Review: _____No. of Sick leave since
                 last review_____
Date of Last Merit Increase _____Length of Employ_____
List any Commendations or Disciplinary Actions Since Last Review:

Rate Each 1= Outstanding   COMMENTS: Use this space to
Factor   2= Excellent   describe employees strengths and (Check one) 3=
Satisfactory   weaknesses, work well done and plans   4= Improvement
Needed for work improvement. **Overall
5= Unsatisfactory   rating of Unsatisfactory or Outstanding
                   must be substantiated by comments.

Appearance 1 2 3 _____
Attendance 1 2 3 _____
Knowledge of Work 1 2 3 4 5 _____
Quality of Work   1 2 3 4 5 _____
Quantity of Work   1 2 3 4 5 _____
Initiative   1 2 3 4 5 _____
Dependability   1 2 3 4 5 _____
Attitude   1 2 3 4 5 _____
Relationships with People 1 2 3 4 5 _____

Rating Score_____ Rating _____(overall)

Rated By: _____ Title: City Manager Date:_____

Date Reviewed with Employee: _____
I understand that a score of less than 23 is classified as a satisfactory evaluation.
This report has been discussed with me and I have received a copy. I agree ,with my
rating ( ) I disagree ( ),
          or I want to appeal my .rating ( ).

Employee Signature _____

E. EMPLOYEE PERFORMANCE REVIEW MANUAL

1. Definition: The Employee Performance Review System is a uniform procedure which permits the evaluation of services performed by employees of the City

2. Purpose: The purpose of the Employee Performance Review system is to permit supervisory personnel to evaluate the performance of employees in the accomplishment of their assigned duties and responsibilities by established standards. The evaluation of the performance of employees is to determine how and to what extent employee performance relates to the standard position requirements.

It is very important that you, the supervisor, give this employee an honest and fair evaluation. Everyone has faults and no one is perfect. Do not turn in an evaluation with all excellents checked, unless this employee can walk on water.

This information is collected with the object of improving employee performance, and thereby improving the various services rendered to the community.

a. It indicates to the employee how his past performance has been evaluated by his immediate supervisor, brings out his strong and weak points, serves as the basis for discussion of how he can improve his performance and provides for the counseling of the individual employee.

b. It calls attention to the need for training employees whose reviews reveal that their work performance could stand improvement and may indicate the special working area in which intensive training is required~ It may be used as a basis for granting a merit increase in salary which is intended as a reward for more than satisfactory performance.

c. It may be used to estimate an employee's potentialities for promotion or may indicate that a transfer is desirable.

d. It may be useful for hearings concerning disciplinary action.

3. Scale of Values: The rating scale is made up of rating values which are listed on the performance review form in the columns. The scale permits values for each factor considered.

These rating values which make up the scale are:

a. **Unsatisfactory**: An employee who fails considerably in meeting the minimum performance requirements of the position to which he has been assigned shall be rated in the Unsatisfactory column for the factors applicable.

b. **Needs Improvement**: An employee who fails to meet the established standards of the position shall be rated in the Improvement Needed column. Employees in this category can, with additional effort, bring their performance up to a satisfactory level.

c. **Satisfactory**: An employee who fully meets the performance standards of the position to which he has been assigned shall be rated in the Satisfactory column for the factors applicable.

d. **Excellent**: An employee whose performance has been above the standard performance requirements of the position to which he has been assigned shall be rated in the Excellent Column for the factors applicable.

4. Evaluation Factors: The evaluation factors are the criteria by which an employee's performance is measured. These factors are listed and defined below:

a.   **Quantity of Work**: To determine a standard quantity of production for a particular job, the rating authority must understand the quantity of work factor in terms of the actual job. The employee should only be rated on the volume of work that is subject to his control. For example, a typist may be able to type twenty letters a day, but if her supervisor only gives her ten letters, the volume of work is beyond her control. The quantity of work is measured by comparing the work performed to the established standard.

b.   **Quality of Work**: This factor is concerned with accuracy, completeness, neatness and effectiveness of work performed. The standard is that quality of work which is desirable in the particular occupation or class of work which is acceptable to the department or division head. The quality of work is measured by comparing the work performed to the established standard.

c.   **Work Habits**: The several different areas that together make up an employee's work abilities. Each individual category shall be rated, and then an overall rating should be made. The overall rating shall depict how well an employee works.

1)   **Dependability**: This factor is concerned with the employee's attention to his work in the absence of direct and indirect supervision. An employee who does not shift the burden of difficult assignments and who is reliable at all times tends to display dependability. The ability to meet deadlines is another indication of this trait.

2) **Job Knowledge**: This factor is concerned with the employee's over-all knowledge of the subject matter and technique necessary for full job performance. The care of property and materials used by the employee in his daily work, the observance of rules, recommended procedures, and safety regulations should be considered in rating this factor. Proper care and use of equipment should be expected of all employees regardless of its value. An employee's ability to observe rules, follow instructions, use effective supervisory techniques, carry out duties in accordance with approved procedures and conform to safety regulations is vital in rating the performance of work habits. In the overall evaluation of this factor, does the employee organize, arrange, and conduct his work in an efficient manner compared to a standard which meets the approval of his department head?

3) **Punctuality**: Does the employee arrive at work, meetings, and appointments on time or early consistently? If so, he/she should receive a good rating in this area. By the same measure, if an employee is late to work 2-3 times a month, and has problems keeping established appointments then the employee should receive an appropriately lower rating.

4)   **Initiative**: This factor is concerned with resourcefulness, self-reliance, willingness to accept and ability to carry out responsibility, and the adaptability of the employee to his work assignments.
It is possible for an employee who is not too experienced or too highly skilled to display initiative. An employee who attempts to solve problems, suggest improvements, and requests additional assignments when completed tends to display the factor of initiative.
Engaging in training courses and encouraging others toward productive use of time also indicates initiative.

5) **Attendance**: This factor is concerned with the employee's attendance, punctuality, and time devoted to actual work. The rater should consider presence on the job when required, punctuality in reporting to work and/or promptness in reporting to assignments, including such items as absence without leave, excessive sick leave, etc. Excellent or outstanding attendance may be noted in the section of the review form reserved for comments.

6) **Appearance**: This factor is concerned with the overall appearance of the employee measured with type work performed. Excellent or outstanding appearance of the employee may be noted in the section of the review form reserved for comments.

7) **Safety**: How safety conscious is the employee? Does he take chances with his own life, city property, city vehicles? Is he careless? These are all factors that should impact upon the rating in this category. If the employee has had 4 accidents in the past year, he probably is not too safety conscious.

8) **Talkativeness**: Is the employee too talkative? Does he/she spend a great deal of the time, and consequently the city's time gossiping? It is fine to be polite and friendly, especially to citizens, but a twenty minute conversation is beyond politeness when the employee is taking up city time.

d. **Interpersonal Relations/Communication Skills**Again, each of the subcategories shall be rated, with an overall rating assigned for this category. The primary purpose of this area is to attempt to rate or score the employee's abilities to get along with others as well as being able to discuss concepts and ideas with others. Can this employee explain to other employees his/her thoughts and ideas on a particular subject? Can he/she transmit his ideas so everyone can understand?

1) **Attitude Reflected in Behavior**: This factor deals with the employee's feelings towards his/her job, fellow employees and the organization for which he works. An employee who is flexible in his/her thinking, is conscious of his/her job responsibilities, and looks for new and better ways of doing things in order to improve the function of the organization for which he/she works tends to display an acceptable attitude towards his/her job. Conversely, an employee who resists authority and is antagonistic about necessary changes in procedure tends to display a poor attitude towards his/her job.

2) **Interactions with Employees**: This factor is concerned with an employee's ability to get along with associates and his/her degree of effectiveness in dealing with supervisors. In most cases, complaints of employees or incidents arising may attract the attention of the supervisor to those employees among whom poor relations exist, but the attention of the supervisor is not easily attracted to those employees among whom good relations exist.

3) **Interactions with Citizens**: The citizens are our customers. Any of you that were ever employed in retail business, I'm certain, have heard the phrase, "The customer is always right." We know that this is, in many cases, an impossibility; no one can always be right. It is important, however, to keep the customer, the citizen, happy. When they complain, listen and tell them you will report it. Always be polite. If an employee handles himself/herself well with the citizens, then the rating in this category should reflect that.

e. **Flexibility/Adaptability**: How well does the employee adapt to changing situations? Change is all around us and constant. Even if we don't change, the world changing around us causes our environment to change, so we change. But, some of us fight change; we want things the way they used to be. Realistically, this can never happen. Just because we do not like change, does not necessarily mean that we fight change. Change is inevitable; it's coming, and nothing we can do will stop it. Does the employee fight new systems and ideas? Does the employee give a new program his/her best effort? Or does he/she just say, "We never used to have to do this."?

As before, each subcategory shall be scored and then an overall score for the category assigned.

1) **Job Changes**: As discussed above, when the job changes, due to whatever reason, does the employee continually complain about wanting the old job back? Be it a change in the employee's assignment, or a change in just the type of work within the assignment, etc.

2) **Changes in Job Procedures**: When the job remains the same, but the way the job is to be performed is different, it is a change in procedures. Often times changes in procedures are made for safety reasons. Other times a new procedure is more time and/or energy efficient. Does the employee try to continue to work the old way? Is it difficult to teach an old dog new tricks? If so, then the employee should not receive a high rating in this area.

3) **Changes in Personnel**: When a new person is hired, does this employee try to make him/her feel welcomed, or does he make life difficult? When another employee is promoted, does this employee accept that promotion, or 'bellyache' about it?

f. **Ranking**: How does this employee stack up against your other subordinates? It is important that you give a fair and honest evaluation of each employee. This ranking section will be a key element in any recommendation for incentive pay raise. You can, however, only have one number one man, one number two, etc. If every evaluation you turn in is ranked first, you, and we, have a problem.

g. **Administrative Comments**: Most of the administrative information on the review form is self-explanatory; the name, the date, the department, etc. As a matter of fact, most of the administrative information will be filled out for you before you get the evaluation form.

All Employee Performance Review forms will be typed, by a deputy clerk, prior to being turned in to the City Manager for review.

h. **Steps in the Review Process:**
1) Blank review form with employee's name and information typed in is given to he employee's supervisor within five working days of the employee's hiring anniversary.

2) Supervisor will have five more working days to complete the review form.

3) By ten working days after the employee's hiring anniversary, the review form will have been typed and submitted to the City Manager for review.

4) At the City Manager's pleasure, but within twenty working days after the employee's hiring anniversary, the supervisor and the City Manager, or his representative, will discuss the review process, all three individuals in the room simultaneously.

5) After this review session, the employee may appeal this review to the City Manager. This appeal must be typewritten and submitted to the City Manager within seven days of the aforementioned review discussion. (See Appeal Process, below)

6) The Review form, and the Appeal, if applicable, will be placed in the employee's personnel record folder. The employee will have been given a copy of same during the Review discussion.

5. Total Rated Value: The total rated value of an employee shall be computed according to the formula below.

EXCELLENT	18 thru 20
IMPROVEMENT NEEDED	10 thru 13
SATISFACTORY	14 thru 17
UNSATISFACTORY 5 thru 9	

Only the five major categories will be utilized for Rated Value Computation. The fourteen subcategories are designed to assist in the evaluation process, and do not increase the score.

6. Employee's Rating Review: It is mandatory that the person rating the employee discuss the evaluation report thoroughly and completely with the employee, in the presence of the City Manager, or his representative. After the evaluation report has been discussed, the employee shall sign the review form. The employee whose rating is unsatisfactory shall be informed in writing on the evaluation form in that section reserved for comments as to the specific reasons he was rated unsatisfactory.

The employee shall be fully instructed with respect to the standard requirements of his positions, and regarding the methods, procedures, techniques and practices which must be applied in order to bring his performance up to the standard level. The rating authority shall give the employee his copy at this time. In no case shall any rating authority reveal to any employee the contents of any review other than the employee's own.

7. Appeal Process: The employee has the right to appeal a rating, if he feels the rating is not a fair evaluation of his potential. To appeal such a rating, the employee shall write, in a standard letter format, the reasons why he feels the rating is unjust. Additionally, the employee must cite specific examples supporting his view that the rating is unfair. This letter of appeal shall be presented to the City Manager, in typewritten form for inclusion with the review form into the employee's personnel record folder; this must take place within seven calendar days of the rating review discussion.

The review form will most probably not be altered, or changed, but the appeal will be stapled to same. The City Manager may, at his discretion, change the review rating of the employee, The City Manager is, however, only required to attach the appeal to the review form.

8. Conclusion: The usefulness of any Employee Evaluation depends almost entirely upon the understanding, impartiality, and objectivity with which ratings are made. Care and skill used by rating authorities in rating employees are measures of supervisory ability in directing the work of subordinates. It must be remembered that RATING EMPLOYEE'S PERFORMANCE IS A CONTINUING PROCESS OF DAY-TO-DAY OBSERVANCE AND NOT MERELY AN EXTRA ACTIVITY WHEN RATINGS ARE MADE!

SECTION XV   INCENTIVE PROGRAM

Since the city administration and the commissioners want to encourage the continuous self-improvement of all City employees, the City of Anycity therefore, has instituted an Incentive Program designed to reward those employees who have made personal sacrifice in order that they might better themselves both to their personal benefit and the benefit of the City.

A. Eligibility
All full time permanent City employees are eligible for the Incentive Program. Schooling/education requirements that are part of the minimum requirements of a job

position can not be considered as contributing factors to the Incentive Program. This Program is designed rather, for those types of training that are above and beyond the minimum requirements for a position in the City employment system.

For example, a Water Department employee serving in a technician position who studies, tests and consequently receives his/her Class "C" Operator's Permit will be promoted under this Incentive Program. A technician is classified as a position #24. A water plant operator is classified as a position 27. For argument's sake, assume the technician was classified as a D-24. Once he/she gets his operator's permit, he/she will be reclassified to a A-27. This is a promotion, but does not include an incentive pay raise. The department head must recommend the employee for an incentive raise on the form provided herein. Incentive pay raises will be granted in conjunction with the new fiscal year, commencing each October 1st.

B. Administrative Requirements
When an employee's training completion has qualified him/her for a higher classification, the Personnel Action form recommending promotion must be filled out by the department head and forwarded to the City Manager. This only increases the classification and in actuality decreases the step; the pay remains the same. In order to elevate the step, i.e. increase the salary, the department head also needs to complete an Incentive Pay Raise Recommendation form and forward it to the City Manager.

C. Categories Qualifying for Recommendation
Department heads should recommend employees for an incentive pay raise when any of the following occurs. (Whether the said training qualifies the employee for a promotion in classification should have no impact upon whether or not the employee receives an incentive pay raise):

• Employee completes a training course of 80 classroom hours, or more. Said course completion certificate shall accompany the recommendation form.

• Employee completes a college degree program resulting in receipt of an associate degree, bachelor's degree or master's degree. Diploma shall accompany recommendation form.

• Employee completes a correspondence course equal to 80 classroom hours, or more. Completion certificate shall accompany recommendation form.

• Employee passes a state or national test causing employee to receive a certain professional recognition for such passage. Proof of satisfactory testing results shall accompany recommendation form.

• Employee has performed his/her duties in an exceptional manner throughout the year/employment. Employee's Performance Review Rating Sheet should reflect a rating of "Usually exceeds standards" in virtually every category for the department to recommend an incentive pay raise under this category.

D. Incentive Pay Raise Recommendation Form

TO: City Manager   FROM: Department Supervisor
Date:
Subject: Recommendation for Incentive Pay Raise

Employee: Position Title:
Position Classification (range and step):

I recommend the above named employee be given an
Incentive Pay Raise because

(use additional paper if needed)   Dept. Head Signature
Supporting documents attached ( )yes ( ) no

Approved: _____is granted an Incentive Pay Raise
                    (employee)
which shall be 5% 10% or _____, of his present base pay.

This salary increase will take effect October 1, 19

Disapproved: _____ is not granted an Incentive Pay Raise.

    Signed
      City Manager

    E. Incentive Awards Program
    1.   In addition to the Incentive Pay Raise Program designed to reward education, training, and outstanding work performance, the City of Anycity will also initiate a program designed to recognize those employees who have been employed by the City for a number of years.

    2.   The only requirements to qualify for this program are continual employment with the City of Anycity for the period indicated.

    3.   Awards for specific time in Service:

1 year	City Key Chain
2 years	Belt Buckle, Paperweight, or personal Pen Set
5 years	City Desk Pen Set or City of Anycity Watch
10 years	City Wall Plaque with Engraved Plate
15 years	A suitable sports gift, with City identification
20 years	A gold Watch with City identification.
30 years	Name a building or facility in employee's honor

    4.   Awards will be made at the pleasure of the City Manager, but generally will be presented at the Annual Employee Halloween Masquerade Party (or other suitable occasion in Anycity).

    F. Memorandum: City Policy on Educational Expenses.

                      City Stationery

MEMORANDUM FOR THE RECORD
TO: All Department Supervisors
FROM: City Manager Ken Griffin
SUBJECT: City Policy on Educational Expenses

NOTE: This Memorandum is a reduction into written form of the Educational Policy that I was apprised of upon my becoming employed with the City. I am unable to advise the date of actual origin.

When the budget permits, departments shall have line item accounts for training purposes. Primarily, this money is to be used in order to facilitate the attendance of employees at seminars, etc., related to their employment in the City.

When the Supervisor feels it is in the best interest of the City and when his/her department has sufficient monies in the Training Account, the Supervisor may fund or participate in the funding of an employee attending college or other pertinent after-work hours classes. The funding, or lack thereof, is irrespective of the work schedule required for the employee to meet his/her obligation to the City, compensatory time, etc. These will be dictated by the Department Supervisor.

This MFR should be reviewed in full cognizance of Section XV, of the Merit System Manual.

SECTION XVI: SAFETY AND WORKMEN'S COMPENSATION

A. General
The City Administration and the Commissioners are vitally interested in the safety and well being of all employees of the City.

All employees are required to take every precaution in the prevention of accidents to themselves, their fellow employees and the public.

All employees shall observe safety rules and regulations as issued and shall be chargeable with responsibility for the proper operation of all equipment that is used in the normal performance of their duties.

B. Reporting Accidents
1. It shall be the responsibility of each employee to report immediately to his/her department head any injury to his/her person or to others.

2. It shall be the responsibility of the department head to investigate the circumstances of the accident; to secure the name of employees and/or other persons who witnessed the occurrence; to make such investigations as may appear desirable; to make a written report on the form provided of the information secured; to forward such report to the City Manager, indicating whether the accident was preventable or unpreventable.

3. The City Manager shall evaluate the reports as submitted and make such further investigations and determinations as may be desirable. After such consideration the City Manager shall make final ruling within 24 hours as to whether the accident shall be classified as preventable or unpreventable.

C. Criteria for Ruling
The basic criteria for ruling whether an injury was preventable or unpreventable shall be as follows:

1. Preventable: violations of any safety rules, regulations, requirements or standards shall be deemed sufficient cause for an injury to be ruled to have been preventable. Any obviously unsafe act will be sufficient cause for an accident to be found to have been preventable. An employee injured in an accident which has been ruled to have been preventable shall receive workmen's compensation payments only.

2. Unpreventable. An accident resulting through no fault of the employee, or from unusual hazards or circumstances, in which an employee is injured, may be deemed to have been unpreventable.

D. Disability Leave
1. An employee who is disabled by illness or injury incurred while performing assigned duties, and as a result of such duty performance, shall be entitled to disability leave in accordance with the following policies:
        a. The employee shall submit a written request to be placed in disability leave status to the City Manager, through the appropriate department head. The request shall contain a certification that the disability was incurred in the course of employment, that it

was not the result of a violation of established rules or regulations, and that it was not the result of willful self-infliction or gross negligence or carelessness. It must also include a statement from a physician of the City's choosing that the employee is medically incapable of performing assigned duties.

    b.   The department head shall endorse the request after investigating to determine the validity of statements contained therein, and forward it to the City Manager with a recommendation for approval or disapproval. Approval or disapproval of the request shall be at the discretion of the City Manager.

    c.   Disability leave status shall continue during the period of actual disability, to a maximum of ninety (90) calendar days. During this period the employee shall report to the City's physician for examination at such frequency as the City's physician may require; and any failure to report for such examination, without valid excuse, shall be grounds for cancellation of disability leave status.

    d.   Should a disabled employee be unable to return to work at the expiration of the ninety (90) day period, the case shall be reviewed by the City's Merit System Board which shall then recommend to the City Manager approval or disapproval of a continuation of disability leave status. If approved by the City Manager, the leave status shall continue for the duration of actual disability, up to a maximum of an additional ninety (90) calendar days, after which it shall terminate. If disapproved by the City Manager, the disability leave status shall terminate immediately.

    2.   Upon the expiration or termination of disability leave status, the employee may then use any accrued sick leave available to him/her, in accordance with established policy governing the use of sick leave.

    3.   In addition to the time limitations as set forth in Paragraphs c and d, above, disability leave status may be terminated by:

    a.   The City's physician's certification that the employee is physically able to return to work.

    b.   The City physician's certification that the employee is permanently disabled, in which case the City shall initiate an application for disability retirement under the appropriate retirement or pension system.

    c.   Termination of employment of the employee, for any reason.

    d.   Entry into employment of any kind by the employee, including self-employment.

    4.   While on disability leave status, an employee shall not accrue ordinary leave or sick leave credit.

E. Payment

Should the request for disability leave status be approved by the City Manager, such status shall be retroactive to the first day of lost time; while in such status, the employee shall receive his/her regular pay, based on his pay rate as of the time of disability, less all Workmen's Compensation payments. Such pay shall be deducted from any Workmen's Compensation award to the employee.

F. Safety Panel

    1.   The City Manager shall appoint a three-member safety panel for the City's employees. These members shall serve for a one year period in conjunction with the City's fiscal year. Reappointments or new appointments will be made each October 1st.

    2.   Each accident involving a City employee and/or vehicle will be investigated by this City Safety Panel. The investigation's major purpose will be to establish whether or not the accident was preventable.

    3.   The City Safety Panel will, after their investigations, make recommendations to the City Manager. These recommendations may refer to: proposed changes in City policy to avoid recurrence, disciplinary action(s) to employees, corrective (repair) action to vehicles and/or equipment, use of sick leave or workmen's compensation, etc.

4. Although the City Safety Panel will exist to make investigations and recommendations on City accidents, the City Manager's decisions on any and all action taken will be final.

SECTION XVII   GENERAL REGULATIONS

A. General
1. An employee shall be responsible for reporting a change in his/her address or telephone number to the department head within two (2) scheduled working days of such change.

2. An employee shall be responsible for reporting a change in his/her Form W-4 dependency status to their department head within ten (10) calendar days of such change.

3. No employee shall use the City Hall address for personal mail.

4. It is the policy of the City of Anycity that no employee shall be allowed an advance of his/her earned pay without complete written recommendation of the department head and City Manager.

5. All employees of the City shall carry the required identification card of the City of Anycity.

B. Religious Observance
Employees whose religious convictions require time off to observe religious holidays may arrange with their department head for time off without pay, or time off to be made up within three (3) calendar months.

C. Temporary Transfers
Employees may be temporarily transferred from one department to another at the discretion of the City Manager when he/she shall find such transfer to be necessary to maintain City services or in the interests of public health, safety and welfare, and budget.

D. Restricted Information
All employees of the City of Anycity shall consider information secured in the course of their work as confidential. Any disclosure of this confidential information to other than legally constituted authority shall be cause for immediate dismissal.

E. City Property
City employees who are issued nonexpendable City property to be used in the performance of their duties shall be required to sign for such property in triplicate:
    One copy to be given to the employee,
    One copy to be retained in the department records,
    One copy to be placed in the employee's service record.

When a City employee returns such City property, a receipt is to be made out in triplicate, with the same distribution of copies.

City employees at the time of their separation from the employ of the City shall be required to return all City property they have signed for. All City property not returned at that time shall be charged for at its cost and the amount of such charge deducted from the final pay check. City property shall include ID Cards, keys, tools, clothes, and any other personal equipment.

SECTION XVIII: THE CITY MERIT SYSTEM BOARD

A. Establishment
A Merit System Board of the City of Anycity is hereby established.

B. Members and Term of Office
The Merit System Board shall be composed of five members who shall be placed in office in accordance with the following procedure:

1. Each member of the City Commission, following his/her election of reelection to office, shall nominate a qualified citizen of the City of Anycity for appointment to the Merit System Board by the City Commission to serve a term of two years.

2. First time appointments made to the Merit System Board under this section: The terms of the Board members shall be the remaining elected term of office of the Commissioner making such appointment.

3. Vacancies on the Merit System Board shall be filled in the same manner as original appointments.

4. In December of each year the Board shall select one of its members to serve as chairman and one of its members to serve as vice-chairman of the Board.

C. Qualifications for Membership
Members of the Merit System Board shall be appointed from the residents and electors of the City, citizens who shall be knowledgeable concerning the functions of municipal government and interested in the promotion of efficient and harmonious personnel relations between the City and its employees. No member of the City Commission and no City officer or employee shall be eligible to serve on this Board.

D. Powers and Duties
The Merit System Board shall have the following powers and duties:

1. To assist the City Manager as the chief administrative officer of the City of Anycity in matters pertaining to the Merit System Rules and Regulations and the interpretation thereof.

2. To make recommendations to the City Manager on problems concerning personnel administration which will improve employment standards in the municipal service.

3. To conduct reviews and hear appeals in regard to any suspension, demotion, dismissal, removal or disciplinary action of a City employee, or on any other matter as expressly provided in the Merit System Rules and Regulations, or as required by law.

4. To perform such other duties as may be requested by the City Manager or directed by the City Commission.

E. Authority
The actions, decisions and recommendations of the Board shall not be final or binding on the City, but shall be advisory only. All statements of facts, findings and recommendations by the Board shall be made in writing to the City Manager who shall forward same to the City Commission, together with his recommendations, for final action by the Commission.

F. Compensation
Members of the Board shall serve without compensation but shall be reimbursed for any authorized expenses which may be incurred in the performance of their duties.

G. Removal

The City Commission shall have the authority to remove any member of the Board from his office for cause whenever, after due notice of hearing at a regular or special meeting of the City Commission, a majority of the Commissioners present voting for such removal. Causes for removal shall include absence from three consecutive Board meetings without valid excuse.

H. Meetings and Procedures

1. All meetings of the Merit Board shall be public hearings open to the public.

2. The Chairman, or Vice-Chairman, or acting Chairman, may administer oaths and compel the attendance of witnesses in the same manner prescribed in the Circuit Court.

3. Minutes will be kept of all public meetings and proceedings and shall include and state the vote of each member on each question, and the motion shall state the reason upon which it is made; such reason or reasons are to be based upon the prescribed guides and standard of the Merit System regarding good personnel administration principles. If a member is absent or abstains from voting, the minutes shall so indicate.

4. The Board shall keep accurate records of its public hearings, together with its minutes and resolutions, and the same shall be open for public inspection at reasonable times and hours.

5. The Board shall hold regular meetings once each month if necessary. If no items are presented for the Board's Agenda at least five (5) days prior to the Board's next regularly scheduled meeting, there shall be no necessity for the Board to meet on such date, and said meeting may be cancelled.

SECTION XIX   DEFINITIONS

Administration - The office of the City Manager

Calendar Day - Any of the seven (7) days of a calendar week

Calendar Week - Any seven (7) consecutive complete calendar days

Calendar Month - Any complete calendar month; or, any consecutive period starting with 12:01 a.m. on any date of one month and ending at 12:00 midnight on the date of preceding number in the next succeeding month

Calendar Year - Any twelve consecutive complete calendar months; or, any consecutive period starting with 12:01 a.m. on any date of one month and ending at 12:00 midnight on the date of preceding number in the same month of the next succeeding year

Certification - Official notice by the Administration to the department head that an eligible has met all requirements for consideration for appointment

Class, or Class of Positions - A group of positions having sufficiently similar duties, supervision requirements, minimum requirements for training, experience, skills and such other characteristics, that the same title, the same test(s) of fitness and the same schedule of compensation may be applied to each position in the group

Class Specification - A written statement of the characteristics of a class of positions including a summary of the nature of the work; illustrative tasks; the requisite knowledge, abilities and skills, and experience and training required of a candidate for the satisfactory performance of the duties of the class

Classification Plan - An orderly arrangement of positions into separate and distinct classes so that each class will contain those positions which are similar in the nature of the work, in duties and responsibilities, and which have similar prerequisite qualifications

Compensation - Wages, salary, fees, allowance, and all other forms of valuable consideration or the amount of any one or more of them paid to an employee, by reason of service rendered in any position, but not including any allowance for expenses authorized and/or reimbursed

Compensation Plan - A schedule of compensation established for the classes of positions so that all positions of a given class will be paid the same wage or salary range established for the class

Demotion - Change of an employee from one position to another position for which a lower minimum and maximum rate of pay is established

Department Head - That person in responsible charge of the operation of a department or office, authorized by lawfully delegated authority to make appointments and to originate or effectively recommend changes in the status of employees

Dismissal - Complete separation of an employee from the City of Anycity for cause

Eligibility List - A list of the names of eligible persons who are qualified and entitled to have their names certified to a department head for consideration for appointment

Employee Service Report - The periodic evaluation or appraisal of an employee's work performance, conduct, attendance and potential

Employment Year - Any twelve (12) months of completed continuous employment, starting with the date of appointment

Layoff - Separation of a permanently appointed employee from a position because of a reduction in the work load available; a lack of funds; abolishment of the position; material change in the departmental organization; or for other related causes

May - The word "may" is to be interpreted as permissive.

Noncompetitive Positions - Positions that cannot be measured, as specified in the Rules and Regulations, including, the general classifications of, but not limited to, unskilled and semiskilled laboring positions; attending, housekeeping, or custodial positions; or as provided in Section III, part K of this Plan

Normal Work Day - The number of hours a qualified employee normally works on any given day, allocated as indicated in Section IV, A.1, of these Rules and Regulations

Normal Work Week - That period of time a qualified employee normally works, in a calendar week, allocated as indicated in Section IV, A.1, of these Rules and Regulations

Open Competitive Test - An examination which permits persons to compete who meet the requirements of the official announcement and the appropriate class specifications and which is not restricted to persons currently permanently employed by the City of Anycity

Original Employment List - The names of those persons who have qualified by examination under these Rules and Regulations, open to all who possess at least the minimal prerequisite qualifications

Overtime - Overtime is the required performance of work in excess of the allocated work schedule, as authorized by the department head.

Part-time Position - A position which is established with a work schedule having fewer hours or days of work than the official work schedule to which the class of positions is allocated; or which has scheduled hours and/or days of work only during certain months of the year

Permanent Employee - An employee who has been regularly and legally appointed to a position after satisfactorily completing the required probationary period

Permanent Position - A position with the town which is established without limiting its duration

Position - An employment involving an aggregation of duties to be performed and responsibilities to be discharged by one person, whether temporary or permanent, part-time or full time, occupied or vacant

Positioning - The process of ascertaining, analyzing, and evaluating the current duties, responsibilities and requirements of a position for the purpose of determining its relative place in the classification plan

Probationary Period - A working test period and an integral part of the evaluation, testing and/or examination process, following a probationary appointment, during which the probationary employee is required to demonstrate fitness for the position by satisfactory performance of the duties of the position and by satisfactory conduct and attendance as prior conditions to receiving a permanent appointment

Promotion - Change of an employee from one position to another position for which a higher minimum and maximum rate of pay is established

Promotion List - A list of classified permanent employees who have qualified for promotion under these Rules and Regulations

Promotional Test - A competitive evaluation, test and/or examination in which competition is open only to permanent employees who meet the requirements of the official announcement and the appropriate class specifications

Qualified employee - Any person permanently appointed under the provisions of these Rules and Regulations

Reclassification - The action taken to officially change an existing position to an appropriate class location because of a change in the duties, responsibilities and/or requirements of the existing position, or because of an amendment of the classification

Reemployment List - A class list of the names of classified permanent employees who have been laid off and who are eligible to have their names certified to an appointing authority under these Rules and Regulations

Resignations - The voluntary termination of employment by an employee

Shall - The word "shall" is to be interpreted as mandatory.

Suspension - Enforced leave of absence without pay of an employee for disciplinary purposes; or, with or without pay during the investigation of alleged misconduct by the employee

Temporary Appointment - Appointment for a limited period of time to a position for which there is no existing appropriate list of eligibles, or no acceptable certified eligibles

Transfer - Change of an employee from one position to another position for which the minimum and maximum rate of pay is the same

Transfer List - The names of classified permanent employees who have requested transfers from a department, whose current service report ratings are satisfactory or better and who have met the requirements of these Rules and Regulations

Vacation Leave - A period of time when a qualified employee receives pay when absent from assigned duty, granted in confidence with and subject to the provisions of these Rules and Regulations

Working Day - Any calendar day, Sunday through Saturday inclusive, excepting days observed as official holidays, or during a state of emergency

SECTION XX: SAMPLE ORDINANCES

A. Sample Ordinance Enacting New Personnel Regulations

ORDINANCE NO..___   First Reading _____
                                     Second Reading ____

AN ORDINANCE OF THE CITY OF ANYCITY,
REVISING CODE OF ORDINANCES, ANYCITY,
APPENDIX C, RELATING THE PERSONNEL POLICIES
FOR CITY EMPLOYEES; AMENDING SUBPARAGRAPHS
(e), (f) AND (9), SECTION 10.2. OF ORDINANCE
NO. 821, CITY OF ANYCITY, DELETING
CERTAIN EMPLOYEES FROM EXCEPTIONS TO THE
MERIT SYSTEM; ADDING SUBPARAGRAPH (d) TO SEC-
ION 10.4.3. OF ORDINANCE NO. 821, CITY OF
ANYCITY, RELATING TO MERIT SYSTEM
APPEALS; PROVIDING ADMINISTRATIVE DIRECTION,
PROVIDING INTENT; PROVIDING FOR SEVERABILITY;
AND ESTABLISHING AN EFFECTIVE DATE.

WHEREAS, the City of Anycity Board of Commissioners is most interested in providing the most current personnel policies for the administration of personnel matters within the City of Anycity; and,

WHEREAS, the Board of Commissioners believes that it is most important to provide for the proper and equitable treatment of the City employees;

NOW, THEREFORE, be it Enacted by the people of the City of Anycity:

Section 1. Appendix C, Code of Ordinances, City of Anycity, is amended to read:
(Substantial rewording of Appendix. See Appendix C dated October 1, 19??, for present text)

APPENDIX C
PERSONNEL REGULATIONS

Section 0.01. Policy.

It is the intention and policy of the City that a proper and efficient personnel program be maintained as an indispensable and necessary prerequisite to professional administration of the business affairs of this City. It is the further intention and policy that a fair, equitable and uniform system of public employment must exist in order to attract good public servants and provide them with an opportunity for normal and useful employment.

It is the intention and policy that the departments be structured in a line and staff organizational relationship whereby each employee be directly responsible to only one supervisor. The authority for the management of each department is vested solely with the department head. The City Manager will counsel and direct the line organization but will not normally supplant the authority of department heads, but may do so if required. In accordance with the provisions contained in the Charter of the City of Anycity, all Department Supervisors are directly responsible to the City Manager. The City Manager is directly responsible to the Board of City Commissioners.

The Board of City Commissioners and City Manager do not hereby relinquish any authority vested in them but delegate authority to the extent provided in the Charter of the City of Anycity.

Section 0.02 Intent.

It shall be the intent of the Board of City Commissioners and other elected officials that:
A. The employees of the City of Anycity be productive persons who perform a useful purpose.
B. There shall be no employee on the City payroll for whom there is no employment need.
C. There shall be no individual, group or factions in the City employ who shall create disharmony, unrest, disquiet, institute rumors or by any other act cause dissension and inefficiency in City Government.
D. All department heads and employees shall comply with and assist in carrying out the personnel program, including the furnishing of records and information at the request of the City Manager.

NOTE: This Appendix refers to employees as "he". For the purpose of this policy, "he" will be considered a generic term, to include female employees.

Section 0.03. Scope.

The personnel policy, regulations and procedures, as adopted, shall apply to all personnel under the jurisdiction of the Board of City Commissioners and City Manager.

Section 0.04. Conflict.

A. Any item in this entire personnel policy that is in conflict with the Charter of the City of Anycity is voided.

B. Any previous city policy on subjects covered in this policy as of (date of enactment), is hereby rescinded.

I. GENERAL POLICIES

Section 1.01 Political activity.

A. No employee shall directly or indirectly coerce or attempt to coerce, command, or advise any other employee to pay, lend, or contribute any part of his salary, or any money, or anything else of value to any party, committee, organization, agency, or person for political purposes. Nothing in this subsection shall prohibit an employee from suggesting to another employee in a noncoercive manner that he may voluntarily contribute to a fund which is administered by a party, committee, organization, agency, person, labor union or other employee organization for political purposes.

B. No employee shall use his official authority or influence for the purpose of interfering with an election or a nomination of office or coercing or influencing another person's vote or affecting the result thereof.

C. No employee shall directly or indirectly coerce or attempt to coerce, command, and advise employee as to where he might purchase commodities or to interfere in any other way with the personal right of said employee.

D. Nothing in this policy shall prevent an employee from becoming a member of a political club or organization or attending meetings of such club organizations or of expressing his opinion on all political subjects except those specifically prohibited above, or from enjoying freedom from all interference in casting his vote.

E. No employee shall hold office as a member of the governing board, council, commission, or authority, by whatever name known, which is his employer while, at the same time, continuing as an employee of such employer.

F. The provisions of this policy shall not be construed so as to prevent any person from becoming a candidate for and actively campaigning for any elective office in this state. All such persons shall retain the right to vote as they may choose and to express their opinions on all political subjects and candidates. The provisions of this policy shall not be construed so as to limit the political activity in a general, special primary, bond, referendum, or other election of any kind or nature, of elected officials or candidates for public office in the state or of any county or municipality thereof.

G. An employee choosing to be a candidate for political office will be placed on personal leave of absence on the date of qualifying for election and will so remain while a political candidate.

H. It is the intent of this policy to maintain an impartial city service and to work toward the ideal of a public service that is dedicated to all citizens of the city, to maintain fair and equal treatment and to avoid a conflict of interest.

Section 1.02 Other employment.

Full-time employees are discouraged, but not restricted from engaging in other employment during their off-duty hours. However, city employment must be considered the primary employment, and no employee may engage in outside employment which would interfere with the performance of his duties or be in conflict with the interest of the city.

Section 1.03 Use of city property.

Equipment, facilities, vehicles or property of the city shall not be used by employees for any reason other than city business. Exceptions to this policy will be granted by the City Manager when in the best interest of the City. For example, police officers may be allowed to take their vehicles home when leaving their duty shift, in order to improve their response time in the event of an emergency.

Section 1.04 Conflict of interest.

A. All personnel in a position to influence the city actions shall refrain from business, professional and social relationships which may affect the exercise of their independent judgment in dealing with the city suppliers of goods or services.

B. Employee acceptance of loans, advances, "kick-backs", or of gifts, gratuities and favors or entertainment from a supplier, bidder or other parties doing business with the City Government is improper; such action shall not be condoned. (This section is not meant to prohibit such incidentals as lunch, dinner or minor social activity).

Section 1.05 Disclosure of information.

The City of Anycity, is a Municipal Government and consequently subject to all portions of State and Federal Legislation entitled Government in the Sunshine. Consequently, all disclosures of information shall be within the guidelines expressed in the continuing and ongoing legislation of Government in the Sunshine.

Section 1.06 Family employment restrictions.

No spouse or member of the immediate family of a City employee or of any member of City Commission will be hired, promoted, transferred or retained on a permanent or temporary basis within the Merit System unless such employment is determined by unanimous vote of the City Commission to be in the best interest of the City; is approved by the City Manager and does not violate State Statute (as amended or superseded).

"Immediate family" is defined as blood, marital, adopted or
step-relative in one of the following categories: father,
mother, son, daughter, brother, sister, aunt, uncle, first
cousin, nephew, niece, husband, wife, father-in-law, mother-in-
law, son-in-law, daughter-in-law, brother-in-law, sister-in-law,
step-father, step-mother, step-son, step-daughter, step-brother,
step-sister, half-brother, half-sister or any ward of an employee
living within the same household.

Section 1.07 Code of conduct.

All employees are expected to keep in mind that they are servants of the public and to conduct themselves in a manner which will in no way discredit the City Government, public officials, fellow employees or themselves.

Section 1.08 Collection of money, fines, bonds.

The City Manager, City Clerk, deputy clerks and Finance Director are the only personnel authorized to collect and disburse city funds. Collections of fines, forfeitures and bonds by the police department personnel is authorized and will be deposited in city hall as soon as possible following collection.

Section 1.09 Sexual harassment on the job.

A. Definition. Harassment on the basis of sex is a violation of Sec. 703 of Title VII, U.S. Code. Unwelcome sexual advances, requests for sexual favors, and other verbal or physical conduct of a sexual nature constitute sexual harassment when:

1. submission to such conduct is made explicitly or implicitly a term or condition of an individual's employment,

2. submission to or rejection of such conduct by an individual is used as the basis for employment decisions affecting such individual, or

3. such conduct has the purpose or effect of unreasonably interfering with an individual's work performance or creating an intimidating, hostile, or offensive working environment.

B. Policy and procedures for sexual harassment complaints. As a part of the City's continuing affirmative action efforts and pursuant to the guidelines on sex discrimination issued by the federal Equal Opportunity Commission, the City endorses the following policy:

1. It is illegal and against the policies of this City for any employee, male or female, to sexually harass another employee by (a) making unwelcomed sexual advances or request for sexual favors or other verbal or physical Conduct of a sexual nature, a condition of an employee's Continued employment, or (b) making submission to or rejections of such conduct the basis for employment decisions affecting the employee, or (c) creating an intimidating, hostile or offensive working environment by such conduct.

2. Any employee who believes he or she has been the subject of sexual harassment should report the alleged act immediately, (within 24 hours after the alleged harassment occurs) to the City Manager or the Personnel Office. An investigation of all complaints will be undertaken immediately. Any supervisor, agent or other employee who has been found by the City, after appropriate investigation, to have sexually harassed another employee, will be subject to appropriate sanctions depending on the circumstances, from a warning in his or her file up to and including termination.

The City recognizes that the question of whether a particular action or incident is a purely personal, social relationship without a discriminatory employment effect requires a factual determination based on all facts in this matter. Given the nature of this type of discrimination, the City recognizes also that false accusations of sexual harassment can have serious effects on innocent women and men. We trust that all employees of the City will continue to act responsibly to establish a pleasant working environment free of discrimination. The City encourages any employee to raise questions he or she may have regarding discrimination or affirmative action with the City Manager.

Section 1.10 Literacy tests.

Literacy tests may be administered as a part of the recruiting and job interview process when a candidate is being considered for employment with the City. If such a test is administered, the test must be one as provided by the said Board of Education to determine whether the students have the minimum of a sixth grade reading level. A test not regularly administered by the said county Board of Education may not be substituted for such a test; no arbitrary testing measures will be permitted.

II. EMPLOYMENT CONDITIONS AND STANDARDS

Section 2.01 Original employment.

When a person is initially employed in a position in the City service, either on a full-time basis or a part-time basis, he shall be employed in one of the following types of original employment status:

1. Permanent employee;
2. Probationary Permanent Employee;
3. Temporary employee.

A. Definitions of types of original employment:

1. Permanent: Permanent employment will be made to a classification for permanently budgeted career positions.

a. A permanent employee shall be eligible for all City fringe benefits immediately upon establishing a continuous service date.

b. A permanent employee is one who has satisfactorily completed his probationary period.

2. Probationary Permanent Employee: A probationary permanent employee shall be an individual hired to fill a regularly Commission funded position, during his/her initial three (3) months of employment and not a permanent employee that has been placed on probation as a disciplinary action.

3. Temporary.
a. Temporary employment may be made when the work of a department requires the services of one or more employees on a seasonal or intermittent basis.
b. A temporary employee shall not be eligible for City fringe benefits.

B. Employment of department heads; The City Manager shall review and approve the employment or promotion of a department supervisor.

Section 2.02 Probationary period.

A. The first three (3) months of City service, promotion or transfer shall be considered a probationary period for all employees. Upon approval by the City Manager, an employee's probationary period may be extended up to an additional three (3) months. All sworn personnel in the Police Department and firefighter personnel in the Fire Department shall nave a special six (6) month probationary period which may be extended by an additional three (3) months as previously provided herein.

B. If the employee is found to be unsatisfactory during his probationary period following employment, he may be terminated. If he wishes to appeal the termination, he must comply with the provisions of the Merit System in order to appear before the Merit System Board. During the Probationary Period, the only disciplinary action a Permanent Probationary Employee will have the right to appeal to the Merit System Board is termination. Other disciplinary actions by a Supervisor may be appealed to the City Manager, but no further. A regular Permanent Employee may appeal any disciplinary action to the Merit System Board, as provided for in the Merit System. If the employee is considered satisfactory for another available position, he may be transferred and will begin a new probation period.

C. An employee in probationary status may not be eligible for certain fringe benefits, until the probationary period is satisfactorily completed.

Section 2.03 City service.

A. Continuous service:
1. An employee's continuous service date shall be established as the most recent date of hire and may not precede the date of actual job performance.
2. Authorized leaves of absence and layoff to the extent provided by personnel policy shall not be considered a break in service. All other separations shall be considered a break in service effective at the end of the employee's regular shift on the last day of work.
3. Any unauthorized leave without pay for more than three (3) consecutive workdays shall be considered a break in service.

B. Creditable service: Creditable service shall be construed as service during which the employee was on the payroll of the City.

C. Basis for change of status: In considering employees for promotion, demotion, layoff, recall from layoff or transfer, job performance shall be the sole criterion. Job performance being equal, continuous service shall be the criterion.

III. PAY PLAN

Pay scales are set by the Board of City Commissioners and will not be altered or changed unless by express permission of the City Manager.

A. Pay raises: The practice of across the board or blanket pay raises for all city employees will be discontinued.

Merit raises will be given to employees on the basis of initiative, capability, supervisory ability, loyalty and dedication to the interest and progress of the City of Anycity. Seniority will have a bearing only when all of the above factors are equal. These raises will be in 5% increments, as provided for in the Merit System (adopted by Ordinance Number xxx).

Cost of living raises will be considered by the Board of City Commissioners and acted upon at their discretion.

The Board of City Commissioners will annually review salaries and may, at their discretion, raise or lower salaries as necessary.

B. Police officers incentive plan: Will be administered as established by State Legislation [or as provided in your state].

IV. NORMAL OVERTIME PROCEDURES

Section 4.01 Overtime work.

A. Statement of policy: The City of Anycity will continue to comply with mandated sanctions of the U.S. Department of Labor, not only with regard to overtime, but all other policies as well.

1. The employment and work program of each department should be arranged so as to reduce to a minimum the necessity for overtime work, except in emergency situations.

2. It is intended, however, that employees should be expected to work, in a reasonable period, beyond regular working hours or during lunch periods when necessary to complete work assignments .

3. Activities such as time spent in taking training courses, travel and voluntary overtime shall not be considered as authorized overtime work.

B. Overtime payment: (Emergency) Overtime payments shall be on the basis of one and one-half (1-1/2) times the employee's rate of pay.

C. Compensatory time:

1. When an employee is required by proper authority to work beyond the normal working hours for his position, he may be granted compensatory time off on a one and one-half (1-1/2) multiplier basis for the extra hours which he worked. Compensatory time must be taken prior to the end of the work week or one pay will be paid to the employee at the rate of time and a half times his normal rate of pay, in accordance with standards set by the U.S. Department of Labor.

2. Compensatory overtime must be authorized by the department head prior to the performance of overtime work and should be credited to the employee as soon as practical following the overtime work.

3. Each department head should make every effort to allow employees to use their earned compensatory leave as promptly as is mutually convenient for the department and the employee, however, an employee may be required to use his earned compensatory leave at any time.

4. A record of earned compensatory time will be maintained by the department head.

V. HOLIDAYS

Section 5.01 Official holidays.

The following are holidays which shall be observed by all departments in which functions can be discontinued without adversely affecting required services to the public.

New Years Day, January 1	Memorial Day, as applicable.
Independence Day, July 4.	Labor Day, first Monday in September.

Thanksgiving Day, designated Thursday in November

Friday after Thanksgiving	Christmas Eve, December 24.

Christmas Day, December 25.

Additionally, one floating holiday to be used as City Board of Commissioners sees fit when holidays fall one day from a weekend.

Section 5.02 Eligibility.

All employees on the active payroll on the date of the holiday shall be eligible for holiday pay at their regular rate of pay.

Section 5.03 Work during holidays.

Each eligible employee shall be given the number of designated holidays each year. However, if the work requirements of the department is such that an employee is required to work on any of the holidays designated, he shall be credited with compensatory leave equal to 1-1/2 the time which he is on duty.

Section 5.04 Holiday falling on weekend.

When a holiday falls on Saturday, the preceding Friday shall be observed as a holiday. When a holiday falls on Sunday, the following Monday shall be observed as a holiday.

Section 5.05 Holidays during paid leave.

Employees on annual or sick leave during periods when designated holidays occur shall not have the day of the holiday charged against their accrued leave.

VI. ANNUAL VACATION

Section 6.01 Eligibility.

Only permanent employees shall earn annual leave. Temporary, emergency or other part time employees shall not be eligible to accrue annual leave.

Section 6.02 Accrual of annual vacation (based on continuous service-date of most recent hire.)

For all city employees the following vacation schedule will apply. Periods of service must be consecutive in order to be eligible for vacation benefits. Broken periods of service will not be accumulative in order to gain maximum benefits. For seniority purposes, service will be counted commencing with the latest period the employee commenced working for the city. Employees must complete six months of satisfactory service before becoming eligible for leave.

One to seven (7) years - Two (2) weeks vacation.
Eight (8) to fifteen (15) years - Three (3) weeks vacation.
Sixteen (16) years or over - Four (4) weeks vacation.

230

Section 6.03 Use of annual vacation.

A. Annual vacation is intended to be used to provide a periodic vacation. However, earned annual vacation may be used for any other purpose when authorized by the department head.

B. Annual vacation shall be used only with the prior approval of the department head and shall not be authorized prior to the time it is earned and credited to the employee. Written vacation requests shall be submitted on the form provided through the supervisor to the Finance Director.

Section 6.04 Holidays during vacation.

When an official holiday occurs while an employee is on annual vacation, that day shall not be charged against the employee's annual vacation balance.

Section 6.05 Payment of earned annual vacation.

A. The only condition under which an employee can be paid for his unused annual leave is upon layoff or terminal separation from the City service and following six months of satisfactory service. Such payment shall be made at the employee's current rate of pay.

B. In case of death of an employee, payment for unused annual leave shall be made to the employee's beneficiary, estate or as provided by law.

VII. SICK LEAVE

A. All City permanent employees shall earn and accumulate paid sick leave. Temporary, emergency and part-time employees shall not be eligible to earn or accrue sick leave.

B. Permanent employees of the City of Anycity will be credited with one day of sick leave each month, totaling twelve (12) sick leave days per year. At the end of each fiscal year unused sick leave will be carried over up to thirty-six (36) days. Any amount in excess of twenty-four (24) sick leave days will be purchased back from the employee, at the end of the Fiscal year, eight hours pay for each day over twenty-four days accumulated.

C. The employee's personal illness, injury or exposure to a contagious disease; which would endanger others, are examples of occasions when sick leave should be used.

D. Accumulated sick leave may be charged when an employee is on Workmen's Compensation or Disability Sick Leave, to supplement the employees benefit, up to the employees normal rate of pay.

E. Employees are responsible for insuring that their supervisors are notified each day when sick leave is used.

F. Supervisors will require employees to present a doctor's certificate from the employee's personal physician, that the employee is physically or mentally unfit to work when more than three (3) consecutive days of sick leave have been used. Medical justification will not be required for illness or incapacitation of three (3) days or less; however, supervisors will be notified by the employee daily when using sick leave.

G. An employee who is either terminated or resigned will be paid for all accumulated sick leave at that employee's current rate of pay at the time of termination or resignation.

H. The sick leave policy regulations and procedures, as adopted, shall apply to all personnel under the jurisdiction of the Board of City Commissioners and the City Manager.

VIII. DISABILITY SICK LEAVE INSURANCE

A. All City probationary permanent employees shall be eligible for the disability insurance and life insurance the first of the month following thirty (30) days from the date of employment.

B. An employee who is disabled by illness or injury, which incurred sometime other than normal working hours or "off-duty", is entitled to Disability Sick Leave. The disability must not be a result from a self-inflicted injury or negligence. The employee must supply his supervisor with a physician's certification that the employee is unable to perform his duties.

C. Disability sick leave status shall continue during the period of actual disability to a maximum to ninety (90) calendar days. Should a disabled employee be unable to return to work at the expiration of the ninety day (90) period, the case shall be reviewed by the City's Merit System Board which shall recommend that the City Manager approve or disapprove the continuation of disability sick leave status. If approved by the City Manager, the leave status shall continue for the duration of actual disability, up to a maximum of an additional ninety days, after which it shall terminate, as mandated by State Laws (adapt to your local laws). If disapproved by the City Manager the disability leave status shall terminate immediately.

D. During the disability sick leave status time period an employee may use any accrued sick leave or vacation benefits accrued to supplement his disability sick leave benefits, up to the employees normal rate of pay.

E. In addition to the time limitations set forth above, disability sick leave status may be terminated by:
   1. The employee's physician certification that the employee is physically able to return to work.
   2. Termination of employment of the employee, for any reason.
   3. Entry into employment of any kind by the employee, including self-employment.

F. While on disability sick leave status an employee shall not accrue any regular sick leave benefits, or vacation benefits, but shall not lose their seniority in their job position.

IX . WORKMEN'S COMPENSATION

A. It shall be the policy of the City of Anycity to provide Workmen's Compensation Benefits to any employee injured or incurring an illness related to the employee's activity while "on-duty."

B. Injury Reporting. All employee's injuries, of any description or size, shall be immediately reported to the supervisor by the injured employee. The supervisor must ensure that a "Notice of Injury" is completed.

C. An injured employee shall be paid regular salary for the first seven (7) days of his/her in jury. On the eighth day, Workmen's Compensation benefits will commence. The employee may, if he/she chooses, charge his/her accumulated sick leave or accumulated vacation benefits to supplement the Workmen's Compensation benefits up to this/her regular rate of pay. If the employee does not have any benefits accumulated, the employee will only be entitled to the Workmen's Compensation Benefit.

D. In the event an employee refuses medical care, a signed statement to this effect should be obtained from the employee and submitted with the accident report, by the supervisor.

X. LEAVE OF ABSENCE

Section 10.01 Administrative Leave.

A. Court Duty
1. An employee who is subpoenaed as a prospective juror or as a witness shall be granted leave with pay. Fees paid by the court will be retained by the employee.
2. In no case shall administrative leave with pay be granted for court attendance when an employee is the defendant or is engaged in personal litigation, unless such actions are a result of an act performed by the employee as a part of his official duties as an employee of the City.

B. Elections: An employee who lives at such distance from his assigned work locations as to preclude his voting outside of working hours, may be authorized as much time as is necessary, with pay, for this purpose. An employee shall not be granted administrative leave to work at the polls during elections.

C. Meetings: In cases where it is deemed by the department head to be beneficial to the City, an employee may be granted leave with pay to attend such professional meetings or conferences as may contribute to the effectiveness of his employment.

D. Examinations: An employee may be granted leave with pay while taking examinations before a federal, state or county agency, provided such examinations are pertinent to his city employment.

E. Examinations for military service. An employee who is ordered, by his Selective Service Board, to appear for physical examination for induction into the military service shall be granted leave with pay.for this purpose.

Section 10.02 Maternity leave.

A. An employee may be allowed to remain in employment until the condition of pregnancy affects satisfactory job performance. The judgement of the supervisor will be final. His decision will take into consideration the written medical opinion of the employee's physician, the nature of the job regarding physical stress and the employee's ability to perform normal job duties with full efficiency.

B. The details of a maternity leave will be administered under the current policies set forth in the Merit Plan.

Section 10.03 Military leave.

A. An employee who is drafted, or who is ordered to active duty in connection with reserve activities other than short term training shall, upon presentation of a copy of his official orders, be granted leave without pay extending ninety (90) calendar days beyond the date of separation from the military service.

B. All unused leave benefits shall be retained by the employee who shall have the same credited to his record if he applies for reinstatement to his position in accordance with "C" below. During such leaves of .absence. the employee shall be entitled to preserve all rights established by City policy.

C. Upon separation from the military service, the employee must request reinstatement within ninety (90) calendar days after separation. The city may require the employee to submit to a medical examination to determine his fitness to perform the duties of the position to which he may be returning. If the employee volunteers for an additional tour of military duty, he shall forfeit his reinstatement rights.

Section 10.04 Leave of Absence: general provisions.

A. Return from leave of absence: An employee returning from leave shall be entitled to employment in the same department and the same, or equivalent, classification wherein employed when leave began.
B. Insurance coverage while on leave of absence:
The City will continue to maintain group insurance benefits for employees while on leave with pay.

XI. DISCIPLINARY ACTIONS

Section 11.01 Intention.

It is the intention of the City Manager that effective supervision and employee relations will avoid most matters which necessitate disciplinary action. The purpose of rules and disciplinary action for violating such rules is not intended to restrict the rights of anyone, but to insure the rights of all and secure cooperation and orderliness throughout the City service.

Section 11.02 Disciplinary actions.

When it is necessary that disciplinary action be taken the action shall be based upon: the Disciplinary Procedures set forth in the Merit System.

Section 11.03 Disciplinary actions.

[As specified in Ordinance No. ___, the Merit System is an expansion of this appendix.]

Section 2. The City Manager shall make the appropriate administrative changes in the Merit System handbook which are necessary to conform the handbook to Ordinance No. ____, as amended and Appendix C, as amended.

Section 3. This ordinance by revision of Appendix C and amendment to Ordinance No. 821 is supplemented to and should be read with Ordinance No. 821.

Section 4. If any portion of this ordinance is determined to be void or otherwise unconstitutional, the remaining portion of this ordinance shall remain in effect.

Section 5. This ordinance shall become effective immediately upon adoption by the Anycity City Board of Commissioners.

END OF SAMPLE ORDINANCE

B. Sample Ordinance Enacting the Merit System

AN ORDINANCE OF THE CITY OF ANYCITY
RELATING TO ADMINISTRATION; AMENDING APPENDIX
"C" OF THE CODE OF ORDINANCES BY ADOPTING A
CITY MERIT SYSTEM CONTAINING PERSONNEL RULES
AND REGULATIONS FOR CITY EMPLOYEES; PROVIDING'
A GRIEVANCE PROCEDURE; AND PROVIDING FOR AN
EFFECTIVE DATE.

WHEREAS, the City Commission of the City of Anycity deems it necessary and advisable to establish a merit system of rules and regulations for the purpose of personnel administration of the City's employees.

NOW THEREFORE, BE IT ORDAINED THE CITY COMMISSION
OF THE CITY OF ANYCITY, ANYSTATE:

Section 1: That Appendix C of the Code of Ordinances of the City of Anycity is hereby amended by the provision of Section 10 thereof to read as follows:

Section 10: IN GENERAL

Section 10.1 DECLARATION OF PERSONNEL POLICY
Under the authority granted to the City Commission by Article III, Section 12, of the Charter of the City of Anycity the following personnel principles and policies are established:

A. Employment by the City of Anycity shall be based upon merit and shall be free of personal and political considerations.

B. Just and equitable incentives and conditions of employment shall be established and maintained to promote efficiency and economy in the operation of City government.

C. Positions having similar job factors and levels of difficulty shall be classified and compensated on an uniform basis.

D. Appointments and other personnel actions involving a change in employee status requiring the application of the merit principle shall be based upon evaluations, tests and/or examinations.

E.   Every effort shall be made to stimulate high morale by fair administration of this article and by every consideration of the rights and interests of employees, consistent with the best interest of the public and of the City.

F. Continuity of employment covered by this article shall be subject to good behavior, satisfactory attendance and performance of work, necessity for the performance of work, and availability of funds.

Section 10 . 2 COVERAGE
All offices and positions in the employ of the City of Anycity shall be and are hereby allocated to the Merit System excepting only those hereinafter specifically exempted. Those offices and positions specifically exempted are:

A. All Elected Officials
B. All persons appointed to fill vacancies in elective office

C. Members of the Board, Commissions and Committees, serving with or without pay

D. The City Attorney and any Assistant City Attorney

E. The Chief of Police, the Chief of the Fire Department, the Finance Director, the Building Official, the Recreation Director and the Public Works Director .

F. The City Manager; any Deputy of the City Manager

G. Architects, auditors, consultants, counsel, engineers, and all others rendering temporary services.

Unless specifically designated otherwise, personnel policies and rules and regulations apply to all persons employed under the Merit System.

Section 10.3 ORGANIZATION FOR PERSONNEL ADMINISTRATION

Section 10.3.1 ORGANIZATION BY CITY MANAGER

The City Manager shall have the basic responsibility for the Merit System personnel program as set forth in this article. The City Manager specifically shall:

A. be responsible for the effective administration and technical direction of the Merit System personnel programs.

B. appoint, remove, suspend and discipline all officers and employees of the City under his jurisdiction subject to the policies set forth in this article, provisions of the City Charter, and those in State Law; or he may, at his discretion, authorize personnel under him to exercise any of several such powers, in such department or office;

C. fix and establish the number of employees in the various City departments and offices under his jurisdiction and determine the duties and compensation in accordance with the policies set forth in this article and subject to the approval of the City Commission and budget limitations;

D. establish a personnel office for the purpose of maintaining such records as are deemed necessary for the proper functioning of the Merit System;

E. cause to be printed such self-explanatory forms as are deemed necessary for the proper and orderly control and recording of all personnel changes and actions, which shall require the signatures of those properly responsible to initiate and approve personnel actions in order to be valid;

F. recommend rules and regulations, and revisions, and amendments thereto for the consideration of the City Commission;

G. prepare and recommend a position classification plan for all Merit System employees for the consideration of the City Commission and install and maintain such a plan, as approved;

H. prepare and recommend a position compensation plan for all Merit System employees for the consideration of the City Commission and install and maintain such a plan, as approved;

I. establish and maintain a roster of all persons in the Merit System, setting forth each employee, the class/title of his/her position, compensation, changes in class/title, changes in status and such other data as may be deemed desirable or useful;

J. develop and administer such recruiting programs and such evaluating examinations and testing programs as may be necessary to obtain an adequate supply of competent applicants to meet the needs of the City;

K. be responsible for the certification of all payrolls;

L. develop and coordinate training and education programs for City employees;

M. investigate periodically the operation and effort of the personnel provisions of this article and the Merit System Rules and Regulations and at least annually report his findings and recommendations to the City Commission.

N. perform such other duties and exercise such other powers in personnel administration as may be prescribed by law, this article, and the Merit System Rules and Regulations

Section 10.4 GRIEVANCES
Section 10.4.1 DEFINITION

A grievance shall be defined as a problem arising from the interpretation or application of the Merit System Rules and Regulations, which affect the employee personally including matters which involve a loss of pay or seniority.

Section 10.4.2 POLICY

It is the City's policy to consider employee grievances promptly and fairly. Any regular employee who believes that he or she has received inequitable treatment which constitutes a grievance as defined above may use this procedure to apply for relief from that condition.

Section 10.4.3 PROCEDURE

The following procedure shall be followed on all grievances. Time expressed in terms of days shall mean working days

A. Within five (5) days of occurrence of the problem the employee shall discuss the matter with his//her department head. If settlement cannot be achieved within three (3) days thereafter, the problem shall be reduced to writing by the employee and delivered to the City Manager within three (3) additional days thereafter; i.e. the City Manager shall be notified in writing within six (6) days after the employee's meeting with the department head.

B. Within three (3) days of receipt of the written grievance from the employee, the City Manager, or his designee for such purpose, shall meet and confer jointly with the employee and the department head, and hear both sides of the grievance. The City Manager shall render his decision on the matter within two (2) days; thereafter and shall forthwith deliver a written copy thereof to both the employee and the department head.

C. After receiving written notification of the City Manager's decision, an employee may submit a request for further review to the Merit System Board, providing such request is in writing and is submitted not later than three (3) days after receipt of final notification. At its next regular meeting, the Merit System Board will investigate the request and hear the employee and any witnesses. No later than its next regular meeting thereafter, the Merit System Board shall render its decision and submit to the City Commission a written report which shall state the grievance, summarize its findings and give its decision and recommendations on the case. The report shall be forwarded to the City Manager who shall forthwith deliver same to the City Commission together with his final recommendation for final action by the Commission. The City Commission shall render a final decision on this matter at its next regular meeting.

Section 10.5 MERIT SYSTEM RULES AND REGULATIONS
Section 10.5.1 ADOPTION

There is hereby adopted as and for the City of Anycity personnel administration system the attached rules and regulations entitled "Merit System Rules and Regulations" which consist of the following designated phases of the City's personnel program. The City of Anycity adopts this Merit System by reference and incorporates the same into the Code of Ordinances as though fully set forth herein

The Merit System Rules and Regulations shall cover procedures and policies to govern the following phases of the Merit System personnel program.

Announcement of vacancies and examinations.
Acceptance of applications for examinations
Character and conduct of examinations.
Establishment and use of eligibility lists
Certification and appointment from eligibility lists
Hours of work and work weeks, Nepotism and Political Activity
Attendance regulations, City Merit System Board
Holiday regulations, Safety and Workmen's Compensation
Position classification, Incentive program
Position compensation, Employee Service Reports

Transfers, promotions, and reinstatements.
Probation.
Suspension, demotion and dismissal
Leave regulations.
Outside employment of Merit System Employees
Employee service reports and ratings including probations.
Employee review requests
Such other matters as may be necessary and proper to carry out the purpose and intent of this article.

Section 10.5.2 AMENDMENT OF RULES AND REGULATIONS
Amendments of the Merit System Rules and Regulations may be proposed by the City Manager and will become effective upon approval by the City Commission by Ordinance.

Section 10.5.3 APPOINTMENTS
The Merit System Rules and Regulations shall provide for the employment of persons on the basis of merit in conformity with this article.
A. An orderly and systematic method of recruitment to insure that all those employed will be hired on a merit basis and the establishment of eligibility lists for appointment purposes.
B. In the absence of appropriate eligibility lists or acceptable certified eligibles, a vacancy may be filled by temporary appointment, provided that an eligibility list shall be established for such position within twelve (12) months from the effective date of the first temporary appointment.
C. During the period of suspension of an employee, or pending final action of proceedings to review suspension, demotion, or dismissal of an employee, the appointing authority may only temporarily fill the vacancy created.

Section 10.5.4 CONSULTATION WITH EMPLOYEES
The City Manager is authorized to consult with, or receive suggestions from: individual City employees; groups of City employees or representatives of organizations of City employees concerning matters of Merit System personnel policy.
The City Manager may, where it is deemed appropriate, refer any requests from City employees to the City Commission along with his recommendations for its consideration.
On matters within the discretion of the City Manager, he shall give due consideration to the views of employees. Nothing herein, however shall be interpreted as depriving the City Commission or the City Manager of the right to make final decisions on matters for which only they have the ultimate responsibility.

Section 10.6 CLASSIFICATION PLAN
Section 10.6.1 PREPARATION
In preparing the classification plan as required by this article, it shall be the responsibility of the City Manager to ascertain the job factors and levels of difficulty of all positions subject to this article. After all necessary consultations, the City Manager shall prepare a position classification plan which shall group all positions in the Merit System in classes based on their job factors and levels of difficulty.

Section 10.6.2 CONTENT OF THE CLASSIFICATION PLAN
The position classification plan shall set forth for each class of positions or position, a class title, a statement of duties, authority and responsibilities thereof and the qualifications necessary or desirable for the satisfactory performance of the duties of the position.

Section 10.7 COMPENSATION PLAN
Section 10.7.1 PREPARATION

The City Manager shall develop a uniform and equitable compensation plan, consisting of minimum, intermediate, and maximum rates of compensation for each class of positions.

Compensation rates for each class of positions shall be coordinated with the position classification plan and shall be based on requisite job factors and levels of difficulty, general rates of pay for comparable work in public and private employment in the area, or in a significant area, cost of living data, maintenance and other benefits received by employees, and other economic considerations.

Section 10.7.2 INITIAL EFFECT OF COMPENSATION PLAN

On the effective date of new or revised compensation plan, employees receiving less than the minimum rate for their class of position shall be increased to the minimum rate of the compensation range therefore.

Employees receiving more than the maximum rate for their class of position shall continue to receive the same rate of compensation unless an exception is requested by the Department head and approved by the City Manager, in which case such an employee's rate of compensation shall be reduced to the maximum rate of compensation for that classification of position.

Section 10.7.3 ADOPTION AND AMENDMENT OF THE CLASSIFICATION AND COMPENSATION PLANS

The City Manager shall review the classification and compensation plans and after any necessary consultations, shall make such modifications as the City Manager believes to be proper and submit the classification and compensation plans to the City Commission.

The classification and compensation plans as presented, or as amended by the City Commission shall become effective upon passage by the City Commission.

The classification and compensation plans may be amended from time to time in the same manner as that in which they were adopted.

Section 10.8 GENERAL PERSONNEL POLICIES
Section 10.8.1 NEPOTISM

No spouse or member of the immediate family of a City employee, or of any member of City Commission will be hired, promoted, transferred, or retained on a permanent or temporary basis within the Merit System unless such employment is determined by unanimous vote of the City Commission to be in the best interest of the City; is approved by the City Manager and does not violate state laws (as amended or superseded).

"Immediate family" is defined as blood, marital, adopted or step- relative in one of the following categories: father, mother, son, daughter, brother, sister, aunt, uncle, first cousin, nephew, niece, husband, wife, father-in-law, mother-in-law, son-in-law, daughter-in-law, brother-in-law, sister-in-law, step-father, step-mother, step-son step-daughter, step- brother, step-sister, half-brother, half-sister or any ward of an employee living within the same household.

Section 10.8.2 POLITICAL ACTIVITY

Any employee of the Merit System who wishes to accept or seek election or appointment to a political office within the City of Anycity shall resign from the Merit System. Upon indicating such intention by formal declaration, or other evidence of candidacy, his/her employment by the City of Anycity shall immediately terminate.

Nothing in this article, however, shall be construed as to prevent any employee from becoming or continuing to be a member of a political organization or from enjoying freedom from any interference in casting their vote.

Section 10.8.3 SOLICITATION OF CONTRIBUTIONS
No solicitation of funds of any character for any purpose whatsoever shall be permitted by or of employees of the Merit System of the City on the job, except with the expressed prior approval of the City Manager.

Section 10.8.4 STATUS OF PRESENT EMPLOYEES
Any person holding a position included in the Merit System who shall have served continuously in such position for a period of at least six (6) months immediately prior to the effective date of this article, or for such longer probationary period as a department head, may have extended as to any specific employee, shall upon certification by the department head that his/her work performance, attendance and conduct has been satisfactory, assume permanent status in the Merit System in the position held on such effective date without further evaluation, test and/or examination in connection with such certification and shall thereafter be subject in all respects to the provisions of the article and the Merit System Rules and Regulations .

Any person who has held a position included in the Merit System who shall have served continuously in such position for a period of less than six (6) months immediately prior to the effective date of this article shall be regarded as holding probationary appointment only and may be certified by the department head in the same manner when he/she has satisfactorily completed a six (6) month probationary period in such position from the date of the original appointment thereto and shall thereafter be subject in all respects to the provisions of this article and the Merit System Rules and Regulations.

Section 10.8.5 APPROPRIATION OF FUNDS
Section 1: The City Commission shall appropriate such funds to carry out the provisions of this article as they deem necessary.

Section 2: Any portion of Appendix "C", of the City Code of Ordinances, that conflict with this Merit System are hereby rescinded.

Section 3: That there is and have been copies of the said "Merit System Rules and Regulations" which is adopted by this Ordinance by reference, presently on file in the Office of the City Manager of the City of Anycity.

Section 4: It is hereby declared the intent of this Ordinance is that the sections, paragraphs, sentences, clauses and phrases of this Ordinance are severable and if any phrase, clause, sentence, paragraph, or section of this ordinance shall be declared unconstitutional or invalid by the valid Judge or Decree of a Court of competent jurisdiction, such unconstitutionality or invalidity shall not affect any of the remaining phrases, clauses, sentences, paragraphs or sections of this Ordinance. Any section of the Municipal Code of the City of Anycity, not specifically amended, modified or repealed herein, shall remain in full force.

Section 5: This Ordinance shall take effect immediately upon passage by the City Commission.

Section 6: Permission to Codify this Ordinance in the Anycity Code of Ordinances is hereby granted.

APPENDIX D

SAMPLE
EMERGENCY/DISASTER PLAN

This document can serve as a basis for your city's emergency and disaster policies. I drafted this document while working for a city. This concept should be discussed with the City Council/Commission; perhaps it can be adopted administratively, i.e. without an ordinance. Check your state laws. The mayor is a key player is emergency and disaster management, so it is paramount for the city manager and the mayor to work closely on this subject particularly.

At the end of this plan there is an appendix identified as 'C', detailing emergency directives to city employees and their families.

TABLE OF CONTENTS

TABLE OF CONTENTS (continued)

Although some sections are not included in total in this sample,
the topic areas were left for your reference.

Emergency/Disaster Plan
for the City of Anycity

I. PURPOSE

The Anycity City Board of Commissioners firmly believe it is the primary duty of this City Government to provide adequate and necessary services for the health, safety, and general welfare of all our Citizens.

The Board of Commissioners have, therefore, directed the City Manager and his staff to formulate the attached general plan for the management of the City in the event of any disaster or other form of emergency. As in any large scale plan, it is absolutely imperative that all of the citizens cooperate with official City employees to the fullest extent they are able if in fact they should ever be asked to do something for the good of the City. Any 'rights or wrongs' can be addressed after the crisis has passed.

This document is specifically designed to set forth pre-agreed upon areas of responsibility in order to maximize the preservation of life and property in the event of an emergency. Any subsequent changes needed may be made at any time by administrative action of the City Manager or the City Board of Commissioners, but not in the midst of a crisis.

NOTE: This manual will be reproduced and maintained in each department. There will be a smaller-size, outline format, condensed copy made of this document that will be issued to each department for placement in their vehicles for ready reference in the event of an emergency or disaster.

II. AREAS OF RESPONSIBILITY

A. Mayor
The Mayor is empowered to declare an emergency in the City at anytime he/she deems it is appropriate. (You should make a reference citation here to the city charter, city ordinance, and/or state statute that gives the mayor this authority.)
In the event such an emergency is declared, "the Mayor shall become the head of the government and shall exercise those powers delegated to him" under the Anystate State Statutes, and the City Charter. In the absence or disability of the Mayor, the City Board of Commissioners may designate one of their fellow Commissioners as the Mayor for discharging of these duties, by Ordinance or Resolution.
In order to most efficiently and effectively manage the resources of the City in time of crisis, the Mayor shall continue to utilize the City Manager as the Chief Operations Officer for the City. The City Manager shall, however, be directly and singularly responsible to the Mayor until the crisis has subsided. Aside from the Mayor's duties as "head" of the City in time of an emergency, the Mayor will also coordinate the decisions of City policy that may be required from the Board of Commissioners. The Mayor will also have the final decision on all press releases made by the City, and shall issue same through the assistance of the City Clerk and her/his staff.
The Mayor will also coordinate and direct the support required by the City Manager and staff, from the City Consulting Engineer, as well as the City Attorney. The Mayor's place of duty, in time of an emergency, is the Anycity City Hall. In the event that structure is not serviceable, the Mayor will work out of Fire Station #2 (or some other specified location in your city).

B. Commissioners
The Commissioners are encouraged to report to the City Hall, or in the alternative Fire Station #2, in the event of an emergency. The primary function of the Commissioners will be to assist the Mayor. The Commissioners will not go to the scene of any emergency, unless their presence there is specifically requested. The Commissioners can

best serve the City by continuing to make policy decisions, as needed, and assisting the City in the 'big picture' at the Operations Center.

C. City Manager

The City Manager will serve as the Chief Operations Officer of the City in time of emergency, just as he/she routinely does. The major difference is that the City Manager is working only for the Mayor in time of an emergency and not for the Board of Commissioners as a whole. This is designed to make the management of the City more streamlined in the event of an emergency. The Manager is to use his technical expertise, and that of his staff, to 'bring the City through' an emergency with as little damage to property as possible, taking care to protect the lives of the Citizens at all costs. If/when the Manager realizes that the scope of the emergency is more broad than can be handled by the City employees/staff, he shall immediately advise the Mayor and make appropriate recommendations to the Mayor as to where the City should seek assistance Once the Mayor has made a decision, the Manager shall do everything within his power to insure that the decision is administered as quickly and efficiently as possible.

D. City Consulting Engineer

The City Consulting Engineer is employed by the City Board of Commissioners. Consequently, in time of emergency, the Consulting Engineer works directly for the Mayor. In the event an emergency does occur within the City, the City Clerk will make every effort to contact the City Engineer and advise him, or his representative, that the Mayor has declared an emergency in the City and that the Engineer's presence in the City is requested as soon as is possible. The Engineer may elect to send a qualified representative from his firm if it is not feasible for the Engineer to come himself. The City Engineer shall work closely with the Mayor to advise him on any and all matter(s) the Mayor feels is/are appropriate.

E. City Attorney

The City Attorney is employed by the City Board of Commissioners. Consequently, in time of emergency, the City Attorney works directly for the Mayor. In the event an emergency does occur within the City, the City Clerk will make every effort to contact the City Attorney and advise him that his presence in the City is requested as soon as is possible. The Attorney may elect to send a qualified representative from his firm if it is not feasible for the Attorney to come himself.

The City Attorney shall work closely with the Mayor to advise him on any and all matter(s) that the Mayor feels is/are appropriate.

F. Finance Director

The Finance Director shall continue to work directly for the City Manager. In the absence of the City Manager, the Finance Director shall become the Chief Operations Officer for the City In Accordance with the Memorandum for the Record (IAW MFR). In such an event, the Finance Director may delegate duties to subordinate personnel that he/she feels are most competent to handle the individual jobs.

Prior to any such Emergency ever occurring or being declared, the Finance Director shall work closely with the Director of Emergency Operations to ensure that charge accounts are set up at the appropriate retail establishments, that stores of food and supplies are cached in the appropriate Emergency Shelters, to include the three Emergency Operations Centers, as well as the Field Operations Center Command Post; and that all such caches are properly secured and regularly inventoried to ensure their presence when required. The Finance Director shall ensure that contacts are made with the local chapter of the American Red Cross, the local County Civil Defense and Emergency Management Office, and the Anystate Emergency Management Agency to seek guidance, financial assistance, and logistical support, when appropriate and available.

The Finance Director will co-locate with the City Clerk in the City Hall, or in the alternative Fire Station #2, and make appropriate directions to the City Clerk regarding use of the City's administrative support staff. The Finance Director will also assist the Mayor in formulating any documentation that may be required, in the event the Mayor deems it necessary to petition Anycity's state, or the federal government for financial disaster assistance.

G. General government (and all departments not listed separately)
All City employees are required to work for the good of the City in the event of an emergency. Such problems as overtime, compensatory time, vacation, etc. will be equitably settled after the emergency and clean-up has been completed.
In the event of an emergency, or possible or suspected emergency, all City employees will be contacted by the most expeditious means. This may be the "telephone tree" in Section IV (Employee List - not included in this Appendix) of this document, or it may be by a 'net' call on the radio, etc.
If an employee is not called, or has not been called yet, but the employee believes his/her presence may be needed for the good of the City, the employee is hereby directed to telephone City Hall, or come by City Hall personally, to inquire if he/she is needed. In the event there is no answer, the employee may assume that his/her presence is not required.
If, by act of God, the emergency/disaster is severe enough that City Hall is no longer standing, the employee will immediately report to Fire Station #2, at [cite street address], for instructions on where he/she can help.
ALL CITY EMPLOYEES shall take their families to either Fire Station #1, or #2 to ensure their safety. (see Appendix C)
Employees will work under their normal supervisor's direction unless that supervisor directs the employee to work for another supervisor. If the normal department supervisor is not present, the assistant supervisor will take charge of his/her department's personnel. If the assistant supervisor is not present, the most senior employee, by date of service, will take charge of that department's personnel. Department supervisors are charged with insuring their employees are intimately familiar with the chain of command to be followed in the event of an emergency.
ALL EMPLOYEES MUST WORK TOGETHER FOR THE ULTIMATE GOOD OF THE CITY in time of emergency. Any problems that arise during such an event will be addressed only after the disaster and the clean up have been completed.

H. Police Department
Read the comments under General Government (above), with specific directions as follows:

1.   The shift sergeant and the zone officer will identify the emergency or disaster, and notify :
   a.   Police backup and ambulance (state how many are required)
   b.   Fire Department
   c.   S.W.A.T. Team
   d.   Police Captain
   e.   Chief of Police
   f.   City Manager

2. The sergeant will then set-up a temporary perimeter designed to let in all emergency personnel only.

3. The Chief of Police will then decide if it is appropriate for the Police Department to retain control of the site, or whether it should be turned over to the Fire Department.

4. The Crime Scene Unit vehicle will be dispatched to the scene to serve as the Field Command Post Operations Center, if deemed appropriate by either the Chief of Police or the Fire Chief.

5. An Incident Commander will be appointed by the controlling agency (either Police or Fire Department).

The aforementioned perimeter will be established for crowd control, evacuation, traffic control, etc. The perimeter will be established taking into consideration the optimum safety distance feasible under the circumstances at the site.
Control of the perimeter will be assumed by the SWAT Team upon their arrival at the scene.
The SWAT Team, and any other requirements for Police Officer manpower, may be augmented by off-duty and reserve officers.

6. Dispatch Section: If there is only one dispatcher on duty in the event of such an emergency, he/she will call in two (2) additional dispatchers automatically and immediately. If there are are two on shift when such an even occurs, a third dispatcher will be called in to assist. If it appears the crisis is going to continue past the normal shift, all dispatchers will be put 'on-call', and the Captain will ensure that there are at least three dispatchers working at any given time.
The room immediately adjacent to the Dispatch Room (identify and specify the name of this room in your city) will serve as the Primary Emergency Operations Center. The Dispatcher's first priority is to the personnel on the scene of the incident. Second priority, however, is to the management personnel that will be working in the E.O.C., providing them with necessary information and issuing directives/messages from the E.O.C. to the Incident Commander and/or his representatives.

7. General Information: In the event of an emergency, declaration of same will come from the Mayor through the Chief of Police. The personnel that are on shift at the time the emergency is declared will remain on shift until relieved by the Chief of Police.
It is very likely that if such an event is imminent, all Police Officers, as well as other City employees, will be placed on stand-by, preparing themselves to respond when requested and at short notice.

If the situation warrants it, there will be three (3) teams assigned to special details:

TEAM I. Will handle strictly security control (buildings, monitoring motels, etc.).

TEAM II. Will concentrate on assisting in evacuation of low-lying areas by utilizing 4-Wheel Drive (4WD) vehicles or similar vehicles that can operate in high water and muddy terrain. It is conceivable that this team may work closely with the Fire Department if their boat would be useful in evacuation.

TEAM III. Will work traffic control, particularly the intersections with electronic traffic signals that may go out of service in an emergency. This Team and the current duty shift will have the Reserve Officers assigned to them.

The Lieutenant and the Captain will serve in the areas that the Chief deems most appropriate at any given moment.

When appropriate, the on-duty shift will ensure that the business owners of the City have their windows taped, their doors locked, etc. After the business owner leaves his store/office, he will call the Dispatch Section and advise them if he decides to reenter the structure. This will assist the duty shift in verifying the security of the businesses.

Hurricane Procedures or other long term emergencies:

In the event of any long term emergency or disaster, the following lists and team assignments for the Police Department. This 'break-out' may be changed according to the time of "Call out", with reference to who is working.

Duty Shift SGT and three patrolling officers

Team I: SGT and three patrolling officers

Team II: SGT and three patrolling officers

Team III: CPL and two patrol officers

Stand-by: remaining officers

Dispatch Team I:
1. One dispatcher monitoring 911 calls.
2. One dispatcher monitoring the regular Police Department phone calls.
3. One dispatcher monitoring the Police Department frequency.
4. One dispatcher monitoring the Fire Department frequency.
5. One dispatcher monitoring the Public Works frequency.

DISPATCH TEAM II:
Two dispatchers who will relieve any of the others.

I. Fire Department
Read the comments under General Government and the Police Department with specific directions as follows:

Upon arrival at an incident scene, the shift leader will identify the nature of the emergency and give Anycity Dispatch a status report. The shift leader will assume the duties and responsibilities of the Incident Commander until and unless another individual is appointed. In the event the disaster/emergency is fire related, the ranking fire authority on the scene will be the incident commander.
NOTE: Incident Commanders can only be designated by the City Manager, the Fire Chief, or the Chief of Police. No other individual has that authority. If no successor is appointed, the shift leader that is first on the scene will remain in this capacity until the incident is over. The Incident Commander will notify Medcom of a medical emergency/disaster, via Medcom radio channel, local Ambulance Service, or telephone. The Incident Commander will assign the tasks that need to be performed to units and personnel as they arrive on the scene.

Anycity Dispatch will notify corresponding agencies, if necessary, at the directive of the E.O.C. personnel. The Incident Commander will advise the E.O.C. personnel at the earliest possible moment it appears that the emergency/disaster at hand is too large to be handled by City personnel alone.

In time of a declared emergency, news/press releases will only be made by the City Clerk, at the direction of the Mayor, or City Manager.

If an emergency/disaster appears imminent, such as a hurricane, etc., the call for manpower will be given 24 hours in advance, or as early as is practical under the given circumstances. If such a 'warning order' is given, all personnel will be considered to be on stand-by, aside from the normal duty shift, and ready to respond on short notice.

If an employee reports for duty when not on regular shift, he/she will be assigned duties by the ranking officer. All personnel will report, when called, to Station #1, unless that station is no longer a standing structure when you report. You will only report to Station #2 if Station #1 no longer exists.

The Chief may divide the available manpower into three (3) Teams.

TEAM I. Will be assigned to Station #1.

TEAM II. Will be assigned to Station #2.

TEAM III. Will be assigned to support services, as needed; i.e. shelters, evacuation, dispatch, incident scenes, etc.

Each team will have a commanding officer, designated by the Fire Chief, to whom they report and take directives The Fire Department will coordinate with E.M.S., the Red Cross, local County Civil Defense, and the State EMS Office, etc.

The Fire Chief will coordinate with the Dispatch Section and all other City departments.

J. Water Department
Read comments under General Government with specific directions as follows:

In general, the Water Department will have a Water Technician on call at all times. In the event the Technician can not handle the problem, he will automatically contact the Water Superintendent. The Superintendent may call out any and all Water Department personnel, if he deems it appropriate for the good of the City, especially in the event of an emergency.

In the event of a declared emergency, the Water Superintendent will ensure that all of the City's fresh water wells are operational and not contaminated. He will constantly monitor these facilities to ensure this is the way they remain. At any time a well becomes contaminated, or questionable, the Superintendent will immediately direct that well to be shut down. As soon as is practical thereafter, the Superintendent will inform the City Manager and make appropriate recommendations to him as to what course of action the City should pursue.

The Water Superintendent will make prior arrangements to have fuel delivered to the well-site generators on a routine basis, in time of emergency, such that the City can continue to provide services to the Citizens.

In the event that all water facilities are properly functioning during a declared emergency, the Superintendent will leave one man at each of the wells and place himself and all other personnel at the disposal of the Fire Chief, until and unless there is a problem in the Water Department requiring his attention.

The Water Department will ensure that they have powdered HTH (chlorine) on hand at all times for emergency use.

K. Street Department
Read comments under General Government section with specific directions as follows:

The Street Superintendent's primary function is to ensure that the maximum number of roadways remain passable/useable at all times, including removal of fallen trees, emergency repairs to sink holes, attention to drainage problems, etc.

The Street Superintendent will place his personnel at the disposal of the Chief of Police to assist in traffic control, etc., unless and until some street or drainage problem requires his attention elsewhere. The Street Superintendent will also maintain close contact with the Water Superintendent, in the event street work has to be done as a part of a water repair.

Street Department personnel will keep appropriate hand tools on their trucks, when they can be secured, to avoid having to make several runs to a shop area.

L. Sanitation Department
Read comments under the General Government Section with specific directions as follows:

The Sanitation Supervisor will place his men at the disposal of the E.O.C. personnel to assist in as many manpower requirements as is feasible.

After any disaster/emergency, the Sanitation Supervisor will be the primary individual responsible for cleanup and disposal of waste materials generated by the disaster. The Sanitation Supervisor will coordinate closely with the senior Fire Department personnel to ensure the proper handling and disposal of all such wastes.

M. Shop Department
The Shop Superintendent will ensure the mechanical availability of the maximum number of City vehicles at all times, but most especially during an emergency or disaster.

During a declared emergency, the Shop Department building will be manned on a 24-hour basis. In the event that building is destroyed, the Shop Superintendent will relocate his operation to an appropriate location you specify in your city.

As part of the duties of the Shop Department personnel, they will coordinate with ALL DEPARTMENTS to ensure that all vehicles are refueled at least once a day throughout an emergency, and clean up the same.

The City wrecker is designed to handle City vehicles, only. In time of emergency, however, shop personnel may be required to use the wrecker to assist in removing trees from roadways, houses, etc., as well as moving other heavy structures. Regardless of the wrecker's functions, however, the Shop Superintendent will ensure that the shop building remains manned with competent personnel at all times.

The Shop Superintendent also has the duty of keeping the E.O.C.s in good repair, i.e. plywood covering windows, doors operational, etc.

N. Emergency/Disaster Preparedness Coordinator
This Coordinator position is primarily a planning and preparation position. The person filling same, specify incumbent in your city, may not have any Coordinator duties in time of emergency/disaster, depending upon the requirements of his primary, day-to-day job.

0. City Clerk
The City Clerk will serve as a coordinator and conduit for directives to all departments from the City Manager and the Emergency Operations Center. Additionally, the City Clerk will work closely with the Mayor to coordinate and clear all official press releases from the City. Lastly, the City Clerk will ensure that her/his administrative staff is operating in full support of the Finance Director and the City in general.

III. EMERGENCY OPERATIONS CENTERS

The Emergency Operations Center will be manned by the City Manager, the Chief of Police and the Fire Chief. If available, the Director of Emergency Disaster Preparedness may also locate in the E.O.C., although he may be dispatched to the Field Command Post Operations Center, if the incident dictates.

The Primary E.O.C. is the [state location in your city]. It is the responsibility of the Director of Emergency Preparedness to have the E.O.C.s (all [specify number] of them) properly posted with maps and other pertinent information.

In the event the Primary E.O.C. is not useable, but [specify other location, such as City Hall, in your city] is, the City Manager's Office will serve as the Backup E.O.C.. If E.O.C. #2 is not useable, the [specify location in your city] will serve as the Secondary E.O.C..

It is most desirable that the Dispatch Section be collocated with the E.O.C. whenever possible. The Chief of Police will have the responsibility of insuring the Dispatch Section can continue to operate if the Police Station becomes unusable. That capability should already exist in City Hall [or some other appropriate location in your city].

Personnel/employees reporting for work assignments shall report to the City Clerk, in City Hall, or Fire Station #2, and not directly to the City Manager at the E.O.C.. [Adapt this to the situation in your city.]

In the event that the three (3) individuals who operate the E.O.C. were to die, or be otherwise incapacitated during the disaster/emergency, the Finance Director, the Police Captain, and the Fire Captain would take over those duties at one of the alternate E.O.C. sites.

IV. EMPLOYEE LIST
(not included in this Appendix)

V. EQUIPMENT LIST - CITY OWNED
(not included in this Appendix)

CITY STATIONERY

VI. A.   MEMORANDUM FOR THE RECORD

TO: All Department Supervisors
FROM: City Manager Ken Griffin
SUBJECT: Administrative Directive Concerning Purchases/Rentals during Declared State of Emergency

In the event that the Mayor of the City of Anycity has declared a State of Emergency within the City, Department Supervisors are hereby authorized to make such purchases/rentals as they deem necessary to do the job as.signed to them and their department during the State of Emergency.

Such purchases/rentals shall be confined to those items that we do not own in-house, or items that can not be borrowed from sister agencies, etc. If you need an item to accomplish the mission assigned, then get it.

Payment for such purchases/rentals will be coordinated by the Supervisor through the Finance Director.

Whenever possible, the Supervisor should advise the City Manager, or in his absence the Finance Director that the purchase/rental is being made. This is not an approval that need be secured prior to making the rental/ purchase, but rather an information loop that should be made.

This MFR shall be filed in your Emergency Disaster Plan under Section V. Equipment List, City-owned.

VI. B. EQUIPMENT LIST - Private Sector

[You will need to modify the specific details cited herein to conform with the situation in your city.]

A. Refer to the local County listing of prearranged private sector vehicles and equipment. If unavailable, advise Med-Com [or the appropriate hospital coordination agency in Anycity] that you need outside assistance.

B. For assistance from the U.S. Naval Training Base, call: Chief Davis - xxx-xxxx or Ass't Chief Roberts - xxx-xxxx, or other military base near Anycity.
This includes requests for equipment, as well as additional manpower.

C. Additional Equipment sources are also listed in the DER Emergency Contingency Plan; see Appendix C to this document.

VII. EMERGENCY SHELTERS

[You will need to modify the specific details cited herein to conform with the situation in your city.]

A. Approved shelters are manned and coordinated through the American Red Cross. In order to gain access, have Med-Com contact the Red Cross.

1. Approved Shelters
   a. xxx High School
   b. xxx Junior High School
   c. xxx Elementary School

B. The City will pursue getting other structures approved and recognized by the Red Cross. If for any reason the above cited shelters are unavailable, the following procedures shall be followed, to the best ability of the City personnel and availability of the structures and personnel.

1. For the well being of all concerned, every shelter occupied shall have a Police Officer and an Emergency Medical Technician present and in command of the Shelter. These may be Reserve City employees, or qualified volunteers (for instance a Registered Nurse may volunteer and serve in the EMT's stead).

2. Whenever possible, Shelters will be stocked with food and supplies prior to being occupied.

Unapproved Shelters (as of July 1985)
   a. xxxx Community Center
   b. xxxx Recreation/Youth Center
   Area churches
NOTE: This list will be expanded with specifically identified churches, volunteers and/or employees that have preagreed to serve as Shelter Commanders, etc. by Anycity Emergency/Disaster Preparedness Coordinator.

VIII. EMERGENCY PHONE NUMBERS

Agencies to be notified for assistance. Notify local emergency services first.

1. Mutual Aid surrounding Fire Departments.
2. Mutual Aid Police, Sheriffs, Highway Patrol
3. E.M.S. (Local Hospitals, Ambulance Services)
4. Heavy Equipment (Preplanned and available)
5. Any agency you may deem necessary to assist you.

Additional Agencies
(Plane Crash - All agencies should be notified)

1. Medical Examiner, Temporary Morgue   ___-_____
2. Federal Bureau of Investigation   ___-_____
3. Treasury Department (Alcohol, Tobacco, and Fire
Arms Division)   ___-_____
4. Secret Service   ___-_____
5. U S. Postal Service   ___-_____
6. National Transportation Safety Board   ___-_____
7. F.A.A. (Federal Aviation Authorities)   ___-_____
8. I.F. Military Plane, Military Authorities   ___-_____
9. Department of Emergency Mgmt. 24 hrs/day   ___-_____

IX. HANDLING OF WASTES AND HAZARDOUS CHEMICALS

(NOTE:) [Notify appropriate state/regional agency.] (They call EPA etc.; in case of emergency they notify appropriate agencies ref: Hazardous Waste , Toxic Materials etc.) If you cannot reach the appropriate agency, call the numbers listed below.

WASTE DISPOSAL SITES
xxxx

APPROVED HAZARDOUS WASTE SITES
xxx

X. RADIO FREQUENCY LIST
(not included in this Appendix)

APPENDIX A
(not included in this Appendix)

APPENDIX B
(not included in this Appendix)

APPENDIX C
to the Emergency/Disaster Plan:

Directions/Information for Families of Employees

In the event of any Emergency or Disaster, City employees are invited and encouraged to bring their family members (immediate family only) to either of the City Fire Stations or appropriate location(s) as identified by Anycity's government. This will enable the employee to better serve the Citizens of Anycity, by having piece of mind knowing that their loved ones are safe.

If by chance, one of your family members wishes to help in the disaster (limited to people over 15 years of age), this is fine. Be sure younger members of the family are entrusted to someone else's care, specifically, not just dropped off at the Fire Station unsupervised.

Prior to leaving your home, you should secure your home properly to limit the effect of damaging winds. Board up or tape all exposed glass doors or windows if the pending emergency/disaster is a hurricane or tornado. Remove any and all articles from outside your home that might be carried away by high winds: i.e. lawn chairs, tables, bikes, mowers, grills, etc.

Make sure you have at least a flashlight and a radio with fresh batteries. Perhaps an extra set of batteries would be wise to have on hand.

Stock up on canned goods and nonperishables that require little preparation. If you elect to come to one of the Fire Stations, bring some of the food with you when you come. This is not a requirement but merely a request for the good of everyone concerned.

Water supplies will be CRITICAL:
        - use water for drinking purposes, ONLY.
        - if you know a storm is imminent, store as much water as possible in containers, and sinks and bathtubs.

If you are coming to a shelter, BRING the following with you:
- blankets and bedding for your entire family.
- flashlights
- any required medications
- change of clothing for each member of the family

DO NOT BRING PETS! As much as we know how an animal can become a real member of the family, we just can not have pets in an emergency shelter. You will have to leave them at home, preferably in an inside room (one with no external walls) and pray for the best.

Do not wait until the last minute to decide to leave your home and come to the shelter. You may find yourself stranded between both and exposed to the elements. It's better to have come to the shelter unnecessarily than to wish that you had; an ounce of prevention is worth a pound of cure.

WARNING
IF YOU STAY HOME, DO NOT ATTEMPT TO LEAVE AFTER THE STORM HAS BEGUN. HURRICANE FORCE WINDS CAN KILL!

Immediately following a disaster and many emergencies, many roads will be blocked, possibly with man-made barricades, or possibly with fallen trees and other debris as well as power lines, which can kill. Please cooperate with us, and each other, until all hazards have been removed.

APPENDIX E

SAMPLE CITY MANAGER
EMPLOYMENT CONTRACTS

These documents may help the new city manager in his/her dealings with prospective employers.

I. SAMPLE CONTRACT A

THE STATE OF _____
COUNTY OF _____

MEMORANDUM OF AGREEMENT

Effective July 1, 19 ~, as a condition of employment with the CITY OF _____ in consideration therefor and in consideration of the monthly payment to me by the CITY OF _____ of the following:

1. An amount equal to twelve percent (12%) of my salary, monthly, or an amount, monthly, equal to the monthly cost of my ICMA Retirement Fund Program, whichever is higher, to be paid to a portable retirement plan (s) at manager's direction;

I hereby agree to withdraw all monies in my (name) Municipal Retirement System account upon my termination of employment and waive any and all claim to said account and to the CITY OF _____ Retirement Income Plan account.

The above Agreement is further made in consideration of the following payment to me by the CITY OF _____

a. Annual salary of _____ Dollars as City Manager of the CITY OF _____

b. Severance pay of six (6) months' salary in the event of termination of employment by the CITY OF _____

c. A full-size leased automobile comparable to a Ford Crown Victoria, every two (2) years, for personal and City business use, including gas, oil, and maintenance. Liability insurance shall be furnished under CITY OF _____and/or lessor's policies covering business and personal use of [name of City Manager] and dependents.

d. Vacation of eighteen (18) days per employment year.

e. Sick leave credit of twenty-four (24) days, with regular employee accrual and maximum.

f. All City business-related expenses justified by itemized receipts.

g. All travel and per diem expenses associated with conferences and professional meetings related to City business and/or professional training.

h. Health insurance according to CITY OF _____ normal coverage.

i. Life insurance by the CITY OF _____ in the amount of $100,000.00.

j. Physical examination annually thru health insurance plan.

This contract is subject to renegotiation after one year, July 1, 19___.

254

All Agreements by me shall be binding upon my heirs, executors, administrators, estates, legal representatives, agents and assigns.

Dated:
ACCEPTED BY AND FOR THE CITY OF _____

_____
Mayor

Dated:

ATTEST:

_____

APPROVED AS TO FORM:

_____
City Attorney

II. SAMPLE CONTRACT B

STATE OF _____
COUNTY OF _____
MEMORANDUM OF AGREEMENT

Effective October 1, 19 ~ as a condition of employment with the CITY OF _____, in consideration therefor and in consideration of the monthly payment to me by the CITY OF _____ of the following:

1. An amount equal to twelve percent (12%) of my salary monthly, or an amount, monthly, equal to the monthly cost of my ICMA Retirement Fund Program, whichever is higher to be paid to a portable retirement plan(s) at the Manager's direction; and

I hereby agree to withdraw all monies in my_____ Municipal Retirement System account upon my termination of employment and waive any and all claim to said account and to the CITY OF_____ Supplemental Retirement Income Plan (SRIP) account.

I further agree, in order to secure this Agreement by me and as a condition of employment, that any amounts owed by me pursuant hereto and not paid within sixty (60) days, may be deducted from any pay and benefits due me by the CITY OF _____ which pay and benefits may be withheld until satisfaction of these obligations. The balance, if any, owed shall remain as an obligation against me. The terms of this Agreement are contractual and not a mere recital.

The above agreement is further made in consideration of the following payment to me by the CITY OF _____

a. Annual salary of _____ Dollars and as City Manager of the City of _____.

b. Severance Pay of six (6) months' salary in the event of termination of employment by the CITY OF _____

c. Full-size leased automobile comparable to a Ford Crown Victoria, every two (2) years, for personal and City business use, including gas, oil, and maintenance. Liability insurance shall be furnished under CITY OF _____ and/or lessor's policies covering business and personal use of the Manager and his/her dependants.

d. Vacation of eighteen (18) days per employment year.

e. Sick leave credit of thirty (30) days, with regular employee accrual and maximum.

f. All City business related expenses justified by itemized receipts.

g. All travel and per diem expenses associated with conferences and professional meetings related to City business and/or professional training.

h. Membership in the _____ City [athletic] Club.

i. Membership in the University of _____ Club or _____ Racquet Club, at the City's option.

j. Long-term disability plan, at the Manager's option, to be specified and agreed to by the CITY OF _____

k. Health insurance according to CITY OF _____ normal coverage, with coverage for the Manager's dependents included.

1. Life insurance according to CITY OF _____ normal coverage.

m. Physical examination annually.

n. Moving expenses from _____ , to _____

o. One (1) round trip air fare for two (2) from [former city] to [current city].

p. Purchase of the Manager's present home (in previous city, if relocating) at a price based on the average of two (2) appraisals accepted by the CITY OF _____

All agreements by me shall be binding upon my heirs, executors, administrators, estates, legal representatives, agents and assigns.

APPROVED AS TO FORM:

    City Attorney _____
Dated _____
ACCEPTED BY AND FOR THE CITY OF _____
                        Mayor _____
Dated _____

ATTEST
_____

APPENDIX F

SAMPLE ORGANIZATIONAL WIRE DIAGRAM

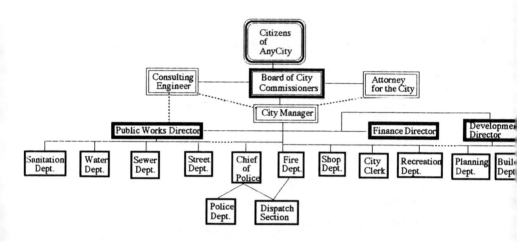

APPENDIX G

SAMPLE CURB CUT
ENGINEERING DETAILS

These details provide specifications for installing a smooth transitioning driveway curb cut into a rolling curb section. Without this type of curb cut, the drainage will not function properly. Some citizens may pour concrete or asphalt into the rolling curb, in order to lessen the bumpiness of the entrance to their driveway. Such material only hinders drainage. A curb cut is the only way to secure a smooth transition into the driveway, and simulataneously keep the curb-gutter drainage flowing properly.

258

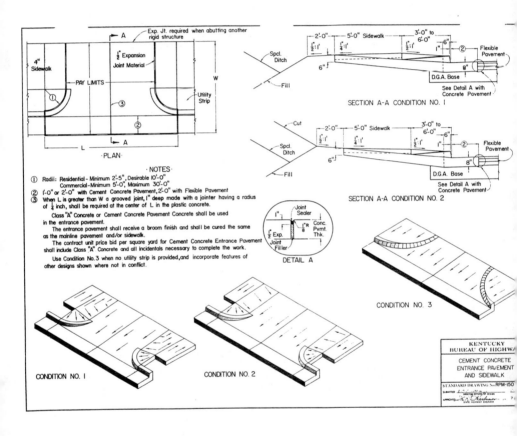

·PLAN·

A — Exp. Jt. required when abutting another rigid structure

4" Sidewalk

$\frac{1}{2}$" Expansion Joint Material

PAY LIMITS

W

Utility Strip

L — A

SECTION A-A CONDITION NO. 1

Spcl. Ditch

Fill

2'-0" — 5'-0" Sidewalk — 3'-0" to 6'-0"

$\frac{1}{2}$":1' $\frac{1}{4}$":1' $\frac{1}{2}$":1' 1"

6"

Flexible Pavement

8"

D.G.A. Base

See Detail A with Concrete Pavement

SECTION A-A CONDITION NO. 2

Cut

Spcl. Ditch

Fill

2'-0" — 5'-0" Sidewalk — 3'-0" to 6'-0"

$\frac{1}{2}$":1' $\frac{1}{4}$":1' 6" $\frac{1}{2}$":1' 1"

6"

Flexible Pavement

8"

D.G.A. Base

See Detail A with Concrete Pavement

· NOTES ·

① Radii: Residential - Minimum 2'-5", Desirable 10'-0"
   Commercial - Minimum 5'-0", Maximum 30'-0"

② 1'-0" or 2'-0" with Cement Concrete Pavement, 2'-0" with Flexible Pavement

③ When L is greater than W a grooved joint, 1" deep made with a jointer having a radius of $\frac{1}{4}$ inch, shall be required at the center of L in the plastic concrete.

Class "A" Concrete or Cement Concrete Pavement Concrete shall be used in the entrance pavement.

The entrance pavement shall receive a broom finish and shall be cured the same as the mainline pavement and/or sidewalk.

The contract unit price bid per square yard for Cement Concrete Entrance Pavement shall include Class "A" Concrete and all incidentals necessary to complete the work.

Use Condition No. 3 when no utility strip is provided, and incorporate features of other designs shown where not in conflict.

DETAIL A

Joint Sealer

1"

$\frac{1}{8}$" R

Conc. Pvmt. Thk.

$\frac{1}{2}$" Exp. Joint Filler

CONDITION NO. 3

CONDITION NO. 1

CONDITION NO. 2

KENTUCKY BUREAU OF HIGHWAYS

CEMENT CONCRETE ENTRANCE PAVEMENT AND SIDEWALK

STANDARD DRAWING No. RPM-150

SUBMITTED
DIRECTOR DIVISION OF DESIGN

APPROVED
STATE HIGHWAY ENGINEER

259

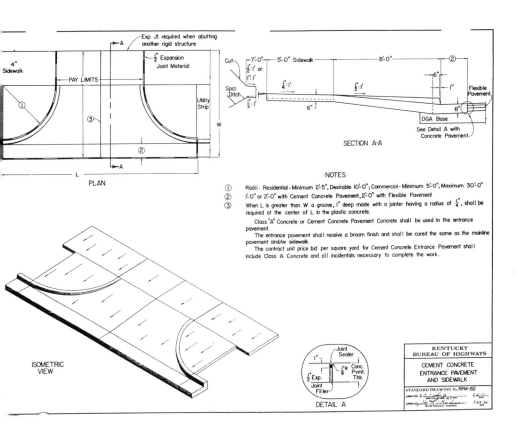

PLAN

Exp. Jt. required when abutting another rigid structure

4" Sidewalk

PAY LIMITS

$\frac{1}{2}$" Expansion Joint Material

Utility Strip

W

L

A

SECTION A-A

7'-0"   5'-0" Sidewalk   8'-0"

Cut

Spcl. Ditch

$\frac{1}{4}$:1'

$\frac{1}{2}$:1'

6"

6"

1"

8"

Flexible Pavement

DGA Base

See Detail A with Concrete Pavement

·NOTES·

① Radii: Residential - Minimum 2'-5", Desirable 10'-0"; Commercial - Minimum 5'-0", Maximum 30'-0"

② 1'-0" or 2'-0" with Cement Concrete Pavement, 2'-0" with Flexible Pavement

③ When L is greater than W a groove, 1" deep made with a jointer having a radius of $\frac{1}{4}$", shall be required at the center of L in the plastic concrete.

Class "A" Concrete or Cement Concrete Pavement Concrete shall be used in the entrance pavement.

The entrance pavement shall receive a broom finish and shall be cured the same as the mainline pavement and/or sidewalk.

The contract unit price bid per square yard for Cement Concrete Entrance Pavement shall include Class A Concrete and all incidentals necessary to complete the work.

ISOMETRIC VIEW

Joint Sealer

1"

$\frac{1}{8}$"R

Conc. Pvmt. Thk.

$\frac{1}{2}$" Exp. Joint Filler

DETAIL A

KENTUCKY
BUREAU OF HIGHWAYS

CEMENT CONCRETE
ENTRANCE PAVEMENT
AND SIDEWALK

STANDARD DRAWING No. RPM-152

APPENDIX H

SAMPLE UTILITY CUT
ENGINEERING DETAILS

These details provide specifications for the asphalt reparation of streets after utility companies have inserted a pipe or other line under the publicly dedicated street. If these specifications are not followed, the portion of the asphalt over the utility cut will 'float' with the weather's temperature variations. The result is a depression in the street, which most citizens perceive as a bump. This bump can not be successfully repaired, only prevented. The solution is the adherence to these specifications at the time the initial utility cut is created.

These specifications are taken from the City of Louisville, Kentucky, as adopted by the City of Hurstbourne.

INSERT GRAPHIC

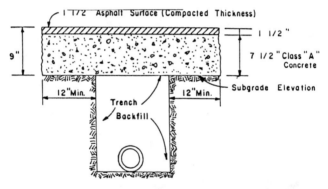

1. Trenches shall be excavated to a width not to exceed 12" on each side of the pipe diameter of 24" or less and not to exceed 15" on each side of the pipe for pipe diameters greater than 24". Trench walls shall be as nearly vertical as possible.

2. Backfill shall be dense graded aggregate or sand. Dense graded aggregate shall be placed in maximum 6" loose lifts and mechanically compacted. Sand may be compacted by placing in maximum 12" loose lifts and then flooded or jetted in place where satisfactory drainage is provided for free water.

3. Backfilling up to subgrade elevation shall be completed prior to excavation for the additional 12" of concrete on each side of the trench.

4. Permittee will be held responsible during the ensuing five years for proper backfilling and replacement of surface. During the five years period after the cut is made, any pavement settlement shall be immediately repaired in an approved manner at the expense of the permittee.

5. Concrete pavements shall be repaired in the same manner as described in this detail except that the thickness of concrete shall be the same as the surrounding pavement.

APPENDIX J

I.C.M.A. AND ITS STATE AFFILIATES
AND OTHER PROFESSIONAL ORGANIZATIONS

The International Headquarters of the International City Management Association may be contacted at:

ICMA
777 North Capitol Street, NE
Washington, DC 20002-4201
(202) 626-4600

The following list of addresses is published with permission of the International City Management Association, Washington, DC.

State Municipal Leagues

Alabama League of Municipalities, P 0 Box 1270, Montgomery 36102

Alaska Municipal League, 105 Municipal Way, Suite 301, Juneau 99801

League of Arizona Cities and Towns, 1820 West Washington Street Phoenix 85007

Arkansas Municipal League, P 0 Box 38, North Little Rock 72115

League of California Cities, 1400 K Street, Sacramento 95814

Colorado Municipal League 1500 Grant Street. Suite 200, Denver 80203

Connecticut Conference of Municipalities 956 Chapel Street, New Haven 06510

Delaware League of Local Governments, P 0 Box 484, Dover 19903

Florida League of Cities. P 0 Box 1757, Tallahassee 32302

Georgia Municipal Association, 34 Peachtree Street, Suite 2300, Atlanta 30303

Association of Idaho Cities, 3314 Grace Street, Boise 83703

Illinois Municipal League, P 0 Box 3387, 1220 South 7th Street, Springfield 62708

Indiana Association of Cities and Towns, 150 West Market Street, Room 600 Indianapolis 46204

League of Iowa Municipalities, Suite 100, 900 Des Moines Street, Des Moines 50309

League of Kansas Municipalities, 112 West 7th Street, Topeka 66603

Kentucky League of Cities, Suite 100, 2201 Regency Road, Lexington 40503
606 257-3285

Louisiana Municipal Association, P 0 Box 4327, Baton Rouge 70821
504 344-5001

Maine Municipal Association Local Government Center, Community Drive, Augusta 04330   207 623-8429

Maryland Municipal League, 76 Maryland Avenue, Annapolis 21401

Massachusetts Municipal Association, 60 Temple Place, Boston 02111

Michigan Municipal League P 0 Box 1487 Ann Arbor 48106

League of Minnesota Cities, 183 University Avenue East, Saint Paul 55101

Mississippi Municipal Association, 455 North Lamar, Jackson 39202

Missouri Municipal League. 1913 William Street, Jefferson City 65109

Montana League of Cities and Towns, 130 Neill Avenue Helena 59601

League of Nebraska Municipalities, 1335 L Street, Lincoln 68508

Nevada League of Cities, P 0 Box 2307, Carson City 89702

New Hampshire Municipal Association, P 0 Box 617, Concord 03302

New Jersey State League of Municipalities, 407 West State Street, Trenton 08618

New Mexico Municipal League. P 0 Box 846, Santa Fe 87504

New York Conference of Mayors, 219 Washington Avenue, Albany 12210

North Carolina League of Municipalities. P 0 Box 3069. Raleigh 27602   S

North Dakota League of Cities, P 0 Box 2235, Bismarck 58502

Ohio Municipal League. 40 South Third Street. 5th Floor Columbus 43215

Oklahoma Municipal League, 201 NE 23rd Street, Oklahoma City 73105

League of Oregon Cities, P 0 Box 928, Salem 97308

Pennsylvania League of Cities, 2608 North Third Street, Harrisburg 17110

Rhode Island League of Cities and Towns, 38 Transit Street. Providence 02903

Municipal Association of South Carolina, P 0 Box 11558. Columbia 29211

South Dakota Municipal League, 214 East Capitol Pierre 57501

Tennessee Municipal League, Room 317. 226 Capitol Boulevard. Nashville 37219

Texas Municipal League. 211 East 7th Street, Suite 1020. Austin 78701

Utah League of Cities and Towns, University Club Building. Suite 1240, 136 East South Temple, Salt Lake City 84111

Vermont League of Cities and Towns 52 State Street, Montpelier 05602

Virginia Municipal League, P 0 Box 12203, Richmond 23241

Association of Washington Cities, 1076 South East Franklin Street. Olympia 98501

West Virginia Municipal League, 1615 Washngton Street, East, Charleston 25311

League of Wisconsin Municipalities, 122 West Washington Avenue, Madison 53703

Wyoming Association of Municipalities, P 0 Box 2535. Cheyenne 82001

A related organization is the American Society for Public Administration.
ASPA
1120 G Street, NW
Washington, DC 20005
(202) 393-7878

Another related organization is the National League of Cities.
The National League of Cities
1301 Pennsylvania Avenue, NW
Washington, DC 20004
(202) 626-3180

APPENDIX K

PROFESSIONAL CODES
OF ETHICS

The ICMA Code of Ethics is published with the permission of the International City Management Association, Washington, D.C.

CODE OF ETHICS

The purpose of the International City Management Association is to increase the proficiency of city management, managers and other municipal administrators, and to strengthen the quality of urban government through professional management. To further these objectives certain ethical principles shall govern the conduct of every member of the International City Management Association Who shall:

1 Be dedicated to the concepts of effective and democratic local government by responsible elected officials and believe that professional general management is essential to the achievement of this objective.

2 Affirm the dignity and worth of the services rendered by government and maintain a constructive. creative. and practical attitude toward urban affairs and a deep sense of social responsibility as a trusted public servant.

3 Be dedicated to the highest ideals of honor and integrity in all public and personal relationships in order that the member may merit the respect and confidence of the elected officials, of other officials and employees, and of the public.

4 Recognize that the chief function of local government at all times is to serve the best interests of all of the people.

5 Submit policy proposals to elected officials, provide them with facts and advice on matters of policy as a basis for making decisions and setting community goals, and uphold and implement municipal policies adopted by elected officials.

6 Recognize that elected representatives of the people are entitled to the credit for the establishment of municipal policies; responsibility for policy execution rests with the members.

7 Refrain from participation in the election of the members of the employing legislative body, and from all partisan political activities which would impair performance as a professional administrator.

8 Make it a duty continually to improve the member's professional ability and to develop the competence of associates in the use of management techniques.

9 Keep the community informed on municipal affairs; encourage communication between the citizens and all municipal officers; emphasize friendly and courteous service to the public; and seek to improve the quality and image of public service.

10 Resist any encroachment on professional responsibilities, believing the member should be free to carry out official policies without interference, and handle each problem without discrimination on the basis of principle and justice.

11 Handle all matters of personnel on the basis of merit so that fairness and impartiality govern a member's decisions, pertaining to appointments, pay adjustments, promotions, and discipline.

12 Seek no favor; believe that personal aggrandizement or profit secured by confidential information or by misuse of public time is dishonest.

This Code was originally adopted in 1924 by the members of the International City Management Association and has since been amended in 1938, 1952, 1969, 1972. and 1976.

The ASPA Code of Ethics is published with the permission of the American Society for Public Administration, Washington, D.C. © by ASPA.

American Society for Public Administration
Code of Ethics

• Demonstrate the highest standards of personal integrity, truthfulness, honesty and fortitude in all our public activities in order to inspire public confidence and trust in public institutions.

• Serve in such a way that we do not realize undue personal gain from the performance of our official duties.

• Avoid any interest or activity which is in conflict with the conduct of our official duties.

• Support, implement, and promote merit employment and programs of affirmative action to assure equal employment opportunity by our recruitment, selection, and advancement of qualified persons from all elements of society.

• Eliminate all forms of illegal discrimination, fraud, and mismanagement of public funds, and support colleagues if they are in difficulty because of responsible efforts to correct such discrimination, fraud, mismanagement or abuse.

• Serve the public with respect, concern, courtesy, and responsiveness, recognizing that service to the public is beyond service to oneself.

• Strive for personal professional excellence and encourage the professional development of our associations and those seeking to enter the field of public administration.

• Approach our organization and operational duties with a positive attitude and constructively support open communication, creativity, dedication and compassion.

• Respect and protect the privileged information to which we have access in the course of official duties.

• Exercise whatever discretionary authority we have under law to promote public interest.

• Accept as a personal duty the responsibility to keep up to date on emerging issues and to administer the public's business with professional competence, fairness, impartiality, efficiency and effectiveness.

• Respect, support, study, and when necessary, work to improve federal and state constitutions and other laws which define the relationships among public agencies, employees, clients and all citizens.

Adopted by ASPA National Council
March 27, 1985

GLOSSARY

Arterial street - a major roadway within a city. An arterial street carries the heaviest loads of traffic within a city.

Cellular telephone - a new technology telephone that works similarly to a "wireless" radio, thus permitting the existence of a phone in a vehicle, or even brief case. This service is available in most metropolitan areas; there is an equipment fee, a monthly access fee, and air time sold by the minute.

Civic group - any one of a number of volunteer organizations with the expressed purpose of aiding their respective communities, or some element within the community. Ex: Civitans, Jaycees, Lions, Kiwanis, Rotary, etc.

Climatological - pertaining to the weather of a given area.

Codification - the recapitulation, generally in a predetermined format, of a city's ordinances. Upon codification, every ordinance within a city is categorized into numbered sections arranged by topic similarities.

Collector street - those roads within a city that carry traffic to arterial, or major streets.

Current mortgage exemption - a reduction in the property assessment amount assigned to a particular property in some states. If a property has a current mortgage on it, the assessment is reduced by a specified flat fee. Thus, the property taxes paid to the government are reduced.

Encumbrances - a financial term relating to the practice of ear-marking certain monies in the specified amount necessary to pay for a particular item or service at the time when that service was ordered, but prior to receipt of the service or product. Encumbrances are a method to prohibit the accidental over-expenditure of budgetary accounts as a result of the time delay between ordering and paying for services.

Federal Emergency Management Agency (FEMA) - the office of the U.S. government specifically created for the purpose of providing emergency management guidance and training to all other governmental entities. FEMA offers assistance in Emergency and Disaster Service training, as well as flood plain management and identification.

Fire Protection Handbook - a text periodically published by the National Association of Fire Chiefs in which general and technical information is published and updated.

GED (General Educational Development) - a document attesting to an individual's having attained the equivalent of a high school diploma without the individual's having technically completed traditional high school classroom training. The GED is earned by successfully passing a multiphase test.

GNMA funds - those securities that are available for purchase through the Government National Mortgage Agency. Commonly referred to as "Ginny-maes". GNMA Certificates are fully backed by the federal government. Sometimes, however, a GNMA pool is referred to as an actual GNMA certificates; when this is done, the pool issues certificates which do not have the same credit-backing as does an actual GNMA certificate.

Homestead exemption - a term peculiar to some states' real property assessment policies and procedures. Generally, if a homestead exemption is recognized, it provides for a flat rate reduction in the assessed value of a home and property, if said property is occupied by the owner, and/or the owner is over 62 or some other legislatively specified age, or a veteran of the U.S. armed services.

HTH - a grade of chlorine commercially available, usually sold in conjunction with swimming pool supplies. HTH can be used as a disinfectant and counteragent to sanitary sewer spills and/or overflows.

Mulch - any one of several different materials used to place at the base of plants, in order for the plant beds to better retain moisture; mulch may be wood chips, bark chips, gravel, etc.

PUD, Planned urban development - a detailed subdivision which mixes residential and commercial land use into a single subdivision development. A PUD is often a zoning district in its own right, because it mixes land uses. Sometimes a PUD will start in one area with single family housing, advance to multiple family housing, then to light commercial development, and perhaps to heavy commercial use all within a single, comprehensive subdivision plan. A PUD may employ such unusual zoning techniques as zero lot-line developments which may not be allowed in any zoning district other than a PUD.

Setbacks - a specified distance from the road right-of-way for the location of the outside edge of a building.

Zero lot line - a special subdivision technique in which buildings (normally houses) may be built right on the edge of the lot, without any setbacks being required. Some townhouse developments are zero lot line developments.

268

problem in open system of, 78; street sweeping as aid to, 77; system capacity to accommodate storm events, 79; use of ditches in open system of, 79; use of flood walls to stop flooding, 78; use of grade-all in construction of, 81; use of headwalls, 79; why it is a growing problem, 77
DRC (development review committee): makeup and duties, 80; planner as chairperson of, 128; planning commission acting as, 127
Driveways: specifications for construction of, 134
Dump fees: defined, 111. See also Fees; Tip fees

Effluent/influent: discussed, 108
Elected officials. See Officials, elected
Eligibility: certification and appointment (C) from lists of, 186; of employees (C), 182; of employees for promotional exams (C), 185; establishment and use (C) of lists of, 186; for examinations (C), 182; kinds (C) of lists of, 186; sequenced (C) lists of, 187
Emergency/disaster plan: approved and unapproved emergency shelters (D), 250; city areas of responsibility (D), 242; city clerk's responsibilities (D), 242; city engineer's responsibilities (D), 243; city manager's responsibilities (D), 243; commissioners' responsibilities (D), 242; consulting engineer's responsibilities (D), 242; contacting support agencies (D), 251; dispatchers' responsibilities (D), 245; early calls for manpower (D), 245; emergency/disaster preparedness coordinator's duties (D), 248; emergency supplies and aid (D), 243; finance director's responsibilities (D), 242; fire department's responsibilities (D), 246; general government department's responsibilities (D), 244; handling of wastes and hazardous chemicals (D), 248; listing of available private equipment (D), 250; mayor's responsibilities (D), 242; must be printed and available (D), 242; notification of employees (D), 242; police department's responsibilities (D), 244; press releases (D), 242; purpose (D), 242; sanitation department's responsibilities (D), 248; settling of employment problems (D), 244; shop department's responsibilities (D), 248; street department's responsibilities (D), 247; table of contents (D), 240; water department's responsibilities (D), 246
Emergency/disaster preparedness coordinator: duties and responsibilities (D), 248
Emergency Medical Services. See EMS
Emergency Medical Technician. See EMT
Emergency Operations Center. See EOC
Emergency shelters: approved and unapproved (D), 250; supplies to be brought by evacuees to (D), 251
Employees: aid from their families in emergency/disaster (D), 251 and labor unions, 14; annual bull sessions for, 26; anonymity of applicants protected (C), 184; appeal process per performance review manual (C), 210; assignment of call numbers to, 149; attendance and holiday regulations (C), 190; care of pets in emergency/disaster (D), 251; categories qualifying for incentive pay raise (C), 213; causes for removal (C), 196; certified and uncertified, 22; city policy on educational expenses (C), 214; code of conduct for (C), 225; compensatory and/or overtime (C),192, 200, 215; conflict of interest (C), 227; disability leave and rules for pay (C), 215; disciplinary actions against (C), 230; discipline (C) of, 195; disclosure of information (C),216; duties of, in parks and recreation department, 138; eligibility (C), 184; eligibility for promotional examinations (C), 186; employment conditions and standards (C), 226; employment problems during emergency/disaster (D), 244; employment records of, 10; and families in emergency/disaster (D), 251; general regulations under merit plan (C), 217; handling of restricted information (C), 217; holiday compensation (C), 190; hours of work/work week, full- and part-time (C), 188; importance of high school diploma or GED, 23; importance of response to citizens, 48; incentive program (C), 212; jobs in maintenance department, 139; leave policies (C), 199; literacy test in job interview (C), 226; may consult with manager (C), 235; need for professional, in maintenance department, 139; no hangout for, in maintenance department, 139; noncompetitive eligibility for positions (C), 185; notification in emergency/disaster (D), 242; other employment (C), 224; outside employment (C),

Striper: for painting lines on streets, 88
Striping: or marking of streets, 88
Subdivision/development regulations. See Regulations, subdivision/development
Subdivisions: amending of regulations for development and, 131; application and filing
    fees for development review assessment of proposed (A), 169; areas to address in
    regulations for development and, 131; impact study needed before approval of, 134;
    landscaping and buffer strips indicated on plans for, 135; lots and utilities properly
    shown and sized on plans for, 134; payment of fees upon petition for proposed, (A)
    169; planning for sidewalks in, 133; regulations for development and, adopted by
    ordinance, 131; should be approved in phases, 132; specs for streets in, 134
Sunshine laws: as applied to city merit board (C), 225; know your state's, 154
Supervisors (staff): incentive award for, 159; relationship with city manager, 7
Surety bond. See Bond
Surplus: revenue investment, 34
Surplus property programs: source for city purchases, 44
Suspension: defined (C), 222; of employees (C), 195
Swale: defined, 78
SWAT (special weapons and tactics) team: duties in emergency/disaster (D), 245

Tap fees. See Fees
Target budgeting: defined and discussed, 33
Taxes: ad valorem, defined, 30; city's liability for billing of, 31; city not only collector of,
    32; exemption from property, 29; gasoline, and street and drainage system
    maintenance, 94; on insurance policies as source of revenue, 32; millage, defined
    and discussed, 31-2; payroll, as source of revenue, 32; raise, or raise fees, 98; real
    property, defined and discussed, 29-31; sales, and state, as source of revenue, 32;
    sales, on utility company sales, 32
Taylor, Robert: his ideas on land-use regulations, 130
Telephone numbers: need for list of important, 163
Telescopic boom excavation equipment: illustrated, 82
Tip fees: defined, 111. See also Dump fees
Traffic impact study: needed before subdivision approval, 134
Training: cross, 19-21; cross, of supervisors, 20-1; leadership, of supervisors, 21; needed
    in use of radios, 149; needed for special job, 22; opportunities for hands-on, 24;
    problem participants in, 24; supervisory classes/seminars in, 19; techniques and
    gimmicks in, 22-3; time and physical arrangements for, 23-4; use of recorder w/tape
    or video, 22-3; of water department personnel, 95
Transcript: need for verbatim, of city meetings, 55, 155
Transfer: and transfer list, defined (C), 187
Trash collection. See Garbage collection
Treasurer. See Finance director
Treatment plant operators I-IV: job description (B), 178

Urban planning: defined, 127
Utilities: provision for, on subdivision plans, 132, 134
Utility cuts. proper handling of (H), 260
Utility fees: importance of ordinance for, 53. See also Fees

Vacation: annual and/or pay in lieu of (C), 229; leave defined (C), 222; leave policies (C),
    198
Vehicles: advisability of departments sharing, 145; bumper numbers for city vehicles,
    141; discussed, 141-8; electric car for meter readers, 145; importance of city decal
    on, 147, 160; Indianapolis Plan for police, 143; inspection by maintenance
    department, 139; inspection of, by city manager, 142; number and type needed, 142;
    numbers on roofs of police, 146; police requirements for, 146; special crime scene
    requirements, 146; specifications for pickup trucks, 144; uniform paint for city
    owned, 147; unmarked, 143